To Rip, We hope you can <u>see</u> some architecture
beneath the snow.....! It's
Much love from Ko and I

English Architecture

OVERLEAF

St John's College, Cambridge: the gatehouse; 1511–20.
The semi-fortified entrance to the older part of the
college, built by the master-mason William Swayne.
Similar towered gatehouses are found in other colleges,
at St James's Palace, London, Hampton Court and
mansions of the Tudor period such as Layer Marney
(page 86).

The National Trust Book of
English Architecture

J.M. Richards

W. W. Norton & Co.   New York · London

Contents

Picture
Acknowledgments

The author and publishers would like to thank the following individuals and institutions for permission to reproduce their photographs (numbers in italics refer to colour illustrations):

John Bethell: frontispiece, 10, *18*, 22 top, 24, *40* bottom, 84, 98, 99, 106, *109*, *110–11*, 122, 136–7, 148, 158, 166, 177, *181* bottom, *182–3*, 188, 193, *217, 219, 220*, 229, *237*, 251, 262.

Edwin Smith: 13, 32, 45, 46, 57, 66, 74, 75, 78, 82–3, 114, 115, 130, 138, 165, 175, 178, 201, 207, 211 top, 211 bottom, 242, 273.

A. F. Kersting: 15, 21 left, 21 right, 28, 29, 30, 31, 35, *38–9*, 42, 43, 49, 52, 59, 63, 64, 68–9, 71, 72–3, 76, 79, 81, 86, *90–91*, 93, 97, 100, 102, 104, 105, 108, *112*, 116, 118–19, 121, 124, 127, 129, 132–3, 140, 142, 144–5, 146, 150–51, 152–3, 155, 156–7, *161*, 174, 176, 180, *184*, 185, 187, 189, 195, 198, 203, 204–5, 213, 214, *218*, 226, 230, 232, *240* bottom, 244, 247, 248, 252, 254, 255, 257 top, 265, 271, 274, 275.

Michael Holford: *17, 40* top.

Crown Copyright, Department of the Environment: 19, 20.

Eric de Maré: 22 bottom, 135, 172, 239, 234–5.

James Austin: 23, 259.

Aerofilms Ltd: 26, 208–9.

Weidenfeld Archives: *37* (photo John Hedgecoe), *38* left (photo Werner Forman), *92*, 126, *164*, 186 (photo Swain), 190.

National Monuments Record: 41 (S. Smith Collection), 222.

Christopher Dalton: 50, 54, 55, 58, 60, 61, 123, 147, 171, 194, 202, 225, 243.

The National Trust: *89*, 95, 364.

By Gracious Permission of Her Majesty The Queen: 103.

Angelo Hornak: *110* left, *162–3, 238–9, 240* top.

British Rail/Oxford Publishing Company: 168.

The Architectural Press: 173 (photo Eric de Maré), 210 (photo A. T. Kelly), 247 bottom, 258, 260, 261 (photo London Transport Executive), 272 bottom (photo Brecht-Einzig Ltd), 276 (photo Henry Snoek), 278.

Stafford Linsley: *181* top.

Lancashire Library: 186.

John Donat: 196, 227, 272 top, 277.

Department of Planning, Leeds City Council: 206.

Country Life: 221 (photo Alex Starkey), 249.

Crown Copyright, Greater London Council: 224, 228.

John Trelawny-Ross: 236.

Norwich Union Insurance: 246.

J. M. Richards: 256 (photo Dell and Wainwright).

The Boots Company Ltd: 263.

Brecht-Einzig Ltd: 266.

Hertfordshire County Architects Department: 268 (photo David Houghton).

Picture research by Julia Brown

Diagrams by Peter White

Foreword

MAIDEN CASTLE and Stonehenge are among the grandest monuments in Europe, but they are only on the fringe of history. We know little about their construction and use, and it is best to regard them as belonging to prehistory and to begin a consecutive account of architecture in Britain with the buildings of the Anglo-Saxons – the first intelligible buildings erected by the English for the English. The Roman buildings that preceded these were the product of an alien culture. Moreover only fragments remain; when the Romans left in AD 410 the buildings they had put up were abandoned and many destroyed for the sake of the materials in them. Several centuries of Roman occupation left little more in the way of a permanent legacy than the location, names and layout of the towns the Romans founded as military centres and the roads that connected them.

It is the intention in any case that this book should not concern itself with fragmentary remains, but with buildings that can be seen and – since architecture is the art of enclosing space – can be entered. Buildings we know about only from illustrations, however recently they may have been replaced or demolished, are for the same reason excluded as far as possible. A few are mentioned by name if they were the best examples of some trend that needs commenting on or of some important architect's work.

It is convenient to date and classify buildings according to their style, and it is not many years since style was considered to be the whole of architecture. Changes of style were observed and recorded like changes in the weather, with far too little reference to the causes of change, social and technical. Today we look at architecture and the styles it evolved as elements in a broader picture and so, although this is a book about buildings, some attempt has been made in its pages to relate the various types of building described to the social history of their period and to the changing demands made on them.

For this and other obvious reasons the buildings ordinary people used every day – their own small houses and the local parish church, shopping street and railway station – together with the regional variations they showed until recently are, in so far as space allows, included as well as the major, the consciously original, monuments. If the latter claim the most attention, that is not only because of their intrinsic importance but because new architectural influences, especially those from overseas, have for the most part first shown themselves in cathedrals and palaces and in the other prominent landmarks of our cities. Through them we can best follow the actual processes of change before seeing how new ways of building and new architectural fashions filtered downwards to the lesser buildings and became familiar to a wider range of master-craftsmen and designers.

Even so these successive processes, the introduction of something new and its assimilation into everyday practice, could be described by reference to hundreds of different buildings. In a short book like this it is impossible to name more than a few, or every paragraph would be choked by lists of names and locations. Only the most significant buildings are therefore described and a few others mentioned which seemed to the author to exemplify clearly the styles and developments he was trying to summarize. Many important buildings are not, inevitably, referred to at all. In deciding which of many alternative examples to mention, the attempt has been made to select them from as many parts of the country as possible in order to give the greatest number of readers an opportunity of seeing them with their own eyes.

The space given to the different periods of English architecture may strike the reader as unbalanced. This is deliberate. Many history books stop short some time in the nineteenth century, but a very large number of the buildings we see and use date from less than a hundred years ago; it is these that determine our architectural environment. For this reason, and because the Gothic cathedrals and the work, for example, of Wren, Vanbrugh, Nash and the other famous architects of earlier periods have so many books devoted to them already, this book includes relatively more about the nineteenth and twentieth centuries up to the point when the

difficulty is encountered of writing history while it is still being made. The amount of attention given to each period is, that is to say, more nearly proportionate than in most histories to the amount of building of the period that competes for the citizen's attention today.

Architects' dates are given only when their names are first mentioned. When a single date is given for a building it is normally the year of its design or commencement, which is the most significant date in relation to the style a building exemplifies or the trends it illustrates; the date of completion is added only when the period of construction was long or when there is some other reason to regard it as significant. In referring to architects with titles, the latter are used throughout, irrespective of whether the title had been acquired – usually a knighthood awarded – at the time referred to. This is in order to avoid the continual repetition of phrases like 'William Chambers (later Sir William)'.

Although this is a book about English architecture, some important or illuminating examples in Wales and Scotland are included when their style originated in England, as it did in the greatest of the Welsh castles and in the classical buildings of Edinburgh, since architects like the Scottish Adam brothers had the same Italian training as the English architects of their day. It is fair to regard these and some other Welsh and Scottish buildings as rooted in English culture.

Another problem which arises from any attempt to write about English architecture in isolation is that for long periods England was culturally a part of Europe, and its architecture and the influence that shaped it cannot be fully understood except in relation to the larger European picture. Even when England went its own independent way its relationship with Europe remained significant, and the reader is recommended to study the European background as well.

This is a short book in which to cover English architecture alone. There are specialized books on every period to which the reader who wants fuller information is referred. The most useful are listed in a bibliography at the end, where there will also be found a glossary of architectural terms used in the text.

J.M.R.

Part One

The Age of Religion

Chapter 1

Early Church Building: Saxon and Norman

WE begin in the seventh century AD with the earliest of the few Anglo-Saxon buildings that survive. These are all churches and have survived because they were built of stone, which was exceptional; for the Anglo-Saxons, who settled in England after the break-up of the Roman Empire, were forest-dwellers by habit and the building material they knew best was wood. The England they came to was mostly forested also. They continued therefore to make most of their buildings of wood, except where there were Roman buildings handy whose stones and tile-like bricks they could reuse; or else they built with mud strengthened with wood (wattle and daub). Their roofs were of thatch. Even the Saxon fortifications were no more than earth banks with palisades of wooden stakes driven into the ground.

Christian churches existed in England in late Roman times but we know nothing of what they were like or whether they influenced the many new churches built in the seventh century when the Anglo-Saxon English were converted to Christianity by the missionaries led by St Augustine. The latter probably began by building monasteries and churches of wood, like the assembly-halls, described in *Beowulf*, in which their chieftains had been accustomed to hold court. But they soon began to use stone as being more lasting and imposing. They were taught how to do so by masons brought over from the Continent or, in the case of the churches in Northumbria, from Ireland where Christianity was already flourishing.

The expert and craftsmanlike use of wood nevertheless continued. It was used not only for domestic and similar buildings but in the new stone churches for roofs and screens and furnishings of all kinds. Stone and wood remained in fact the basis of the tradition of church building which continued to provide England with its most distinguished works of architecture for nearly another thousand years, that is, right up to the Reformation. The Saxon

Parish church, Iffley, Oxfordshire; about 1170: the west end. The church was given to the parish by a rich patron and is typically late Norman, with its deeply recessed round-arched doors and windows enriched with zigzag sculpture. The upper windows are separated by twisted columns with carved capitals. The circular window is an insertion of 1856 but there was evidence of a similar window in the same place when the church was first built.

churches, even when of stone, were however small and primitive; more so than appears from the examples that survive because these have all been altered and improved. They were plain rectangular buildings with small windows, usually arched, sometimes triangular. There is a group of them in Kent, where the Christian Church established its headquarters at Canterbury (at first adapting, exceptionally, a Roman building for its services). These Kentish churches had apses at the east end and an arcade separating nave from chancel. In Northumbria, where there is another group, the buildings were long and narrow with square-ended chancels. Sometimes they had side-chambers. None of the early Saxon churches had towers.

Good examples of Saxon, or basically Saxon, churches in south-eastern England are to be found at Canterbury (St Martin's) and Bradwell, Essex; in the north at Escomb, Jarrow (this was Bede's own church) and Monkwearmouth. Between the two groups is the most impressive of all: that at Brixworth, Northamptonshire, founded about 670. There was a second wave of church building in the tenth century, after the Viking invasions and the reconstruction of the country under King Alfred. Examples are Earls Barton, Deerhurst and Bradford-on-Avon, the last being an enlargement of a Saxon church of the earlier period. Sompting Church, Sussex, has an unusual tower with a gabled spire of German type – a sign, perhaps, of increasing Continental influence.

At this time more interest was shown in decoration, exemplified by the strips of stone that make patterns on the walls of Earls Barton tower, reminiscent of timber construction, and the spiral columns in the Saxon crypt at Repton. Wood was still being used as well as stone, as can be seen from the one timber-built church that survives from Saxon times – that at Greensted, Essex, where the nave walls are split oak logs. Here the body of St Edmund rested on its journey from Bury St Edmunds, so the church can be precisely dated: 1013.

Notwithstanding these first crude attempts at decoration, the Saxon churches remained primitive in style and construction until a far more sophisticated and technically skilful way of building came to England with the Norman conquest. It is therefore called Norman, but although brought over by the Normans it was neither created by them nor peculiar

to them. It was a local version of the Romanesque style common to the whole of Europe, a style of massive walls and round arches, descended from the Carolingian and, more remotely, from the Roman and Early Christian remains to be seen all over southern Europe throughout the Dark Ages. The Romanesque style as adopted by the Normans was first evolved by the monks of Cluny in Burgundy, where in the middle of the tenth century they established a reformed version of the Benedictine Order.

A few buildings in this style had been put up in England before the Normans came. Edward the Confessor, whose mother was Norman and who had lived among monks in Normandy until he was twenty-five, was an admirer of everything Norman as well as a devotee of religion. He rebuilt Westminster Abbey in 1050–65 in the style of the great French abbey churches at Caen and Jumièges, but nothing of his work there remains. He took up his own residence at Westminster (instead of at Winchester, the old royal capital of Wessex), thereby causing Westminster to become the administrative centre of England while the role of the city of London remained wholly mercantile, to be dominated shortly afterwards by the Tower constructed by the conqueror William.

After the Conquest the Normans set about building energetically. They despised the primitive structures they found when they landed and replaced them by buildings in their own style as well as constructing new churches and monasteries (and of course fortresses – for these see the next chapter) in extraordinary numbers. They built in stone even when the material had to be brought from far away – Canterbury Cathedral uses Caen stone from Normandy – and many of their buildings were very large, introducing elements into the English land-

Saxon church, Brixworth, Northamptonshire. Apart from its timber roof and furnishings, this is an almost unaltered example of an early Saxon church interior of the end of the seventh century. The arches are formed of reused Roman tiles and those along either side once opened on to aisles, now demolished. The church, which was founded by monks from Peterborough, was damaged in Danish raids in the ninth century but then restored. The triple window at the west end lights a chamber inserted at this time (early eleventh century) in the upper part of the porch. The latter was heightened in the Middle Ages to form a tower.

scape of a size and character it had never contained before. Most of the new English abbots and bishops were Normans and the building enterprises they started made an important contribution to the process of assimilating the Normans and their civilization into English life and thus bringing England within the main – the Latin rather than the Germanic – stream of European culture.

The great Norman churches were nearly all built for one of the religious orders, at first the Benedictine, then the more puritanical Cistercian. They had massive plain towers and thick walls. Inside they had arcades of huge, closely spaced cylindrical columns with a second smaller arcade above and, above this, clerestory windows to admit light from over the aisle roofs. Within twenty years of the Norman Conquest, the flat bare surfaces of Saxon buildings thus gave way to an elaborate articulation of parts: arches, columns, wall-shafts together creating an organized geometrical system, out of which the later styles of medieval architecture were to develop. The larger Norman churches had transepts with towers over the crossing, and usually a pair of towers at the west end. Ornament grew richer as the skill of the stonemasons increased. It ranged from the geometrical patterns incised into the surfaces of columns and emphasizing the curves of arches to carved capitals and sculpture-filled tympanums over the doorways of even modest parish churches.

It is chiefly in the naves of some of the greater churches (built as abbey churches around the end of the eleventh century but maintained since the Reformation as cathedrals) that this rich but massive pattern of building can best be seen today. The chancels of the same churches have in many instances been rebuilt. In England the naves were of great length – longer than any of their Continental prototypes. Among the major early Norman churches were the cathedrals of Canterbury and Winchester and the Benedictine abbey churches of St Albans, Ely and Worcester, all built in the 1070s and the 1080s. Although little remains of the Norman work at Canterbury (begun by Lanfranc, the first Norman archbishop, who was Italian by birth and had previously been abbot of Caen), the transepts survive at Winchester. They were part of a new cathedral begun by Walkelin, the first Norman bishop, in 1079. The whole of the nave as well as the transepts survive at Ely where Abbot Simeon,

Walkelin's brother, began rebuilding the abbey church in 1090. Norwich, Gloucester, Chichester, Rochester, St Albans and Peterborough cathedrals all have splendid Norman naves built early in the twelfth century; so have Tewkesbury and Romsey abbeys. A well-preserved example on a smaller scale is St Bartholomew's Church at Smithfield, London, where the choir is also Norman. Also in London a complete jewel of Norman architecture is the little chapel of St John in the Tower with its stone barrel-vaulting.

Of all the Norman buildings in England, however, Durham Cathedral, begun in 1093, is the noblest. Durham was a city of outstanding political importance, the last ecclesiastical bastion before the Scottish border, the seat of a prince-bishop and the capital of a vast area virtually repopulated by the Normans after William had half exterminated its rebellious people. Its cathedral shares with a powerful castle a precipitous rock in a loop of the River Wear. Durham Cathedral is the one English building of this period to make an original contribution to the development of Romanesque architecture; for the builders of its nave evolved, in 1128, the ribbed vault, which was a great technical improvement on the cylindrical barrel-vault on which stone-built roofs had hitherto relied. It appears to have been the first example in Europe and since it allowed the weight of the roof to be supported at isolated points instead of on continuous walls, it may be regarded as one of the main starting points of the development of the structural methods that created the later glories of Gothic architecture. Ribbed vaulting was soon adopted in northern France but it does not seem to have been used again in England for half a century and it did not become usual until well into the thirteenth century.

Durham Cathedral: the Norman nave looking east. The most completely Norman cathedral in England, Durham was begun in 1093. The huge cylindrical columns typical of the period have geometrical ornament cut into the surface of the stone, including the Normans' favourite chevron pattern, first used at Durham. The columns alternate with compound piers with recessed arches, between which wall-shafts rise through the triforium to support the vault. Norman naves usually had timber roofs. Durham had a stone roof from the beginning, not the Romanesque barrel vault but a ribbed vault which in 1128 when it was built was more advanced than any in Europe.

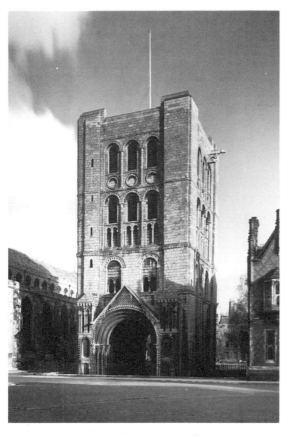

Bury St Edmunds, Suffolk: abbey gateway. Bury was the most powerful monastery in East Anglia, of Benedictine foundation and revered as the burial place of King Edmund in 910. It was rebuilt soon after the Conquest, more splendidly it was said than any monastery in England except Glastonbury. Only ruins remain of its Norman and later buildings except two gateways, one of which is in the Decorated style of the fourteenth century. The Norman gateway shown here, begun in 1121, faces the west door of the abbey church. It is nearly 90 feet high and has walls 6 feet thick. Its windows have carving of a shallower type than, for example, at Iffley Church and were probably executed with an axe rather than a chisel. The main archway originally had a carved tympanum but this was removed in 1789 to allow the passage of farm wagons.

OPPOSITE
St Mawes Castle, Cornwall; about 1543. One of a string of castles built by Henry VIII along the southern coast of England during the invasion scare of 1538–43. They were not residences as well, being designed solely to house artillery. (See page 31.)

Tewkesbury Abbey, Gloucestershire: from the north-west. A Benedictine abbey church, Tewkesbury was built between 1087 and 1150 with a nave arcade of tall cylindrical columns from which now springs a fourteenth-century vault. The aisle windows seen in the picture are also fourteenth-century. The square central tower is typically Norman of the twelfth century, decorated with shafts and chevron-ornamented arches between the bell-openings and with blind arcading on the stage between. The pinnacles and battlements were added in 1660. On the lowest stage of the tower can be seen the outline of the original high-pitched roof, replaced by the present roof of lower pitch in 1593.

local conditions became more settled. Although of course far smaller than the great churches described above, they used the same vocabulary of successively recessed arches spanning between circular columns, the same round-headed windows and the same geometrical ornament on chancel arches and porches. There are examples all over the country. Among the best are the parish churches at Iffley, Oxfordshire; Barfreston, Kent; Kilpeck, Hereford

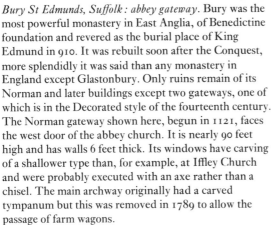

and Worcester – notable for its suggestion of Scandinavian influence – Melbourne, Derbyshire; Stow, Lincolnshire, and Cambridge (St Benet's and the Holy Sepulchre). The last is one of five circular churches built by the crusading orders of knights to echo the rotunda of the Holy Sepulchre in Jerusalem.

By the beginning of the thirteenth century the Gothic style (the subject of Chapter 3) had arrived in England, mainly through the building activities of the monks of the Cistercian Order. It came after a transitional period during which the austerity of the true Norman architecture was modified and its structure progressively elaborated. A degree of lightness was introduced, of which the first evidence, perhaps, is the Galilee porch (intended as a Lady Chapel) that was added to the western end of Durham Cathedral as early as 1170. Here the five aisles are divided by arcades supported on groups of slender columns. It is in marked contrast to the massiveness of Durham as a whole, inside and out, and a reminder that influences on English architecture came from Europe generally as well as from Normandy in particular; for the style of the porch is more that of the Cluniac Gothic of Burgundy, just as the richly sculptured west door of Rochester Cathedral (1150) resembles the Romanesque style of Aquitaine.

In contrast to the severity of the early Norman work there was also, at the end of the twelfth century, more use made of surface ornament. On the

LEFT ABOVE

Kilpeck Church, Hereford and Worcester: south door. This small parish church serving a remote rural village dates from the third quarter of the twelfth century and is an unusually rich example of late Norman architecture. It has elaborate and very well preserved carving at the west end, along the cornice, round this south door and – inside the church – round the chancel arch. The carving surrounding the door is notable for its evidence of Scandinavian influence.

LEFT

Church of the Holy Sepulchre, Cambridge; 1130. This Norman round church is one of the five churches that survive out of a number built in the early twelfth century by the Orders of crusading knights on the pattern of the Church of the Holy Sepulchre in Jerusalem. (The others are the Temple Church, London; a chapel at Ludlow Castle, Shropshire; and churches at Little Maplestead, Essex, and Northampton.) Its upper storey was heavily restored by Anthony Salvin in 1844.

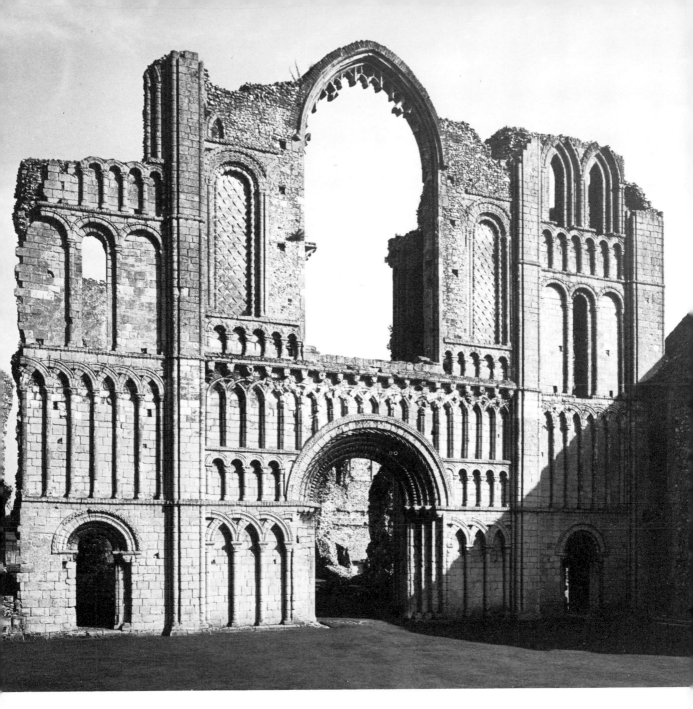

west fronts of Ely and Lincoln, inside the chapter-house of Bristol Cathedral and at Castle Acre Priory in Norfolk (one of the many monastic buildings which, although ruined, still reveal the richness and skilled craftsmanship achieved at this time), the ornament takes the form of interlacing arches, giving a foretaste of the pointed arch that was to be Gothic architecture's characteristic device, both structurally and aesthetically.

Castle Acre, Norfolk: priory ruins. This was a Cluniac priory, founded in 1090. It stands just outside the town and castle on the banks of the River Nar. The west front, shown here, built in 1140–50, is typical of the extravagantly decorative style favoured by the Cluniac Order and illustrates Norman architecture verging on the Gothic. The great window above the main door is of later date but the tiers of blind arcading with intersecting arches are decorative devices of which this transitional period was very fond.

Chapter 2

Fortresses of the Feudal Age

I T is one thing to defeat the army of another country, as Norman William did in 1066, and quite another to occupy that country and set up in it a widespread administrative system – in this case an improved and more highly organized version of the feudal system already established in Saxon England. Under the Normans there was greater emphasis on military service in return for grants of land by the lord or baron, and William retained control of the system – and thus of all England – by building castles, from which he and his newly appointed French-speaking lords, with the help of their armoured cavalry, dominated the countryside and its people and which served as strong-points in troubled times.

The heavily fortified castle was something new to the Anglo-Saxons. The experts the Normans brought with them began immediately after the Conquest to erect these strong-points in key positions, at first of earth ramparts and wood, soon however to be replaced by stone. A few of the most important early castles, including the Tower of London and Colchester Castle, were of stone from the beginning. The usual form was that known as motte-and-bailey, with a central keep surrounded by a ditch, beyond which was an open area (the bailey) defended by a rampart and another ditch. The motte, or mound on which the keep stood, reached from the bailey by a bridge, was sometimes built up artificially; more often the castle was sited where a hill or rock gave it a naturally commanding position.

As many as forty-nine castles are mentioned in the survey known as Domesday Book, made in 1086. There were almost certainly more, distributed all over England. Many have now gone or survive only as a shape in the ground, which was once the motte, or as a heap of stones; many were subsequently extended and rebuilt. But enough remain in nearly their original form to convey an idea of the style and appearance of a typical Norman castle. Hedingham, Essex, is a good example of the square Norman keep.

Hedingham Castle, Essex; 1140. One of the best preserved examples of the square Norman tower keep, rivalled only by Rochester. These two were the first stone castles to be built in England after the Tower of London. Hedingham, built by the Earl of Oxford, is faced with white Barnack stone and stands alone on its motte, the surrounding fortifications of the inner and outer bailey having disappeared. For easier defence the entrance is at first-floor level. A single ornamented arch, originally protected by a low building of which only some ruined stonework remains, leads into a large hall divided by an arch that spans the whole width of the building. The main stair is in one of the corner turrets, which reach nearly 100 feet above the ground.

25

Dover Castle, Kent; 1180s: from the air. Built high on the cliffs on the site of a Norman stronghold by Henry II, Dover has a square keep enclosed by two rings of fortifications, each consisting of walls with towers at intervals, an arrangement unique in Europe at this time and influenced by the castles the crusading knights had encountered in the Holy Land. It marked the beginning of the change to a system in which towered curtain walls, rather than a keep, provided the main defences. Beyond the outer ring of walls is a ditch, following the line of Iron Age earthworks. It is spanned by a bridge guarded (right of picture) by a gatehouse. This, the Constable's Tower, was added by King John after 1216 when King Louis of France nearly forced his way into the castle through the original gateway on the north, which had been unwisely sited facing the one point from which the castle is commanded by higher ground.

It rises clear from the ground, its height and bulk accentuated by the small size of the round-arched windows that pierce its smooth stone walls. Other Norman keeps of this type are at Rochester and

Norwich. Still another is the White Tower at the Tower of London, where the keep, however, is surrounded by fortifications of several later periods. An unusual feature of the keep at Norwich is the three storeys of blind arcading between the buttresses on the outside walls, which have no other than a decorative purpose. Normally the stonework of castles was purely functional.

All these castles consisted basically of simple towers defended by walls and ramparts. But as the Norman kings were succeeded by those of other dynasties, castle architecture changed, not however, as in the case of the cathedrals and monasteries, because new styles were introduced as a result of fashion, of aesthetic and religious aspirations and of developing masonry techniques; in the castles they were the result of new methods of attack and defence. An important influence was the Crusades, which brought English lords and their retainers into touch with the castle-building methods of other countries and the techniques of siege warfare. Stone altogether replaced wood, even for roofs, since wooden roofs could too easily be set on fire. Walls rather than the keep became the main defensive element, although a central stronghold might remain as a last refuge. Gatehouses assumed increasing importance. At Richmond, Yorkshire, built in 1172, a square stone gatehouse altogether replaces the keep.

At Richmond, too, a high curtain-wall makes an early appearance. The transition to the new style can however best be seen at Dover, the great castle built by Henry II between 1168 and 1185 on the site of first Saxon and then Norman castles. Dover retained the square central keep, strong enough to serve as a fortress in itself, but it was enclosed within a curtain-wall with towers, which itself has a walled and towered bailey beyond. Thus the outer works of castles became more elaborate, with fortified gateways and towers making approach more difficult, at the same time as the solid central tower was gradually replaced by an enclosed court with a variety of buildings round it linked by curtain-walls. Towers and corners were rounded to make it more difficult to undermine them by sapping, and their layout was designed to eliminate dead areas hidden from the defenders' missiles. There was no standard pattern however; the form of a castle was mainly determined by the nature of the terrain.

Inside the castle comfort took second place. Windows remained small and stairways narrow so as not to weaken the walls into the thickness of which they were built. The castle had to provide for all the needs of its inhabitants. Besides living quarters there was a chapel, armouries, stores of all kinds, stabling for horses, the castle's own water-supply. The living quarters were primitive and largely communal, for in the great hall, located in the keep or the principal tower, the lord and his retainers ate and many of the latter slept. The number of private chambers – sleeping-rooms for the lord and his family – was very small. The hall was usually on the first floor, above a lower vaulted floor. Nevertheless its multiple use makes it the ancestor of the hall of the medieval manor-house and of the main living space of all but the smallest houses for centuries to come.

Furniture in the hall was scanty: trestle tables and benches, chairs for those privileged to sit on the dais at one end, the 'cupboard' at the side of the dais on which the family wealth in silver vessels was displayed. From the end of the thirteenth century

the previously plastered walls were hung with woollen tapestries to keep out the cold. These were imported from Paris or Arras until manufacture in England began in the fifteenth century. They were not permanent fixtures but were carried from castle to castle.

Imposing examples of late Norman and early Plantagenet castles are Bamburgh, Northumberland, Arundel, Sussex – much added to later – Carisbrooke, Isle of Wight, and Pevensey, Sussex, the last little more than a ruin now but important in its time as the natural landing-point for an invasion of England – the point indeed that William the Conqueror had chosen. Henry II was one of the great builder kings. As part of his programme of pacifying and unifying the immense territory over which he ruled, which included most of France as well as England, he discouraged and even destroyed privately owned castles and built a number of his own in regions such as the north of England where a strong royal presence was desirable.

Castles of his time, or soon after, that are still in a good state of preservation include Framlingham, Suffolk, Conisbrough, South Yorkshire (built by Henry's half-brother) and Goodrich, Hereford and Worcester – smaller but exceptionally complete, except for the crumbling upper parts of its towers, and most dramatically situated. Henry also enlarged and improved some of the key royal castles of earlier reigns – Dover has already been mentioned. His son Richard brought back from the Crusades experienced castle builders who elaborated still further the castle's response to the special conditions of siege warfare. He greatly enlarged the Tower of London, like Dover on the new concentric plan.

In Wales there were some powerful castles in early times, such as those at Chepstow, Skenfrith and elsewhere up and down the border, but the finest Welsh castles were built by a later Plantagenet king, Edward I, after his conquest of the country between 1276 and 1295. A number of these are still remarkably complete; in fact as a result of Edward's building activities Wales, even more than Yorkshire and Northumbria, is the place to see well-preserved medieval castles occupying magnificent sites. His castles are concentric in plan like those of the Crusaders, with high curtain-walls flanked by round towers and elaborately defended gateways, as at Caerphilly. Some, like Harlech and Kidwelly, have

Plan of Caernarvon Castle and its walled town.

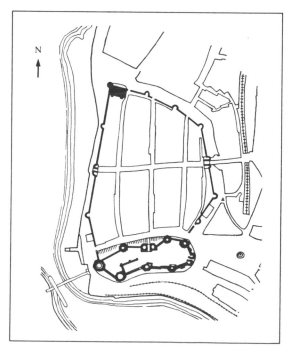

Caernarvon Castle, Gwynedd, Wales; 1283–1323. The largest of the castles built by Edward I following his campaigns to subdue Wales between 1276 and 1295, Caernarvon was designed by Edward's castle expert, James of St George, whom the king had brought back from the Crusades in 1273. The castle forms the south side of a walled town, newly laid out at the same time. It stands between the town and a wide river, and is separated from the town by a moat crossed by a drawbridge. Here is the main gate, powerfully defended. There is another gate at the eastern end. Besides these towered gates, the high curtain-wall is defended by seven intermediate towers, some with turrets, linked by a complex system of passages and fighting platforms.

an inner and an outer curtain-wall. Other spectacular Welsh castles of this period and type are Caernarvon, Beaumaris on Anglesey and Chirk, of similar pattern to Beaumaris. Some were supported by newly laid out walled towns, a new element in the wild Welsh countryside.

Edward's son and grandson extended their authority to Scotland and then over much of France. They built new castles in England and extended old ones to conform to the fashion for multiple towers and curtain-walls and to make them more resistant to new methods of attack. Edward III employed a specialist in castle building, William of Wykeham, who was later responsible for much ecclesiastical building, notably at Winchester and Oxford, and may be said to have been the first holder of the office, which exercised great architectural influence in later centuries, of Keeper of the King's Works. In the mid-fourteenth century he rebuilt the king's existing castle at Windsor as a vast fortified palace. It remained unchanged thereafter, except for the addition of St George's Chapel by Edward IV in 1474, until it was remodelled by George IV in 1824.

Unlike his Norman predecessors, and unlike Henry II, Edward III encouraged the strengthening

Bodiam Castle, Sussex; 1386. A private castle, built by one of Edward III's generals who was given permission to build it ('licence to crenellate') because of the French invasion threat – the sea was then twelve miles closer. It is set in a wide moat and is symmetrical in plan, with all its defensive strength in the walls, which have round corner towers and square intermediate towers, one of the latter being enlarged to form a gatehouse. On the inside of the walls were a chapel, a great hall (facing the gatehouse), kitchens, lodgings, etc. – all now ruined – surrounding a square courtyard.

of privately owned castles, especially in the south of England, after the French wars had turned against England and there was fear of invasion. Royal permission had however to be obtained before such work was begun. Licence to crenellate, it was called, after the crenellations or battlements on the roofline which were the mark of a house built primarily for defence. Bodiam, Sussex, is an exceptionally well-preserved example of a private castle constructed at this time, near enough to the south coast to require strong protection. Bodiam was begun in 1386. It is surrounded by a moat so wide that the castle appears to stand on an island in a lake. It is symmetrical, with curtain-walls defended by circular towers at each corner and by square towers in the centre of each side, one of which is the gatehouse. It thus marks the introduction of consciously formal architecture, a contrast to the informal (and to us more romantic) grouping of towers and battlements more usually associated with castles, especially those that have been added to over the centuries.

The rectangular courtyard form of castle, with no dominating keep, became common at the end of the fourteenth century and in the fifteenth, but sometimes large towers were added, resembling the earlier keeps, for the occupation – and greater safety – of the owners, since mercenary soldiers whose

Herstmonceux Castle, Sussex; 1441: the gatehouse. A late medieval castle with a curtain-wall, towers and a powerful gatehouse commanding the bridge over the moat, Herstmonceux was built by Roger de Fiennes of the household of Henry VI. It provided a secure residence but by this time possession of castles no longer dominated warfare. The use, as at Herstmonceux, of brick for the walls showed that a castle was not expected to resist the new heavy artillery.

loyalty could not always be depended on had largely succeeded feudal retainers. Such towers can be seen at Ludlow and at Warwick; also at Tattershall, Lincolnshire, which is notable for being of brick, almost unprecedented as early as 1434. Herstmonceux, another Sussex castle built not long afterwards, and intended like Bodiam for the defence of the south coast, is also of brick and has an unusually powerful gatehouse in a symmetrical facade.

However during the fifteenth century the strength of castles generally, and their key role in the process of acquiring and maintaining power, was being radically changed by gunpowder and by the use of cannon as a siege weapon. Feudal lords in their relatively modest castles could not so easily flout the royal authority, which was now supported by siege-trains and the resources to manufacture ever larger cannon. Although the process of centralizing power was delayed by the Wars of the Roses and the widespread lawlessness resulting from them, the development of the castle as a specialized architectural form based on the techniques of warfare that had grown up with it was coming to an end. The use of brick, mentioned above, was an indication of the castle's changing role. It is not the most suitable material for resistance to cannon-fire. Fortification, nevertheless, remained in the form of towers and crenellations – part of the vocabulary of architectural display – long after it ceased to be militarily functional (see Chapter 7).

The need for castles for local defence returned on one occasion. A threat of invasion from across the Channel between 1538 and 1543 impelled Henry VIII to construct a number of fortresses along the east and south coasts, designed, usually on a geometrical plan, to house artillery, not as residential seats of power as in the past. Surviving examples are at Deal and Walmer in Kent and at Pendennis and St Mawes in Cornwall. The Napoleonic Martello towers served the same purpose two and a half centuries later.

Fortified structures other than residential castles must be included in this chapter. Especially in times of unrest, many besides feudal lords found it necessary to defend themselves and their property. Although monasteries were not often fortified in a full military sense, they surrounded themselves with walls, entered through gatehouses (Battle, St Albans, Bury St Edmunds), and several bishops, some of whom were simultaneously feudal barons, found it advisable to live in a strongly defended palace like that at Wells, Somerset, or even a castle, as at Durham and Farnham, Surrey, the residence of the Bishop of Winchester. The Oxford and Cambridge colleges, though far from turning themselves into fortresses, provided themselves with gateways defensible enough to discourage marauders.

Finally, in the fourteenth century, after which England was no longer an almost wholly agricultural country but increasingly a trading country, drawing wealth thereby from overseas, still another form of fortification was given more attention and became more sophisticated, learning many lessons from the preceding years' experience of castle building. The market towns, which were the main source of commercial wealth, and the merchants residing in them, whose political power was beginning to grow, demanded protection. A few market towns had been walled since Saxon times, but now many others built stone walls with towers and fortified gateways that could be closed at night, replacing the earth and timber defences that were all they had previously possessed unless they still had the remains of Roman walls, as at Colchester. In several ancient English towns the enclosing walls still stand, although they have partly crumbled, gaps have been made for the passage of modern traffic and the town has expanded far beyond them. Well-preserved examples are York, Chester and Great Yarmouth in England and Conway, Caernarvon and Tenby in Wales. Handsome town gateways remain as part of all these systems of defence; also at Southampton, Monmouth and Norwich.

Plan of Walmer Castle, Kent.

Monk Bar, York. The walls enclosing the city of York were the longest in England: 2¾ miles. They incorporate fragments of Roman and Saxon stonework but the present walls were mostly built between 1250 and the end of the fourteenth century. Monk Bar is one of several surviving gates. The central arch originally had wooden doors and a portcullis, the machinery for which can still be seen on the second floor.

Chapter 3

Gothic Architecture: the Great Abbeys and Cathedrals

THE surge of ecclesiastical building in the second half of the twelfth century began a process of continually refining the structure which reached its climax in the airy cages of stone and glass, unique to England, achieved at the end of the fifteenth century. The initial inspiration came from France; yet taken as a whole the architectural quality of the English cathedrals is higher than the French, whose cathedrals include some major masterpieces, but also many buildings of no great distinction. An additional appeal of the English cathedrals for the student of architecture is their rich variety. In some cases it is possible to read nearly the whole history of English Gothic, as well as of the Norman that preceded it, in one building. Only Salisbury, Lichfield, Exeter and Southwell among English cathedrals were built within a relatively short time and therefore largely in one style.

The main impetus came from the monastic orders. In fact the majority of the present-day English cathedrals began as abbey churches, for the most part Benedictine. Only eight of the twenty-five medieval cathedrals are of the 'old foundation', that is, cathedrals that have always been served by a chapter of secular canons presided over by a dean. These are Chichester, Exeter, Hereford, Lichfield, Lincoln, Salisbury, Wells and York, together with St Paul's, London, no longer a medieval building. Nearly all the rest are monastic in origin. The abbey churches of Canterbury, Carlisle, Durham, Ely, Norwich, Rochester, Winchester and Worcester, were also cathedrals (that is, the seats of bishops) before the dissolution of the monasteries by Henry VIII. They were given the same status as the first-named eight on their 'new foundation' after the dissolution, and were placed under a dean and chapter. On the same occasion five more abbey churches were made cathedrals for the first time: Bristol, Chester, Gloucester, Oxford and Peterborough. The total of twenty-five medieval cathed-

Ely Cathedral: looking westwards from the choir. The ceiling of the Norman nave is painted wood. The richly decorated choir is mid-fourteenth-century. Between the two, over the crossing, is the unique octagon, constructed in 1322 by John Attegrene, master-mason. Above it is a timber vault with octagonal lantern by William Hurley, master-carpenter, completed in 1340. Timber is scarce in the Fens and the corner-posts, 60 feet long, were brought by road from Bedfordshire using teams of draught oxen.

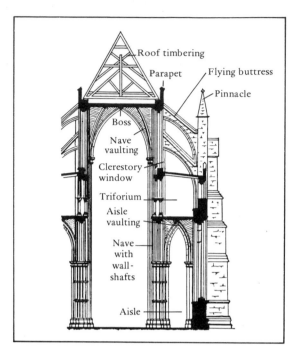

Section through typical Gothic cathedral.

Labels on diagram: Roof timbering · Parapet · Flying buttress · Pinnacle · Boss · Nave vaulting · Clerestory window · Triforium · Aisle vaulting · Nave with wall-shafts · Aisle

rals is made up by St Albans, an abbey church which only became a cathedral in 1878, Ripon and Southwell, which had never been monastic foundations and were also made cathedrals in the nineteenth century, and Southwark, formerly the church of an Augustinian priory, made a cathedral in 1905.

In these twenty-five great buildings the successive phases of English Gothic can be studied feature by feature, but several abbey churches that survived the dissolution are also among England's major medieval monuments: Tewkesbury, Beverley, Sherborne, Bath, Selby, Romsey and others, to which must be added Westminster Abbey, a cathedral for only a few years in the sixteenth century. The monasteries that survived the dissolution lost the greater part of their buildings and their churches stand isolated among the ruins. In some of the greatest the churches are ruined too and no longer in use. Parts of what remain are, however, substantial enough to furnish additional key illustrations of the progress of English architecture: Glastonbury and Tintern in the West Country, Bury St Edmunds in East Anglia (where two great gateways stand among the ruins of what was one of the most powerful Benedictine monasteries in England) and – most spectacular of all – the wonderful group of Cistercian establishments in Yorkshire now all ruined to some degree. These include Fountains, Rievaulx, Kirkstall and Bolton.

We must not therefore think of England's great abbey churches in the state we see them now, as crumbling ruins peacefully set down in a barely inhabited countryside, but as the focal centres of busy communities from which influence on the lives of everyone in the region spread incessantly outwards. The secular (that is, the non-monastic) cathedrals, too, were in most cases the centre of the life of the town or city in which they stood – sometimes indeed the cause of its foundation – the bishop being, politically and socially, the dominating local personage. Nevertheless the internal layout of cathedrals and abbey churches was not derived from the needs of any lay congregation but was planned for processional and choral services and for the daily offices required of their own clergy. Their architecture can only be understood in relation to these. In recent years a number of medieval parish churches have been made the seats of bishops and given the status of cathedrals to serve growing centres of population, but not having been designed as cathedrals or abbey churches they cannot be compared with the others. The parish church, serving a lay congregation, is the subject of another chapter.

Fully developed Gothic in the style already flourishing in northern France started at Canterbury. In 1175, after a fire had destroyed the eastern part of the Norman cathedral, William of Sens began rebuilding the choir in a style which not only incorporated the pointed arch – the essence of Gothic – but explored simultaneously the decorative and the structural possibilities to which it opened the way. Canterbury was not the first place in England to exploit the pointed arch, nor was it exceptional in following French models, but nowhere else were the

Canterbury Cathedral: the choir. This is a landmark in English architecture – the first appearance of fully developed Gothic, an importation from France by William of Sens in 1175. The change it introduced was not only in the style but in the nature of the structure: the thrust of the vaults is resisted by a balanced system of piers and buttresses, a significant step forward from the more static structures of the Normans.

splendours that Gothic architecture was soon to display suggested so long before the end of the twelfth century, nor the system of superimposed arcades, with the piers between them strengthened by buttresses extended at right angles, which in Gothic architecture superseded the Norman system of substantial load-bearing walls. The thrust of the vaults was increasingly to be taken, instead of by walls and piers, by pinnacled and flying buttresses.

Several years before the great leap forward at Canterbury, however, the pointed arch, the importance of which lies in its permitting much greater flexibility in the relation of height to span than the round Norman arch, had been brought from France to England by the monks of the Cistercian Order. It appears in combination with typical Norman features in several of the Order's Yorkshire monasteries; at Fountains (*c*.1135), for instance, and at Kirkstall (*c*.1150). In such abbey churches we can see the bulky cylindrical pillar being gradually transformed into the compound pier typical of Gothic. At Roche Abbey (*c*.1160) there are vaults supported on wall-shafts and walls composed of tiers of pointed arcades, making it the first truly Gothic building in England.

The building of these great Yorkshire abbeys, mostly in remote valleys, were remarkable feats of organization for which there can have been no local precedents. At Rievaulx, to take one example, a canal over a mile long was specially cut for the transport of stone. Yet the severity and restraint enjoined by the Cistercian Order on its builders kept them to a great extent, especially in the north of England, from fully exploiting in their architecture the aesthetic potentialities of Gothic. The choir at Canterbury, adventurous to a degree and therefore a landmark in the history of English architecture, is Gothic at its most French. But it was not long before English Gothic developed characteristics of its own, some equally daring and original. A typically English Gothic emerged at Worcester (1170), at Wells (*c*.1180), in the retro-choir at Chichester (1187–99) and at Lincoln (begun 1192). In the nave at Worcester are the first clustered shafts, reinforcing the vertical emphasis of the new style.

The planning of most of the newly built English cathedrals, moreover, developed on different lines from the French. In contrast to the French-style chevet, or cluster of chapels, at the east end, to be seen at Canterbury and afterwards at Westminster

OPPOSITE

Westminster Abbey: from the roof of the Houses of Parliament. This view illustrates the layout of a great abbey church and its monastic buildings. These span several centuries. In the distance are the twin western towers rebuilt by Nicholas Hawksmoor in 1745. Nearer are the cruciform roofs of the abbey church, with flying buttresses supporting the high stone vaults: first the nave, finished later than the rest (not till the end of the fifteenth century); then the choir, built from 1245 onwards when Henry III began the process of rebuilding the Norman abbey that stood on the same site. Westminster Abbey is very French in its proportions and plan, and below the east end of the choir can be seen the chevet – or cluster of chapels – a typically French feature. Extending beyond these is Henry VII's Chapel, added in 1503, surrounded by the stone pinnacles that weigh down its buttresses. To the left of the church are the chapter-house and cloisters, both of 1249, and to the left of these the site of the monastic buildings, of which only fragments remain incorporated in ecclesiastical dwellings and in parts of Westminster School. (The monks' dormitory, for example, is now the school hall.)

OVERLEAF LEFT

Westminster Abbey: ceiling of King Henry VII's Chapel. The chapel was built in 1503–12 as an addition to the east end of the thirteenth-century abbey church by Henry VII and completed by Henry VIII as a chantry chapel for his father. It is richly sculptured, the climax being this daringly constructed ceiling of fan-shaped stone pendants behind which the ribs of the groined roof disappear.

OVERLEAF RIGHT

York Minster: from the north. This flank view of the whole cathedral except the nave and western towers illustrates the several periods during which it was built. At left is the Lady Chapel with its pinnacled buttresses (1361–1423); then, obscuring most of the choir, the chapter-house and its vestibule (1280–90) with their Decorated windows; then the gabled end of the north transept (1225–55) with tall lancet windows – typically Early English. These are the famous 'five sisters' filled with 'grisaille' glass of 1250–75. Behind the transept rises the central tower (1408–23 but not completed until the 1470s – the very end of the Perpendicular period).

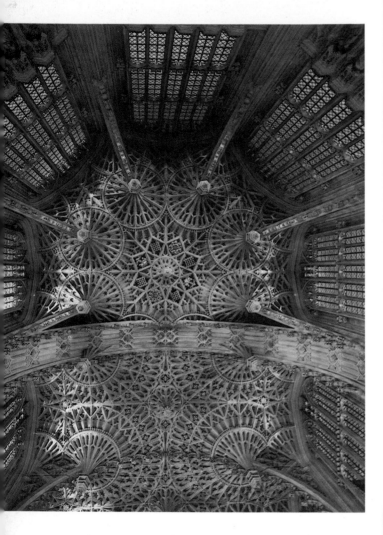

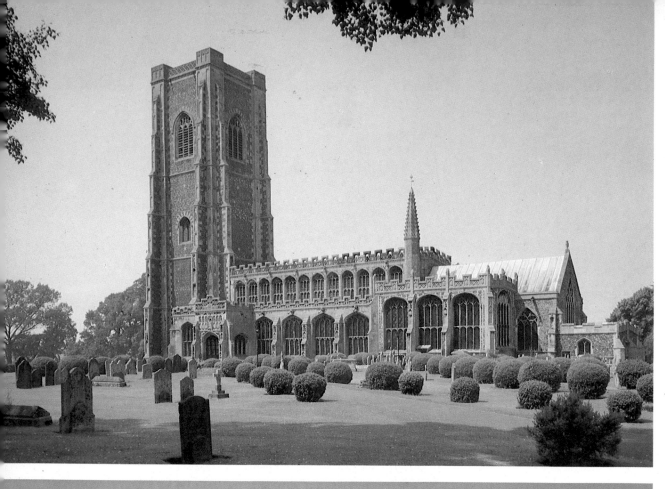

Lincoln Cathedral: from the north-west. The cathedral dominates the landscape from its high ground in the centre of the city and would do so even more dramatically if it still had the spires that crowned its three towers in the Middle Ages. Lincoln is the supreme example, inside and out, of Early English architecture, being nearly all of the thirteenth century except for small parts of the west front, which remain from a Norman building of 1092, and except for the upper stages of the towers, which were not completed until 1375.

OPPOSITE ABOVE
Lavenham, Suffolk. One of the most spacious of the large, richly appointed parish churches that East Anglia owes to the prosperity of the cloth trade. This reached its peak in the fifteenth century and so Lavenham Church is for the most part Perpendicular with the characteristic large clerestory windows filling the interior with light. Only the chancel is Decorated. To the south of the latter (right of picture) is a chantry chapel endowed by the Spring family, clothiers of Lavenham, who were among the church's many rich patrons. The tower, of 1486–95, flint with stone dressings, is of impressive height though unfinished. (See Chapter 4.)

OPPOSITE BELOW
Yaxley, Cambridgeshire. The elegant steeple commands the rural landscape. It is Perpendicular, with delicately modelled buttresses, three-light bell-openings and flying buttresses at the base of the spire. The church, containing work of every medieval style after about 1300, has a complex plan with aisles to both chancel and transepts. (See Chapter 4.)

Abbey, most of the English cathedrals built square east ends. Some had a double transept. They treated their interiors as a succession of compartments while the French aimed at spatial unity, and their extreme length contrasted with the French emphasis on height. In spite of their lack of height, however, the English cathedrals stand out from their surroundings as prominently as the French. They are not so closely set round by the buildings of the town; in fact they often stand apart in their own close or monastic precinct.

The supreme example of Early English (as Thomas Rickman named the first phase of Gothic when he differentiated its successive styles in 1817) is Lincoln Cathedral. Wells was the first English cathedral wholly in the pointed style but, exquisite though it is, its interior has not the aspiring quality of Lincoln. At Wells the three-tier nave is still subdivided horizontally; there are no wall-shafts soaring from pier to vault as there are at Lincoln, which is more assured and technically self-confident than anything built at that time in England or France. Lincoln is consistent throughout except for the Norman parts of its west front which are survivals from an earlier structure. And even though it has lost its three spires, its external aspect is one of the most dramatic of any cathedral.

Other English masterpieces from the first years of the thirteenth century include the west porch at

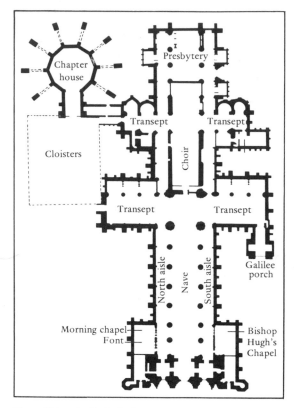

Plan of Lincoln Cathedral.

tween them a triforium that appears compressed and somewhat ungainly.

Early English Gothic had become an elegant, disciplined and clearly identifiable style, seen at its best, though in miniature, in the Lady Chapel at Salisbury's east end. Early English interiors had gained lightness and grace from their vertical lines of clustered columns and tall lancet windows; also from new refinements in stone vaulting, which by now, in nearly all the major churches, had replaced the wooden ceilings hitherto more usual. A surviving example of these wood ceilings, dating from 1220, can be seen at Peterborough Cathedral.

Wells Cathedral: interior of the chapter-house. This is the meeting place of the clergy who administer the cathedral; they sit round the walls. Most chapter-houses are approached through the cloisters but at Wells, where there are none, it is reached by a flight of steps from the north aisle of the choir. Built at the end of the thirteenth century, it has a high vaulted roof supported on a central column. It is polygonal in shape like those at nine of the English cathedrals. Worcester is the earliest (1120) of these; Lincoln the largest. The originally monastic cathedrals of Bristol, Canterbury, Chester, Gloucester and Oxford have rectangular chapter-houses.

Peterborough, the Galilee porch projecting from the west end at Ely and the sculpture-filled west front at Wells. These were followed by an even greater enterprise, the whole cathedral at Salisbury, begun in 1220; for Salisbury was not, like most of the others, a rebuilding, comprehensive or partial, but a fresh start on an unencumbered site, made when Salisbury town was moved down from Old Sarum to the Avon valley. The cathedral was built in a relatively short time – thirty-eight years except for the central tower and spire – and so is consistent throughout. More than most others, however, its interior suffers from the difficulty of fitting the customary three tiers of arches – main arcade, triforium (the gallery at the level of the aisle roof) and clerestory windows – into the moderate height to which the English cathedral builders limited themselves without cramping one or more of them. Among the Early English interiors the nave at Lincoln probably manages this best. At Salisbury there is a handsome nave arcade and a clerestory beautifully integrated with the vaulting, but be-

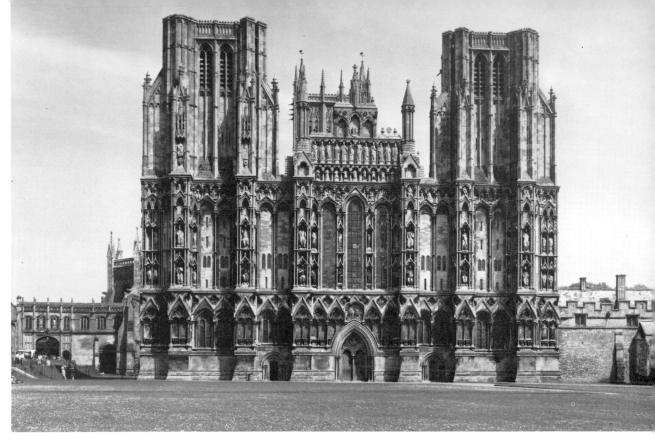

Wells Cathedral: the west front. The early part of the thirteenth century when this was built – it was begun in 1220 – was a period of variety and inventiveness in cathedral west fronts (see also Lincoln, begun 1125, and Peterborough with its three huge arches, built 1193–1220). The front at Wells is rich in sculpture and its great width is relieved from flatness by the square buttresses that project forwards and outwards. The doorways are surprisingly small compared with French cathedrals of similar date, such as Amiens or Reims, where the west fronts are dominated by cavernous porches expressive of the great spaces within and serving as gateways between the town square and the cathedral interior. English west fronts have more the nature of facades or screens and seldom suggest the spaces that lie behind.

Early English exteriors, too, extended upwards in the form of slender towers and spires. Carved decoration had been developed by then to a remarkable degree, as in the foliated capitals of Wells and Southwell. It is therefore somewhat confusing that the term Decorated should be reserved, in Rickman's classification, for the still newer style of the hundred years that followed. It is true, however, that decoration became in those years less restricted in relation to the structure, and the ornament more naturalistic; also that the greatly favoured curvilinear forms, especially after the introduction of the ogee arch, deserve the name Decorated when they are contrasted with the severer rectilinear forms of the next period, called by Rickman Perpendicular.

Perhaps the most significant innovation of the Decorated period was, however, as much structural as aesthetic, and once again it was introduced from France. This was bar tracery, first employed at Reims in 1211: moulded ribs or mullions subdividing the windows and, when they branched or intersected, forming geometrical figures. Besides introducing a new decorative element into the architecture, they permitted the enlargement of the window area. Bar tracery can thus be seen as part of the further progress towards Gothic architecture's ultimate elimination of the wall and substitution of the stone skeleton.

Once more we can identify the first comprehensive use of the Decorated style with a direct importation from France; this was in the new Westminster Abbey, designed in 1245 to replace the Norman abbey. It had an unusual number of typical French features: great height and a chevet of chapels at the east end. But these were not widely imitated elsewhere. As in the case of the Early English style,

43

the Decorated style developed on lines peculiar to England, notably in the Angel choir at Lincoln and in the nave at Lichfield, two of its finest manifestations. In the former especially the large traceried windows already suggest the coming predominance of glass over wall. At Lichfield the problem already referred to of fitting three superimposed arcades into a moderate total height is solved in an interesting way by making the clerestory windows triangular, thus giving them width without an appearance of squatness and still leaving room for a high triforium.

In the nave at York Minster (begun 1291), treatment of the interior walling as one unit was taken a step further by the triforium being enclosed within the outermost frame of the clerestory windows and the latter separated by wall-shafts continuous from floor to vault. The boldest structural experiment – one without precedent – was

Plan of Westminster Abbey.

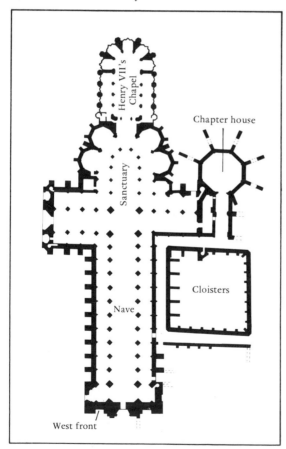

made at Ely. The cathedral's Norman central tower collapsed in 1322 and an octagon of highly original construction was built over the crossing to replace it, crowned by a timber lantern. The Ely octagon, unlike other experiments by the medieval master-carpenters and master-masons, set no subsequent fashion. It remains unique. But another new step forward was made at the same time which was followed up in many other buildings. The falling Norman tower destroyed three bays of the choir, and these were rebuilt with vaults in which lierne ribs (cross-ribs between one main rib and another) divided the vaulted surface into star-shaped compartments. This was the first step leading towards the complex patterned vaults of the next century.

Around the end of the thirteenth century and the beginning of the fourteenth, Exeter and Bristol cathedrals were almost wholly rebuilt. They are the English cathedrals most consistently in the Decorated style, displaying its characteristic smoothly rounded nature, markedly different from the crisper but stiffer simplicity of the preceding Early English style, a difference reinforced by the nave arches not being so pointed. Exeter has a particularly imaginative ribbed vault. Bristol is unusual in being a hall-church, that is, one with nave and aisles of the same height and therefore with no clerestory lighting and with stone arches across the aisles performing the function of the usual buttresses. It is to be noted, incidentally, that except at Westminster Abbey nearly all the pioneering moves that brought Gothic architecture forward into another era took place in cathedrals of the 'old foundation'. The unique position even of the wealthiest monastic houses was beginning to decline with the growth of the orders of preaching friars, the spread of education and the rise of the town-dwelling merchant class.

It may have been noticed that just as the Norman period, together with the beginning of its transition

Gloucester Cathedral: the choir and great east window. Replacing a Norman choir, this was completed in 1350 and is the first structure to show all the characteristics of Perpendicular architecture: panelled walls divided by continuous wall-shafts into emphatically vertical compartments; large windows with tracery in the form of rectangular panels. The vaulting has a complex pattern of lierne ribs. The east window is the largest in any cathedral – so wide in fact that the walls of the choir are splayed outwards at the end to make room for it.

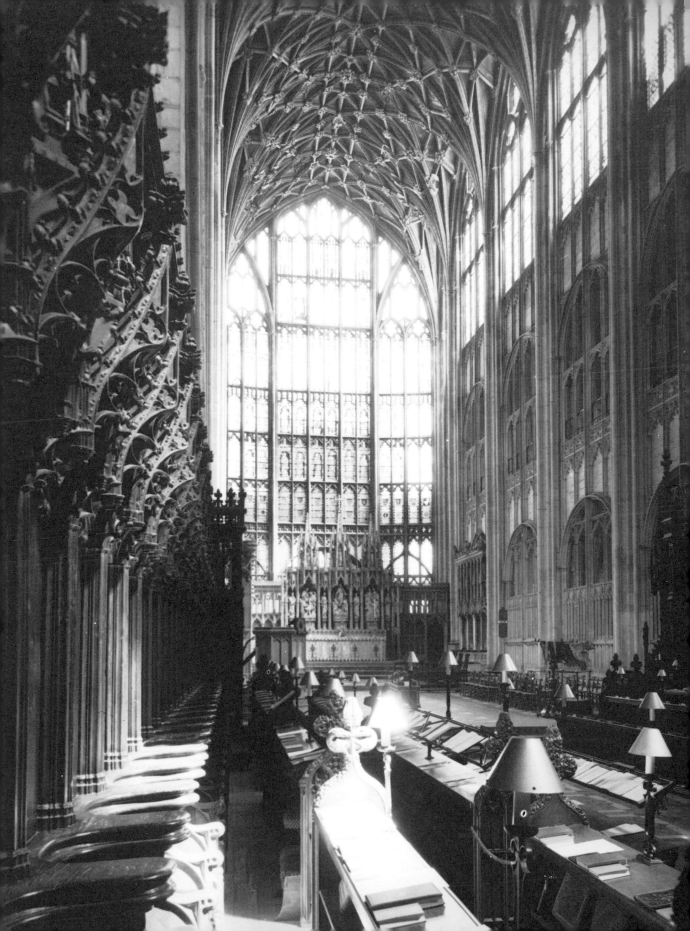

Salisbury Cathedral: the cloisters. Cloisters are arcaded and vaulted walks, enclosing an open quadrangle and connecting an abbey church with the domestic parts of a monastery. They survive in several cathedrals where the other monastic buildings have disappeared. They were usually placed in the angle between the nave and south transept, where it was sunniest and most sheltered. The cloisters at Salisbury are unusual because the cathedral was never part of a monastery; they serve as the approach to the chapter-house. Thirteenth-century like the rest of the cathedral, they have windows with Decorated tracery and are the earliest as well as the largest cloisters in England.

towards Gothic, lasted roughly for a hundred years (1050 to 1150), the Early English and the Decorated each lasted for another hundred. So by 1350 still another change was on the way, although at first it was only gradual; one style merged into another as the bolder masons became more daring while the more conservative preferred the safety of what had been done before. The remarkable thing about the new, late fourteenth-century style is that unlike its predecessors it was not based on innovations from abroad. From the fourteenth century until the sixteenth, when England was pursuing her solitary path into the final phase of Gothic (often separately

classified as Tudor), the Continent had already embarked upon the Renaissance; or in so far as France, by whom England had been continuously influenced, still built in Gothic it was flamboyantly curvilinear – an absolute contrast to the new English style with its emphasis on vertical lines.

England now had fewer cultural connections with the Continent, having lost nearly all her French territories by the end of the Hundred Years War. The English language was coming into use in place of French in parliament and the law courts, although records were kept in Latin and French for some while afterwards, and architecturally England set off in a direction peculiarly her own, creating the Perpendicular style which has a special place in any account of English architectural history, being unique in the world. It is seen at its most impressive in the new nave at Canterbury, begun in 1379 and one of the masterpieces of mature English Gothic. This was designed by Henry Yevele who had become the King's master-mason in 1360. Until his death in 1400 he also worked on a new nave for Westminster Abbey, replacing the Norman nave, but here he allowed himself to be influenced to some extent by the Decorated design of the choir. Along with William of Wykeham and William of Wynford, Yevele is the best known of the master-masons who can be regarded as the forerunners of the professional architect. The names of many others are known, men who worked on the major English churches as far back in some instances as the twelfth century, and some of the buildings for which they were responsible have been identified. The exact part they played is not always clear, but they undoubtedly had the leading role in advancing the art of architecture generation by generation. They moved during their careers from one building site to another and therefore widely influenced the nation-wide spread of the successive styles.

The Perpendicular style's emphasis on the vertical, which the tall arcade of the Canterbury nave well exemplifies, had already been a characteristic of the preceding period with its wall-shafts soaring

Development of Gothic vaulting: (top) Early English rib vaulting at Salisbury Cathedral and Westminster Abbey; (centre) Decorated vaulting at Exeter and Bristol cathedrals with lierne ribs added; (below) Perpendicular vaulting: star vault at St Mary's Church, Recliffe, Bristol; fan vault in the cloisters of Gloucester Cathedral.

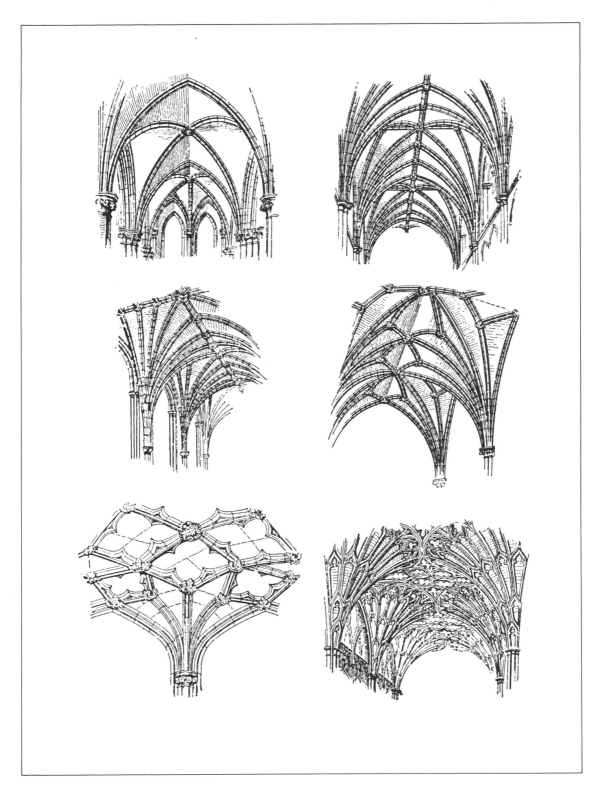

from floor to vault. The new emphasis was equally on the sense of space that refinement of the structure was able to create, and especially on light, which flooded the interiors following a dramatic reduction in the size of piers and other supporting elements. Unity as well as verticality were achieved by panelling nearly every masonry surface, inside and out.

The centuries-long division of the interior walls into three arcaded tiers was overlaid by a new wall-treatment in which the dominating element was the unbroken cluster of ribs between which main arcade, triforium and clerestory were united by the enclosing panelling. This transformation is first seen in the choir at Gloucester (1337–50). By the time the Lady Chapel in the same cathedral had been completed a century later the whole wall had almost become one large window. Choir and Lady Chapel were roofed with vaults made more complex than ever before by a pattern of intersecting ribs with carved bosses, and at Gloucester there emerged as well, in the cloisters begun in 1370, the ultimate in complex stone roofing, the fan vault – a decorative, not a structural, innovation. The choir at Sherborne Abbey was likewise roofed with a fan vault. Contrasting with such richness, Perpendicular window tracery was reduced to regular rectangular compartments, elaborated only by simple cusping.

The later Perpendicular age was also an age of graceful towers. Many cathedrals of earlier date are crowned with towers added or rebuilt in the fifteenth century. Their slender proportions, turretted silhouettes and elaborately panelled walls give an outline to English cathedral (and indeed many other) towns that is far less common on the Continent. Gloucester again is an example. Its central tower was begun in 1450. Equally splendid are the towers of Canterbury, Worcester and York, the central tower at Durham and the twin western towers at Beverley Abbey.

One phase of Gothic remains – again a phase peculiar to England: the Tudor style that developed after the middle of the fifteenth century, that is, at the end of the Wars of the Roses when England at last acquired a far-sighted and enterprising king in the person of Henry VII. Among the Tudor characteristics are the four-centred arch, introduced for use over doors and windows, and the ever more elaborate vaulting. This was no longer a period of great church building activity. Apart from the rebuilding of Bath Abbey (1501–39) and the

addition of a new nave to Ripon Cathedral (1502–22), the most important major ecclesiastical buildings of this time took the form of chapels rather than churches. They therefore did not have to provide the latter's sequence of spaces each with its own function, and the previously sought-after unity of space could be finally achieved, with the loss however of nearly all the sense of mystery that, in the earlier phases of Gothic, had been created by one space being barely visible from another and by gloom being contrasted with brightness. In the grandest of these chapels, that at King's College, Cambridge (begun in 1446), the tendency for the windows to occupy the greater part of the wall surface was taken as far as was structurally possible. Windows, the panelled walls below them and the fan vault of forty-foot span make an indivisible whole. Other examples are St George's Chapel, Windsor, and Eton College Chapel. Henry VII's Chapel at Westminster Abbey (1503–12) has round the outside polygonal buttresses weighted by elaborate pinnacles which also support the flying buttresses above. The vault inside has stone pendants descending from a daring fan-like structure derived from timber roof-construction. This is late Gothic at its most ornate and florid. Another vault of similar character roofs the choir of Christ Church Cathedral, Oxford (1480–1500). There is also a panelled fan vault over the hall stair at Christ Church built as late as 1640, by which date even in England the Renaissance had long taken over. It illustrates the hankering after the picturesqueness and flexibility of Gothic which led England to begin reviving Gothic styles before the end of the eighteenth century. It is a question indeed whether the hall stair at Christ Church should not be classed as a precocious beginning of that Gothic Revival which meant so much to the nineteenth century.

King's College Chapel, Cambridge. Completed in 1515, this represents the climax of English Gothic. It consists in effect of one great space. The walling is the minimum that will support the roof, permitting huge windows that flood the whole interior, 80 feet high, with light. The use of flat, four-centred arches and the fan-vaulted roof are also characteristic of the final, Tudor, phase of the Perpendicular style. The oak screen carrying the organ and dividing the nave from the choir on the far side was made in 1533 by an Italian sculptor and was one of the first works in England in a pure Renaissance style.

Chapter 4

The Parish Church: Regional Variations

Clifton Campville, Staffordshire. A large stone-built church for a small population, mostly of 1300–50; simple in form, including the prominent tower with recessed spire supported by flying buttresses. The chancel is Early English but its large east window is Decorated, with a good example of reticulated tracery.

ENGLAND has about twenty thousand parish churches of which nearly half are medieval – or basically medieval, for a great many have been altered, restored or refurnished at various times. Between them they reflect the many influences that have shaped English medieval architecture, in some ways more fully than do the greater churches – the cathedrals and abbeys – described in Chapter 3, for they embody local as well as national history. The greater churches show some regional variations but the architectural story they illustrate is on the whole a national story – indeed for all but the last century and a half of the Middle Ages, that is, up to about 1450, an international story – whereas the parish churches reflect in many illuminating ways the differences, geological, economic and social, between one region of England and another.

At the time they were built, and for centuries afterwards, the parish churches and their graveyards were the focus of the community life of every town or village. They were designed not only for the glory of God and for parish worship but to show off local wealth, collective or individual. They were embellished inside with monuments, windows and the like commemorating persons of importance. Their interiors are in every sense repositories of local history. There had been parish churches before the Norman Conquest, served by priests who were under the control of the bishops rather than the all-powerful monasteries. Many were rebuilt in the eleventh and twelfth centuries and after the thirteenth they increased rapidly in size and number – especially in size because of the activities of the new orders of preaching friars and the popularity of building chantry chapels (where masses were said for the souls of those they commemorated) within the parish church rather than, as previously, in the local abbey church. In the fourteenth and fifteenth centuries, too, parish churches obtained new financial support from the trade guilds, who set up their own altars and chapels.

51

Sandwich, Kent. The central tower and the tower arches are all that remain of a cruciform Norman church. The chancel is Early English and the nave fifteenth-century; both of flint and stone. The triple nave with no clerestory is characteristic of Kent.

In most English villages the church was – and still is – in the most literal sense of the word the outstanding feature; the largest and by far the oldest building. This was true also in most of the towns (except those which had developed round a prominently sited castle or abbey) until the early nineteenth century when industrial structures like textile mills, and then secular buildings of many other kinds, first began to compete in bulk with the parish church. The church tower still rises above most of these. The tower indeed was a feature of church architecture whose role was to call attention to its presence from afar as well as to summon worshippers by means of the bells it accommodated.

The architectural styles of the English parish church follow the same succession that has already been described in Chapter 3; for the cathedrals and abbeys, the subject of that chapter, were the models from which styles and fashions filtered downwards either through direct imitation or through masons and carpenters who had worked on the greater churches moving about the countryside to work on parish churches also. Variations on these styles common to one area evolved through the masons engaged to build or improve one church being instructed to copy some admired feature in an existing church nearby. Some cathedral chapters and religious houses, moreover, employed a permanent master-mason whose duties included the care of surrounding parish churches. He thus spread throughout the area the latest architectural fashions and technical improvements – or, more often, simplified versions of them, since the parish had not the money to build as elaborately as the cathedral or abbey.

There is no need to repeat here in detail the sequence of styles as it evolved over the centuries; it has already been described in relation to the cathedrals and abbeys. First came the massive-walled simplicity of the Saxon and the round-arched Norman (some parish churches of these periods were mentioned in Chapter 1); then the spare elegance of the Early English style, made suddenly more spacious by the new conception of structure that came in with the pointed arch; then the richer, more flowing Decorated style; then the even more spacious Perpendicular with its pronounced vertical lines, its interiors now flooded with light, and finally the equally wide-windowed Tudor style with its low four-centred arches and nostalgic fascination with heraldry. Only the last style in the sequence is missing in the case of the parish church, for the Tudor period was not a church-building age although churches built in the preceding periods contain many Tudor monuments and other embellishments.

The great age of the parish church was the fourteenth and fifteenth centuries when there were long intervals of civil peace and the growth of trade brought prosperity to many areas. A favourite way of expending the newly available wealth was by building new churches and enlarging old ones. The latter practice explains why so many medieval parish churches contain the work of different periods in the same building.

In many parts of England sheep-rearing, encouraged by the shortage of labour resulting from the Black Death of the mid-fourteenth century,

Development of window tracery: (top left) plate tracery; (top right) geometrical tracery; (bottom left) curvilinear or flamboyant tracery; (bottom right) Perpendicular tracery with a transom dividing the window horizontally.

brought sudden wealth through the export of wool to Flanders, the Low Countries and elsewhere, and some of the finest parish churches in England are to be found in the regions where wool was grown: from Somerset and the Cotswolds right across England to Suffolk, Lincolnshire and the North Riding of Yorkshire. In the fourteenth century weaving, too, became an English industry and there developed a profitable export trade in cloth as well as wool. This new wealth inspired townsmen and villagers, supported by the local merchants and gentry, to build anew, each town or village endeavouring to rival its neighbour in the splendour of its church. In

Fairford, Gloucestershire. This late Perpendicular church is consistent in style throughout because it was totally rebuilt, except for the base of the tower, in 1490–1500 by John Tame, a local wool merchant, and his son Sir Edmund Tame. The beautiful stonework and rich ornamentation, such as the pinnacles along each battlemented parapet and on the tower, suggest that no expense was spared. The church has the very large windows of the period, which still retain their complete equipment of stained glass.

OPPOSITE

Bere Regis, Dorset. Of mixed periods, like so many English parish churches, this is basically a twelfth-century addition to an even earlier church, but it was extended in about 1300 and the fine upstanding tower is Perpendicular – a good example of flint and stone chequer-work. Inside, Bere Regis has the best timber roof in Dorset.

some places far larger churches were erected than the surrounding population can possibly have required.

A great part of the riches of English church architecture is due to the fortunate fact that nearly all the sheep-rearing regions are those possessing a good building stone – limestone for the most part. This is not a coincidence: the band of limestone that runs diagonally across England is not generally an area of rich soils suitable for arable farming but it produces abundant grass for sheep to feed on, and the result is the spacious stone-built churches, with lofty towers and elaborate porches, tracery and carved ornament such as only fine-grained stone – combined with money – makes possible. In areas with richer soils, agriculture may have provided as good a living, but not the same disposable wealth.

The availability of building materials is thus, even

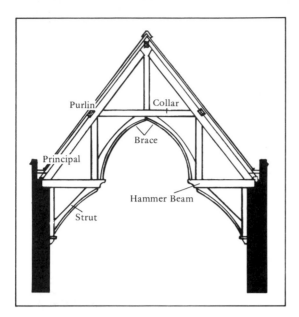

Construction of a hammer-beam roof.

the pitch of nave and chancel roofs became flatter in the fourteenth century with the introduction of lead for covering. Woolpit and Kersey, both in Suffolk, are good examples. There followed the more ambitious hammer-beam roofs of the fifteenth century (Wymondham and Necton, Norfolk, and Needham Market, Suffolk) and finally the double-hammer-beam (Knapton, Norfolk, and Grundisburgh, Suffolk). Mildenhall, Suffolk, has tie-beams alternating with hammer-beams and there are other variations on the theme. Another prosperous area lacking stone but enterprising in its use of timber is Cheshire. (That county's black and white timber-framed houses are noted in the next chapter.) There the tradition is one of flat timber roofs, carved and sometimes painted (Witton and Barthomley). In areas with suitable timber, pitched roofs were covered with wood shingles rather than tiles, which were themselves (when roofs had not been flattened and covered with lead) gradually superseding thatch.

The above are only examples. There is in fact no end to the architectural influence of local materials. The wooded clay-lands of the south-east had a varied architecture based largely on timber. The sandstones of the Midlands produced a stone vernacular style with more rounded forms than that of the harder, close-grained limestone. The granites further north (and in Devon and Cornwall), though too hard to be freely used and far too hard to carve, created a local tradition of simplicity and severity. Stone-tiled roofs and churchyards with slate gravestones indicate in other places the nature of the underlying geology. When the walls of churches were of inferior rubble stone, such as local field-stones, they were usually plastered for better protection from the weather. Plastered walls, however, with fine-jointed imported ashlar for

more than the influence of particular master-masons, the reason why parish churches differ so much between one region and another. Nevertheless, because of the cost and the technical skill required, even in areas possessing good building stone, churches wholly of ashlar (cut stone) are rare. Walls are usually of roughly squared stone, cut stone being used for the corners of towers and buttresses, and for porches, window-surrounds and tracery. East Anglia, the only one of the rich sheep-rearing areas that has no building stone, was for that reason unable to make so fine a display of the stonemason's art; nor could it draw on a tradition of expert masonry. But its wealth enabled it to import the necessary minimum of stone. The towers of the Norfolk churches, though less ornate, are seen from greater distances across the flatter landscape. In compensation for not being able to display such handsomely ornamented towers as those of the Somerset churches in the absence of a suitable building stone, or sculptured porches like those of Gloucestershire, the East Anglian churches are enriched inside by splendid open timber roofs which became a local speciality as well as an art that no country outside England could rival.

The first such roofs were tie-beam roofs, often with curved braces, which were evolved soon after

Necton, Norfolk : hammer-beam roof. East Anglia is famous for this type of carpentered roof, much used in the fifteenth century to span the wide naves and chancels erected in this prosperous region. The Necton roof alternates hammer-beams with plain braced arches. It was customary to decorate hammer-beams (as at Westminster Hall, London, page 76) with carved wooden angels; at Necton there are also upright figures in niches at the springing of each arch. The roof still has much of its medieval colouring. Necton Church has a commanding western tower of correct thirteenth-century pattern but most surprisingly dating from 1865.

Huish Episcopi, Somerset. This has one of the handsome Perpendicular towers for which Somerset is famous. They are all recognizably of the same type but there are minor differences, especially between those in the north of the county – in the Mendips – and those in the south and west – the Quantocks – no doubt the work of different groups of masons. The Huish Episcopi tower is typical of those in the Quantocks. It is 100 feet high and has multi-pinnacled corner buttresses, windows and bell-openings similarly ornamented and the typical Somerset pierced parapet, also with pinnacles. The church was originally twelfth-century but was remodelled in the fourteenth and fifteenth. It is of blue lias stone with Ham Hill stone dressings.

window-surrounds, quoins, buttresses and the like, are not now so common as in the past because the plaster has been removed by church restorers, inside as well as out, to expose poor quality stone walling that was never meant to be seen.

The impressive number of huge East Anglian churches already referred to were mostly walled with flint. Some of the minor Norfolk churches have round towers, a means of avoiding corners that would need stone, and at Hales there is even a curved east end of the twelfth century, all in flint. Such an intractable material as flint evolved nevertheless its own technique of decoration: knapped flint panels set flush into a pattern of stone tracery (the south porch at Kersey and the tower at Eye, both in Suffolk; St Michael at Coslany, in the city of Norwich; the gateway of St Osyth's Priory, Essex).

It should be added that brick, in later centuries the alternative to stone, is found only in a few very late medieval churches. Bricks, though used by the Romans, were not made again in England until the fourteenth century and were not widely used until later still. As a result of trade with Holland they then became common in East Anglia, but less for churches than for houses.

Even when it could be imported, stone remained expensive to work, so the stone-vaulted roofs that are so impressive a feature of the greater churches are a rarity in parish churches. The complex science of vaulting, moreover, cannot have been mastered by any but a few master-masons. A certain amount of stone roofing is nevertheless to be found in the limestone regions, especially in the North Riding of Yorkshire, and a good number of prosperous churches elsewhere have vaulting over small areas such as porches and chapels (there is a fan-vaulted chapel at Cirencester) and the lower stages of their towers.

The clearest indication that a church is in an area with good building stone, or in one with access to such areas by water (the cheapest way of transporting stone), is the possession of an outstanding tower, and among the greatest architectural glories of the parts of England made wealthy by wool are the towers of their parish churches. Again the favoured pattern in each area is different; more so than in the case of other parts of the church since the tower, not having a liturgical function, was especially susceptible to the vagaries of fashion. In Somerset, for example, a distinctive type of tall square tower emerged in the fifteenth century, Perpendicular in its general form but with a characteristic style derived from its elaborate parapets, its tall windows lighting the bell-chamber filled with pierced stonework and its multiplicity of pinnacles (Bruton, Taunton and Huish Episcopi). Other stone-bearing areas show variations on the same theme: sculptured pinnacles at St Neots, formerly Huntingdonshire, hexagonal or octagonal lanterns (Lowick, Northamptonshire; Boston, Lincolnshire).

In Lincolnshire and the East Midlands, more than anywhere else, church towers are crowned with stone spires. They spread from there south-westwards as far as Gloucestershire. Spires go back to the thirteenth century, when the device called a broach was introduced: half-pyramids at the base of the spire, which is usually octagonal, to effect the geometrical transition from the octagon to the square of the tower. Broach spires rising straight from the face of the tower are most typical of the Early English churches of Lincolnshire, Huntingdonshire and Northamptonshire. Later there were parapets concealing the junction of tower and spire, with or without pinnacles, and occasionally flying buttresses to elaborate the junc-

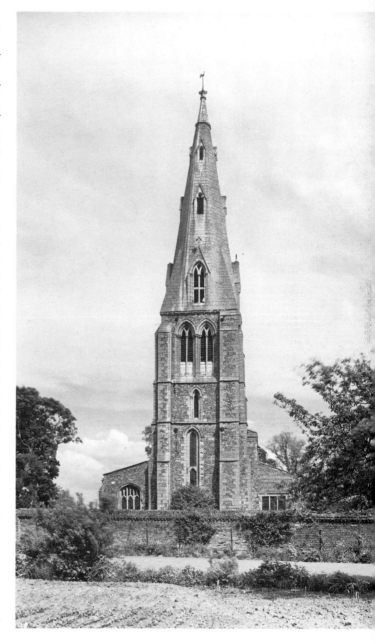

Warboys, Cambridgeshire. This broach spire is a graceful specimen of a type common in Early English churches, especially in the East Midlands. There is no parapet where the spire sits on the tower; instead, the transition from square to octagon is smoothly made by the geometrical device of half-pyramids at the corners. The tower has the rectangular buttresses and lancet windows of the early thirteenth century. The chancel of the church was rebuilt in yellow brick in 1832.

Badley, Suffolk. A humble village church interior, completely unrestored, of the Perpendicular period. It is aisle-less with plastered walls, exposed roof beams and seventeenth-century box pews.

tions, as at Yaxley (see page 40). Small timber spires, covered with lead, can be found in all parts.

The plan of the English parish church can be regarded in its basic simplicity as a descendant of the rectangular Saxon plan, though memory of the latter would have been too remote for copying. The parish church, even the most spacious, is not a smaller version of the cathedral or abbey church since the needs of a lay congregation were quite different from those of monks and secular canons who planned

their churches first of all for the services, devotions and processions required by their vocations. The essential elements of the parish church plan are the nave and the chancel, and some modest churches consist of little else. These are separated, to a greater or lesser degree according to liturgical preferences, or the custom of the time and the locality, by a chancel arch and a – usually wooden – rood-screen.

Denston, Suffolk. A contrast to Badley, this is the interior of a spacious, lavishly endowed fifteenth-century church of which there are many in the regions made wealthy by the cloth industry. It is wholly consistent late Perpendicular (about 1475) with a high nave arcade continuing into the chancel, moulded timber roof and oak benches of the period.

way of extending the church to create space for more altars was however to add transepts later. Other ways were to throw out side-chapels, to add an aisle (sometimes to one side only of an aisleless church) or to make chapels by extending an aisle eastwards. Some strangely shaped plans emerged from such successive additions year after year, in spite of the fact that all church plans began by being symmetrical (see Burford, page 62).

The most usual place for the tower was at the west end. Central towers are not uncommon, especially in south-western areas, and are generally a sign of a parish that was relatively prosperous, or had a wealthy patron, from an early date, for example in the thirteenth century. A central tower cannot be added, and in many cases was removed because the substantial piers that supported it impeded change, and the empty space beneath it, between nave and chancel, could not be fully used. When a west tower is of later date than the rest of the church it may mean that the nave has been lengthened and the tower added at the same time. This was a frequent method of enlarging churches in the fourteenth and fifteenth centuries.

The larger aisled churches had clerestory windows but, unlike the great cathedral churches, no triforium. The presence or absence of a clerestory is again subject to regional variation. It is uncommon, for example, in Kent. In the smaller churches the entrance was usually through the west tower or, in an area that for lack of stone or other reasons did not build towers, in the west end which was emphasized externally by some kind of bell-turret or roof structure, perhaps only of wood. In the case of most larger churches, including the 'wool' churches built anew in the fifteenth century, there was often a south porch leading directly into the nave. Unusually magnificent south porches are at Northleach and Cirencester, Gloucestershire. The latter, built in 1490, has such capacious upper storeys that from the dissolution of the monasteries until the eighteenth century the porch was used as the town hall. In some areas without much stone, such as Surrey and Essex, there is a tradition of elaborate wooden south porches.

Finally, church furniture: its richness, like the scale of the church itself, depended on the wealth of the locality, but also on benefactions from guilds and patrons and of course on the skill of available craftsmen. For these reasons quite poor churches often contain single monuments of surprising elaboration and artistic quality. East Anglia has already been mentioned as being famous for its ambitiously carpentered roofs. It is likewise famous for wooden screens enclosing chantries and chapels (Lavenham and Dennington, Suffolk), and carved pew-ends (Wiggenhall, Norfolk). Other parts of the country specialize in other types of furniture wherever a local school of craftsmen developed and if conditions have allowed enough examples to survive: carved doorways and capitals, unusually intricate tracery, sculptured monuments or stained and painted glass. Through these too, in accordance with the accidents of circumstance, the parish church of today recounts its own history. Sometimes the only evidence that a church is far older than the greater part of its structure is, for example, the survival of a Norman font.

Northleach, Gloucestershire: south porch. Such monumental porches are a feature of many of the Perpendicular 'wool' churches, especially in the Cotswolds. Cirencester has another. Northleach Church was entirely rebuilt in the fifteenth century. The porch has corner buttresses bearing niches for statues and terminating in crocketed pinnacles, and a miniature spire crowning the stair-turret. This leads to a chamber over the porch equipped with a fireplace, the chimney from which is concealed in the buttress and pinnacle alongside the stair.

Chapter 5

The Medieval Dwelling-House

WITH very few exceptions the oldest of the lesser houses, such as farmhouses and cottages, that remain scattered through the English countryside, though often referred to as medieval, date only from the sixteenth century, incorporating perhaps in some cases remnants of earlier buildings. So the history of the humbler house as we can observe it today had hardly begun in the period with which these first chapters are concerned. At the time when the cathedrals, abbeys, castles and parish churches described in the preceding chapters were being built, ordinary people, other than the retainers accommodated in the castles of the great men they served, lived in primitive huts of impermanent materials, built to last no longer than one or two generations. Most were of split logs or wattle and daub (sticks or osiers woven together and covered with clay mixed with chopped straw) and were roofed with thatch or sometimes turf.

From the thirteenth century onwards, however, as conditions became settled enough for country life in the open – that is, away from the heavily protected castles – and as the feudal system with its obligations of military service was adapted to allow the gentry time to cultivate their estates, substantial houses – manor-houses and houses for small land-owners – were built of more permanent materials such as stone (in parts of the country where stone was available) and stout timber framing.

It was still thought necessary that they should be fortified, though not made proof against besieging armies, and a few such houses survive with their defences largely intact; a moat perhaps and a gatehouse leading into a walled courtyard. Some such courtyards had suites of rooms looking into them, with larger windows than those facing outwards, for the process had begun of replacing the communal great hall by separate living-rooms. Nevertheless the hall remained in some form for a long time yet.

House at Swaffham Bulbeck, Cambridgeshire. Half-timber construction with the closely spaced timbers characteristic of the sixteenth century and before, and with plastered infill, probably wattle and daub. The over-sailing upper storey is formed by resting the wall frame on the projecting ends of the floor beams.

The houses that have lasted since the early Middle Ages are naturally those built of stone. But there is one knight's house, dating from the end of the thirteenth century, that is exceptional in being of brick, or, rather, a mixture of brick and flint with stone corners. This is Little Wenham Hall, Suffolk, the earliest known medieval building in which bricks (other than reused Roman bricks) are employed. These however are thought to have been shipped from Holland, with which country the East Anglian ports regularly traded. Brick-making, a familiar craft in Roman times, did not begin again in England until the fourteenth century and bricks were not widely used until the fifteenth.

Houses like Little Wenham Hall, which must at this date have had some outer defences in the shape of enclosing walls and outbuildings, give a clear idea of how simply quite well-to-do people, below the rank of the lord in his castle, were housed. The whole of the first floor is occupied by the living-hall and a chapel, and there is just one private chamber above. There are traceried windows of a type that might have adorned a village church, for there was no stylistic difference between domestic and ecclesiastical buildings. Internally there was no more comfort than in the strictly functional castle.

A somewhat grander house of half a century later, but hardly more comfortable, is the oldest part of Penshurst Place, Kent (1341). Outside it has moulded doorways and ornately traceried windows, which indicate a degree of wealth in the owner that is typical of the trend of the time, for he was not a nobleman but a London merchant, Sir John de Poultney, four times Lord Mayor. Although subsequently enlarged (in the sixteenth century and again afterwards) to convert it into quite a substantial mansion, Penshurst preserves its original core which resembles other fairly prosperous dwellings in being derived less from the Norman castle hall than from the Saxon assembly-hall.

This layout was composed of a single lofty hall with a screen at one end sheltering it from the

Little Wenham Hall, Suffolk; about 1270. A well-to-do gentleman's fortified house, it is of stone, flint and brick – the first known use of brick in England after the Romans. It has a vaulted ground floor but the main rooms, consisting of hall and chapel, are on the first floor reached by an outside stair. There is a sleeping chamber over the chapel.

68

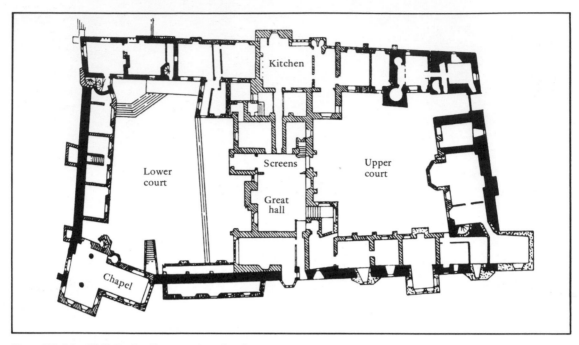

Plan of Haddon Hall, Derbyshire; remains of earliest
castle shown in black.

entrance and from a passage which led, between the buttery and the pantry, to the kitchens. At the opposite end was a dais for the owner and his family. Reached from the dais end were a chamber and family room with perhaps another sleeping-room (called a solar) above it. Remarkably, the same hall layout was carried over almost unaltered into the later and larger manor-house, into the pre-Renaissance palace and into every kind of college hall. It lasted in fact well into the seventeenth century.

In the smaller manor-houses the plan was simplified and consisted of little more than the hall, often without the screened passage (there may have been a light screen to prevent draughts from the entrance), without the formal dais and with just one or two private chambers. The even simpler farmhouse or yeoman's house maintained the tradition of the hall in the sense that the main accommodation was limited to one large room reaching up into the roof. Most such farmhouses have had an intermediate floor inserted since.

At the dissolution of the monasteries early in the sixteenth century, manor-houses multiplied as monastic lands were sold to the gentry and to the increasingly wealthy class of merchants from the towns. Some such houses indeed were built from the stones of ruined abbeys. They were designed for family use and for the administration of agricultural estates, and protected by nothing more than the fences that enclosed their private demesnes. These stood in close proximity to a village, its church and its cottages and farmsteads. Self-sufficient local communities grew up, with the occupier of the manor-house, who probably served as a magistrate, becoming – unlike the lord in his castle in the centuries before – an essential part of the social hierarchy of the countryside.

Penshurst Place, Kent; 1341 onwards: the great hall. Such a hall was the main living space of the medieval house and followed a standard pattern with open roof the full height of the building, dais for the master at one end and screened passage at the other. The passage led to the entrance and beyond it were the buttery, kitchens, etc. When the hall at Penshurst was built halls had no fireplaces, the smoke from the hearth in the centre finding its way out through louvres in the roof.

70

Great Chalfield Manor, Wiltshire; about 1470. This stone-built manor-house was not designed primarily for defence since the Wiltshire countryside was peaceful, but it still has a moat crossed by a bridge guarded by a gateway (which also leads to the parish church). The house has the typical great hall (left of entrance) with screened passage and bay windows at either side of the dais at the opposite end.

The later manor-houses (fifteenth- and sixteenth-century) possessed a far greater variety of rooms. More light was admitted through their much enlarged windows. Strong walls being no longer needed to withstand attack, quite large houses were now constructed of timber framing, especially in areas where stone would have had to be imported. This type of construction further facilitated the

enlargement of the windows and, since window-glass (introduced as a rare luxury at the end of the thirteenth century) was common by now, we find timber-framed houses built with very large windows. (Ockwells Manor, Berkshire, 1465, is a good example.)

In some parts of England, especially in Lancashire and Cheshire in the north-west and southwards from there into Shropshire and Herefordshire, there grew up a rich and spectacular tradition of timber houses with the framing close-set, making geometrical patterns. The most famous of these, Moreton Old Hall, Congleton, Cheshire (1559) has a top floor containing a long gallery like those that were a feature of the still larger Elizabethan palaces described in Chapter 7.

Rufford Old Hall, Lancashire, in the same style

but half a century earlier, has a very highly decorated hall and screened passage and a hammer-beam roof. Even at the close of the Middle Ages houses like those just mentioned, it will be seen, showed no sign of the Renaissance influence that was beginning to penetrate, in however amateurish a form, the mansions and palaces of the nobility. Interior arrangements, however, began gradually to improve, as did the privacy afforded by a greater variety of rooms; yet only at the very end of the sixteenth century were the middle classes living in any kind of comfort. Since the fourteenth century, woollen tapestries, previously imported from the Continent, had been made in England, and in prosperous houses cold stone walls had been commonly warmed by woollen hangings, but with no more need to safeguard the house from being set

on fire by an enemy, the walls could be lined internally by wainscoting or panelling. Comfortable furniture and better heating and sanitation remained for somewhat longer the privileges of the really rich.

The first important improvement to the structure of the house was the introduction of fireplaces and chimneys. Previously the hearth was on the floor of the hall and the smoke had to find its way out through louvres above the roof-timbers. This was still the system at Penshurst in spite of that house's relative opulence. The system probably explains the long continuance of the double-storey living hall, for only when there was a proper outlet for smoke could ceilings be made lower. Domestic fireplaces had existed as early as the thirteenth century, but they were rare and generally served the upper room only. The first chimneys were of wattle and clay, which easily caught fire. Stone chimneys were of course safer, but only when bricks came into regular use in the fifteenth century did the construction of chimneys become usual. From the sixteenth century the chimney became an important architectural feature, dominating the roofline of almost every house more pretentious than a cottage. Kent has a particularly widespread tradition of handsome chimneys. Almost everywhere cut and moulded bricks were used to decorate their caps and bases and their separate shafts were moulded and decorated – even twisted – so that in some houses the chimney-stacks took on an almost sculptural role.

As with parish churches, the architectural styles of houses of every kind, whether cottages, farm-houses or quite ambitious manor-houses, were local rather than national, changing with the building materials most freely available and the craft traditions founded on them. It was not until the fourteenth century that the labourer's cottage and the small farmhouse outgrew the primitive technique of the wattle-and-daub hut. Except where stone was easily dug up and transported, timber was the usual material, beginning in the first place with cruck construction. Crucks were slightly curved tree-trunks, leaning against each other in pairs and meeting at the ridge of the roof. To give head-room, wall-timbers and rafters were built out from these, and from this contrivance timber framing (also called half-timbering) developed as the built-out wall-posts and rafters became substantial enough for the original cruck to be discarded. Crucks can still

73

Cottage at Didbrook, Gloucestershire; about 1520. This illustrates the most primitive method of building in timber, known as cruck construction. Wall-timbers and beams are built outwards from inclined pairs of heavy timbers or 'crucks'.

Cruck construction.

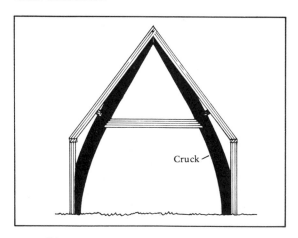

occasionally be seen (there is one, for example, at Didbrook in Gloucestershire) in the gable-ends of early wood and wattle-and-daub cottages.

The timber wall-frames, perched on a brick or stone base, were at first closely spaced. Later, as a result of a scarcity of strong timbers, they were built wider apart and the infill between the timbers became a more important structural element in the wall. The material used for this was wattle and daub or flints set in clay and plastered, or most commonly brick (called brick nogging) either laid horizontally or in a herring-bone pattern. In the south-east the upper part of a cottage was frequently hung with tiles. It was a good deal later, after soft wood had begun to be imported into England in the eighteenth century, that it was faced with the typically Kentish weather-boarding. Other materials were special to certain localities: chalk in the south (known as clunch when used as a building stone); a mixture of brick and flint in the south and Midlands (when the local sandstone was not available); cob in Devonshire, which was a mixture of mud and straw built up in layers, compressed by ramming and covered with plaster and whitewash. A covering of plaster was added to many materials to give extra protection from the weather. In East Anglia especially, the thick plaster protecting the wattle-and-daub infill was panelled and moulded into decorative patterns, a practice known as pargetting. Roof-coverings likewise varied with the locality: stone tiles – the most weather-proof of all but so heavy as to require more substantial roof-timbers – clay tiles, slates or thatch.

In many timber-framed houses, in order to make the upper rooms more spacious, the floor-beams were projected beyond the ground-floor walls and the walls above made to rest on their ends, creating the overhanging upper storeys familiar in ancient half-timbered houses and cottages. This was an especially common practice in the towns owing to the restricted sites. At the same time it strengthened the floors since the weight of the walls on the ends of the beams lifted some of the load from their centre – an indication of an increased understanding of the laws of mechanics on the part of ordinary builders, as distinct from the specialist builders of churches and cathedrals who had long mastered the complex mechanics of masonry construction.

Wood was not solely a rural building material. Except where stone was easily available – and not

Cottages at Brenchley, Kent. These show the forms of cottage construction and the materials typical of the late sixteenth and seventeenth centuries in regions where there was no building stone. Local builders followed these traditional practices for many years afterwards. Widely spaced timbers have brick or rubble stone infill, whitewashed. Tile-hanging gives extra protection from the weather. The half-hipped roof of the tile-hung house is a speciality of the south-east.

always then, because of the cost of transport and skilled labour – the towns that began to develop outside the castle walls and round the growing market centres from the thirteenth century onwards were almost wholly of wood. London was a city of wooden houses until the mid-seventeenth century; hence the devastation caused by the Great Fire. Few medieval town houses remain, not only because of the frequency of fires but because of repeated rebuildings to make better use of expensive sites. There is a good late example at Chipping Campden, Gloucestershire (Grevel House, of about 1400) with a tall bay window, and another of the early sixteenth century at Glastonbury (the Tribunal House) with a

flat-arched door and windows in typical Tudor style. The layout and accommodation of town houses were similar to those in the country except that merchants' houses often had storage space incorporated and, because of the narrow frontages available, they were turned at right angles so that their gable-ends faced the street.

The labourer's cottage, though now more solidly built, still had the most primitive kind of accommodation, arranged on one or two floors. These were usually divided into a number of equal-sized rooms about sixteen feet deep, a dimension based, it is believed, on the required depth of the shed that housed the draught and plough oxen – this shed, and a barn for storage, being the basic structures of every farm settlement. It will be noticed that in every grade of dwelling, from the humble cottage upwards to the rich man's residence, rooms still led out of one another. Separate entrances to rooms from hallways and passages were introduced in the architects' plans drawn up many years later; in fact most domestic apartments could only be reached by passing through another until as late as the eighteenth century.

Chapter 6

Expanding Needs: the First Community Buildings

FOR nearly the whole of the Middle Ages new developments in architecture, with the exception of fortress architecture and of the humblest dwellings, came through the initiative of the church, both structural developments and the styles and fashions related to them – hence the general title of Part One of this book. The history of English architecture is therefore in all important respects the history of ecclesiastical buildings. But towards the end of the period, in late Plantagenet and especially in Tudor times, as the feudal system was gradually discarded, as society became organized in other than military hierarchies and as trade and commerce came to play an increasing part in the national life, towns and to a small extent the countryside began to equip themselves with buildings that were neither churches, monasteries, fortresses nor dwellings.

A few of the earliest buildings that can be so described date however from before this time, but they were still built under the shadow of the church, though neither consecrated nor in all cases located within monastic precincts. These are the tithe barns in which the tithe, or tenth part of the produce of the soil which had to be set aside to provide an income for the church, was brought after harvest-time and stored. Simple in plan and with windowless, stone-walled exteriors, they have quite spectacular interiors almost cathedral-like in their scale, with open timber roofs that show great structural skill. Whatever their original connection with monastic buildings, they mostly stand now in the open countryside.

The most impressive surviving example is probably the barn at Great Coxwell, near Faringdon, Oxfordshire, built around the middle of the thirteenth century to serve as an outpost (of which nothing remains) of the Cistercian Abbey of Beaulieu in Hampshire. There is a fourteenth-century tithe barn at Bradford-on-Avon, Wiltshire, a fifteenth-century one at Tisbury, Wiltshire, two

Westminster Hall, London. First built by William Rufus in 1097 but remodelled in 1394 for Richard II by his master-mason Henry Yevele. The hall is a surviving part of the palace of Westminster and was used for banquets, trials and royal ceremonies. The oak roof of 1394, by the master-carpenter Hugh Herland, is the earliest hammer-beam roof known and the finest in Europe. It spans 68 feet and weighs 660 tons, requiring massive stone buttresses along the outer walls. The timbers are of great size, the posts supported on the hammer-beams (the bracket-like projections from which the other timbers spring – see page 56) being over 20 feet high and 3 feet thick. Tracery fills the spandrels of the arches and carved wooden angels decorate the ends of the hammer-beams.

Tithe Barn, Great Coxwell, Oxfordshire; mid-thirteenth century. Built by Cistercian monks from Beaulieu Abbey, of rough Cotswold stone with ashlar-faced buttresses and two porches, each still possessing its original wooden doors. The barn has an open timber roof carried on timber posts resting on stone bases. It is 152 feet long, 44 feet wide and 48 feet to the ridge of the roof, which is covered with stone tiles. The tie-beams of the roof structure are 30 feet above the floor.

hundred feet long and the largest in England (both originally belonging to the nunnery of Shaftesbury), and another at Glastonbury of about 1500, standing just outside the walls that enclose the ruins of one of southern England's most famous monasteries.

Other medieval buildings related to the cultivation of the land are few. Farm buildings were little more than rude sheds of impermanent materials. Water-mills, using the power of local streams to grind the farmer's corn, were common all over England, having been introduced by the Romans, but the buildings that housed their primitive wooden machinery have been many times replaced

and most of those still standing date from no earlier than the eighteenth century. Where water-power was not available the corn was ground by windmills, but they were a later invention; all the mills mentioned in Domesday Book were either water-mills or cattle-mills. The first mention of windmills in England occurs in 1185 when they still seem to have been something of a curiosity. The earliest type was the post-mill, where the whole upper part of the building revolved on its base to meet the wind – a base which in the first examples was probably partly sunk into the ground. The old windmills, however, like the old water-mills, have been repeatedly rebuilt and no medieval specimens remain.

Moving from agriculture to the disposal of its produce, we find a number of medieval structures in the towns that are more truly community buildings, such as the market crosses that were erected to serve as the focus of a market-place or to shelter those

Market Cross, Chichester, Sussex; 1501. Octagonal, with ogee arches leading into a covered space for the sale of produce. A circular central column supports eight ogee ribs topped by a lantern.

78

buying and selling. Most such structures are now out of use or only serve, as in the case of the market cross at Chichester, Sussex, as the centre of a traffic roundabout. The Chichester cross is one of several that were given a decorative, indeed a surprisingly fanciful, architectural form. Built in 1501, it is octagonal with ogee arches leading into the covered space in the centre, within which is a circular column supporting eight ogee ribs topped by a lantern. Salisbury once had four market crosses but only one, Poultry Cross, survives, similar in design to that at Chichester and a little earlier. Another of the same date, perhaps the finest of them all, is at Malmesbury, Wiltshire. Leighton Buzzard, Bedfordshire, has a smaller pentagonal market cross of the fifteenth century, still with its sculptured figures in niches above the archways – the figures have disappeared at Chichester and Salisbury.

Related to these in their function are such dual-purpose buildings as the fifteenth-century guildhall at Thaxted, Essex, which provides a large covered space for selling produce and above this two storeys of meeting halls for the local guilds, standing on wooden posts. There is a similar building at Ledbury, Hereford and Worcester. Although completed as late as 1655 it is wholly medieval in design, being, like the one at Thaxted, timber-framed with plaster infill – an indication that the new Renaissance styles had hardly begun to penetrate into rural England even in the seventeenth century. The Old Town Hall at Leominster in the same county provides another instance: a richly decorated one of 1633 by the king's master-carpenter, John Abel. Here the once open ground floor has been filled in.

Even before the establishment of local government with the king's officer, the sheriff, the authoritative figure, guilds were housed in imposing buildings, reflecting the growing importance of the trade guilds, especially where one trade dominated the local economy, such as the wool trade from the fourteenth century onwards in the West Country and East Anglia. Lavenham, Suffolk, has in its fifteenth-century Old Wool Hall one of the best-preserved half-timbered buildings in England with the traditional high open-roofed hall. Externally it resembles a prosperous mansion of the period. Similarly the Butchers' Guildhall at Hereford (1621) resembles a prosperous merchant's town house, timber-framed and enriched with bay windows and ornamented gables. York has its early fifteenth-

century Merchant Adventurers' Hall with an interior like a tithe barn.

The so-called Guildhall in the City of London did not serve as such except at the very beginning, but was used for elections, banquets and trials. It was begun in 1411 but the building as it appears today is more neo-Gothic than Gothic since it has been much altered after successive fires. However the great hall (except for its roof) and the crypt beneath it are fifteenth-century; so is the vaulted entrance porch. The equivalent in London of the provincial guildhalls was the separate halls of the many Livery Companies. None of their rich and capacious medieval halls however survives, having all been lost in the Great Fire. Only the Merchant Taylors' Hall in Threadneedle Street retains a crypt of 1375 and a kitchen of 1425.

In the Middle Ages the political functions of the central government were not separately housed. The king and his counsellors were continually on the move with a retinue of clerks and miscellaneous officials; the country was administered from wherever the king's travels took him and when in London from his palace at Westminster. One great building that formed part of this palace is still standing: Westminster Hall, which was for centuries the location of the chief law courts of England. In it also were held state trials, ceremonies and banquets. It is the oldest part of the palace, begun in the eleventh century when the Norman kings moved their residence from Winchester (see Chapter 3) to share Thorney Island, an area of firm ground in the marshes west of London, with the already established abbey church and monastery.

The palace was enlarged piecemeal until the early sixteenth century when Henry VIII moved the short distance to Whitehall. The Norman hall is the only part that remains except the cloister and undercroft of St Stephen's Chapel, a building of great significance because from 1547 the House of Commons continued to meet in it for nearly three hundred years, and because it pioneered the initial phase of Perpendicular architecture. However, the chapel, along with the rest of the palace apart from the hall, was destroyed in the fire of 1834. The glory of Westminster Hall is its open timber roof, built by the master-carpenter Hugh Herland in 1394, when the hall was remodelled by Richard II's master-mason Henry Yevele. It is the earliest hammer-beam roof surviving.

Other community activities that in the later Middle Ages were evolving their own types of building (but not their own styles of architecture – a different style for a different function was centuries in the future) were education and the care of the old. With these we are back within the shadow of the church, for in the early part of the Middle Ages the church was the sole repository of learning and, along with the trade guilds, the source of all charity. Colleges and universities, in fact, had the training of the clergy as their main function. From early in the fifteenth century, however, things began to change. Literacy spread rapidly and before the Wars of the Roses threw the country temporarily into chaos, schools had been founded for the education of the sons of the gentry and the more prosperous merchant class. Several of the most famous of the present-day public schools were founded then: Winchester by William of Wykeham late in the fourteenth century and Eton by Henry VI in the middle of the fifteenth. Education was further promoted by the invention of printing. (William Caxton set up his first press at Westminster in 1476.) Day grammar schools were also set up in increasing numbers, especially in the sixteenth century, from which time school buildings survive in country towns all over England. There are good examples – stone buildings with handsome street frontages – at Ashbourne, Derbyshire (1586) and Chard, Somerset (1583). New colleges were founded at Oxford and Cambridge by royal and religious benefactors.

Several public schools (Winchester, Eton, Sherborne) retain their medieval buildings which were modelled on monastic buildings, as were the original buildings of nearly all the university colleges. The first of the latter, New College, Oxford, was founded – also by William of Wykeham – in 1380, and the others followed the same pattern. Their living quarters were planned round quadrangles or courts, often incorporating cloisters and reached through towered gateways. In prominent positions were the college chapel and the hall for dining. The latter, however, was not taken from the monastery but from the great hall of the medieval manor-house and followed exactly the same arrangement: screened passage at the entrance end with buttery and kitchens beyond; dais at the other end with oriel window (but not the private chambers that were added beyond the dais in the castle and manor-

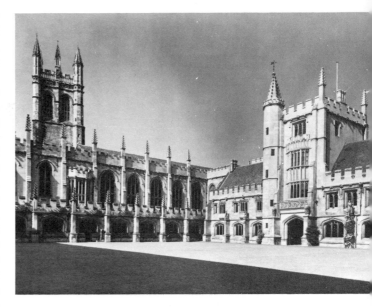

Magdalen College, Oxford; 1474 onwards. The master-mason of this typical cloistered college quadrangle was William Orchard who also built at Eton College. At left is the chapel (its tower begun in 1492 and finished in 1510); further left is one of the windows of the hall, which is on the first floor with a cellar beneath; on the right of the picture is the Founder's Tower, the original gateway to the college.

house as living became more civilized); open timber roof.

This almost standardized hall can be seen also in the Inns of Court in London where lawyers were – and still are – trained. The buildings surrounding these, though for the most part later in date, are laid out on the same collegiate plan. Tudor halls survive at Grays Inn (1556) and in the Middle Temple (1562). This type of collegiate building is however best seen at Oxford and Cambridge. At Oxford the most interesting medieval or Tudor buildings that remain are at New College (already mentioned), at Brasenose, at Christ Church (which has Oxford Cathedral as its chapel, the church of the twelfth-century Augustinian priory that first occupied the site), at Corpus Christi and Lincoln (both possessing domestically scaled front quads) and at Magdalen and St John's (which have more spacious quads, in the last case embattled in the seventeenth century, as was often the practice). The Divinity School is notable for its fan-vaulted ceiling of 1483.

81

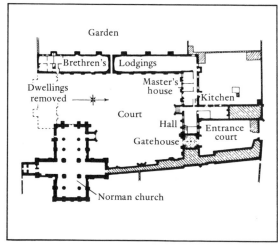

Plan of the Hospital of St Cross, Winchester.

Hospital of St Cross, Winchester; 1445. A pensioners' home planned like a college round two closed courts, in the larger of which is a Norman church. Each house, marked by a tall chimney, contains four brethren's lodgings, two on the ground floor and two on the first, the four sharing a staircase. Each lodging has three rooms. The large doorway at the far end leads up a flight of steps to the hall, the windows of which are on the right of the picture (further right is the gatehouse). The hall has an open timber roof supported on stone brackets in the form of angels.

At Cambridge, colleges with a substantial quantity of medieval and Tudor buildings include Corpus Christi, which has an almost untouched fourteenth-century court, Jesus, where the hall, dating from the foundation of the college in 1497 and refurnished in the eighteenth century, is one of the most distinguished in the university, King's with its famous chapel referred to in Chapter 3, Magdalene with a small fifteenth-century court, Queen's with a fifteenth-century court faced wholly in brick – a material commoner than at Oxford, which stands on the edge of stone-bearing country – and St John's and Trinity, both with large courts, the former of the sixteenth century, guarded by towered brick gatehouses similar to those which formed the entrance to the grander Tudor mansions, such as Hampton Court (see the next chapter) and St James's Palace, London.

A final category of non-ecclesiastical medieval buildings for the service of the community includes the various kinds of charitable institution for the sick and aged. Among them are almshouses, many again laid out on the collegiate courtyard plan since they, too, were originally monastic. Later, however, the trade guilds founded similar institutions, which grew in number after the dissolution of the monasteries created a need to replace the services the monasteries had been accustomed to provide.

One of the completest surviving examples of such medieval institutions – in this case of religious origin and typical in its layout – is the Hospital of St Cross at Winchester, founded in its present form by

Leycester's Hospital, Warwick. Founded in 1571 by the Earl of Leicester, who took over the fourteenth- and fifteenth-century half-timbered buildings of the guilds of the Holy Trinity and St George and incorporated also a couple of old houses. The whole group surrounds the courtyard seen in the picture; along one side is a wooden gallery. The courtyard is entered through a Perpendicular-style stone archway.

Cardinal Beaufort in 1445 as an extension of a Norman predecessor. Like the university colleges it has two courtyards linked by a turreted gateway. In a corner of the inner one stands the high cruciform church of the earlier foundation (finished in 1225), an exceptionally fine – and exceptionally late – example of Norman church architecture.

A contrast to this is St Mary's Hospital, Chichester, part of an earlier nunnery adapted in 1562 to house poor people. They are all accommodated under one roof, in dwelling-rooms ranged along either side of a central hall at the end of which, still part of the same building, is a chapel. The Bede House at Stamford, Lincolnshire, incorporates a similar arrangement. St John's Hospital, Lichfield, Staffordshire, has a street frontage of 1495 largely composed of a row of enormous chimneys, creating a surprisingly modern effect. Typical of the way such institutions changed and grew in accordance with changing needs and resources is Leycester's Hospital at Warwick, founded in 1571 by incorporating some earlier guilds and a couple of timbered houses. The result is an unusually picturesque group.

Almshouses of this period are frequent, generally in the form of rows or quadrangles of cottages, often with a chapel and sometimes with a refectory attached. There are well-preserved examples at Cobham, Kent, and Ewelme, Oxfordshire, the latter (1436) of brick and timber with a cloister round the quadrangle.

Part Two

The Age of Reason

Chapter 7

The Prodigy Houses

THE moment when a castle should be described instead as a country mansion is best defined as the moment when defence was no longer the first consideration in constructing it. This naturally varied in different places and circumstances but can generally be placed around the end of the fifteenth century, by which time the feudal system of raising local armies was far in the past, the Wars of the Roses between rival royal dynasties were over, the Tudors had established a firm government and life in England had become relatively secure. Existing castles were still used for military purposes and even added to, but after this time only on the Scottish borders was the strength of its fortifications vital to the survival of a great house except for a short period many years later during the Civil War. Then the houses of Royalist families all over England were besieged by Cromwell's army and their outdated medieval fortifications proved unable to withstand new methods of assault.

Nevertheless it is not easy to relate the gradual emergence of less scientifically defended country houses to their architecture as we see it now. Although it may appear at first glance that greater comfort and convenience have altogether overtaken the earlier need for defence, especially in such matters as the provision of large windows even on the ground floor, yet many of the older houses may still have been protected by outer walls and gatehouses which have now disappeared. However, we have dealt with fortified manor-houses in an earlier chapter and we are more concerned here with the really great houses, the houses for the most part of the men who ruled England, which were a new and spectacular development during the Tudor, and especially the Elizabethan, periods. Many of these were wholly new; others, like Haddon Hall, Derbyshire, presented and still present to the eye centuries of visible history. In fact the core of Haddon Hall (see page 70) is an almost unchanged

Layer Marney Hall, Essex; 1520: the gatehouse. Built by Sir Henry Marney, Captain of the King's Bodyguard to Henry VIII and Keeper of the Privy Seal. The large windows and the parapets round the turrets are of cream-coloured terracotta made by Italian workmen in the new Renaissance style. The remainder of the structure is brick, in different shades of red, still English Gothic in style.

early fourteenth-century medieval hall. It is surrounded by buildings of various dates up to the seventeenth century, some with bay windows facing outwards – hardly suitable for defence.

Haddon Hall is irregular in outline and romantically crenellated, typical of houses that have grown over the centuries. But a further cause of confusion is that in other houses, newly built in the sixteenth century when the need for fortification was almost entirely a thing of the past – Cowdray, Sussex, and Compton Wynyates, Warwickshire, are examples – architectural features that had been originally devised for military purposes, such as crenellations at the top of the walls, projecting towers, a gatehouse at Cowdray and a moat at Compton Wynyates, were incorporated simply for display and for the status they gave the building. Such houses had the outline of a castle but little more. The frequent use of brick (see also Chapter 2) is another indication that resistance to artillery was no longer a basic need.

Whatever they adopted in the way of pseudo-military features outside, the interiors of these spectacular new houses presented a totally changed picture. Not only did their larger windows bring light into living quarters that in the ancient castles must have been gloomy as well as very draughty; there were sumptuous wall decorations, moulded plaster ceilings, huge sculptured chimney-pieces and relatively comfortable furniture. There were improvements in water supply and sanitation. With the multiplication of rooms a degree of privacy became possible – something that had hardly existed while the hall of the castle and manor-house was the common living and eating place of all its occupants. By the sixteenth century upper-class, and many middle-class, Englishmen had acquired expectations of comfort and convenience that few besides royalty had enjoyed a couple of hundred years before.

The architectural style of the numerous grand houses – 'prodigious' houses as the historian Sir John Summerson has aptly termed them – of the reigns of Henry VIII and Elizabeth was determined, although in a negative sense, by an event of greater significance than the invention of new comforts or even the establishment of domestic security. This was the dissolution of the monasteries by Henry VIII, which brought to an abrupt end the influence of the monastic orders through whom innovations in the arts had for centuries entered England from the Continent. By cutting England off from the main stream of European culture, of which the predominant source had been first the Roman Catholic Church and then the courts and princes subservient to it, England's adoption of the principles of the Reformation restricted English architecture to its own separate channels and greatly delayed the spread into England of the new fashions then taking over in Italy and France – those of the Renaissance. As a result they did not appear fully fledged in English architecture for another hundred years, even though Renaissance influence permeated modes of thought and literature.

In the meantime what Renaissance ideas on architecture did arrive in England came indirectly by way of Holland and Flanders with which countries England principally traded and which were closer to those parts of the Continent already converted to the Reformation. They were spasmodically and in general eccentrically applied; so much so that this chapter should be regarded as intermediate between Parts One and Two of this book. The buildings it describes, although far from religious, are not in the least rational.

How different, and how loyally obedient to the precepts of the Renaissance as understood in Italy, the first steps of the English Renaissance might have been is suggested by the few works – not of architecture but of sculpture – commissioned by Henry VIII before he rejected the authority of the Roman Church: the tomb of his father Henry VII in Westminster Abbey, designed for him by the

OPPOSITE
Moreton Old Hall, Congleton, Cheshire; 1559. A timber-framed manor-house in a boldly patterned style peculiar to the north-west, especially Cheshire and Lancashire. Its only defence is a moat, crossed by a bridge. The house is planned round a courtyard entered through a projecting gatehouse. It has a hall on the ground floor and a long gallery on the top floor. The lowest horizontal timbers rest on a stone base. (See page 72.)

OVERLEAF
Wilton House, Wiltshire: the south front; 1636. Inigo Jones is known to have played a large part in the design of this front, built for the Earl of Pembroke. It was one of his few private commissions – Jones was essentially a court architect – and it had a lasting influence. Echoes of the corner pavilions, for example, can be seen in several later houses. (See page 104.)

Hampton Court, near London; 1515 onwards: the west front. A mansion beside the River Thames, built for his own use by Cardinal Wolsey on a grander scale than any royal palace. His master-mason was Henry Redman. In 1526 Wolsey presented the house to Henry VIII who lived there frequently and between 1531 and 1536 made several additions, including a great hall with hammer-beam roof and a chapel. Henry's master-mason, appointed after Redman's death, was John Molton. The walls and gateways are red brick with a diaper pattern, finished with battlemented parapets and the ornamental brick chimneys of which the Tudors were so fond.

OPPOSITE

Compton Wynyates, Warwickshire; 1520. Tudor country mansion built by Sir William Compton, a London merchant and a favourite of Henry VIII. It is irregular in shape and skyline, in contrast to the formal, symmetrical shape of the great houses soon to go up under the influence of the Renaissance (Sutton Place; Montacute; Wollaton). Compton Wynyates is of mixed materials: brick, stone and half-timber. The battlemented entrance tower is for show rather than defence. A great hall is still included, with the traditional screened passage, but there is also a drawing-room.

Florentine sculptor Torrigiano in 1512, and the oak screen he added to King's College Chapel, Cambridge, in 1531, the work of either Italian or French craftsmen. These are in a pure Renaissance idiom, but they are unique. England has no buildings of similar date and style; only imported decorations. For example the main gateway of the most ambitious residence of this time, Hampton Court Palace, bears high up on the walls small terracotta roundels depicting Roman emperors, by another Italian sculptor, da Maiano, but it is otherwise wholly in the conventional Tudor style with no sign of Renaissance influence.

Hampton Court was begun by Cardinal Wolsey in 1515, that is, before Henry took the fateful step of breaking with Rome. After Wolsey had given it to him in 1529 as a fruitless gesture of appeasement, Henry enlarged it to make it the biggest house in England, giving it a great hall with a splendid timber roof but one that, once again, looked back to the traditional carpentered roofs of the previous century in spite of having some Italian-style enrichments. The palace is laid out as a series of courtyards

93

entered through towered gateways like those of some of the Oxford and Cambridge colleges founded at this time, such as Trinity, Cambridge, founded by Henry himself.

After the Reformation there was little church building and these great houses are the most notable and the most characteristic buildings of the years that followed it. They are, moreover, unique to England, the only possible comparison among buildings overseas being the châteaux along the Loire in central France. They were planned not only for their owners to live in but to receive important visitors, including royalty, and their numerous retinues. They were built for ambitious men with knowledge of the world; for it was one of the essential characteristics of this and the preceding century that knowledge was no longer a monopoly of the Church. Moreover, although these country houses were the centres of great estates, by no means all were built by the successors of the land-owning nobles who had built the now obsolete castles. Many of the proprietors belonged to a new category of powerful administrators. One of the first houses, Longleat, Wiltshire, was built between 1567 and 1580 by Sir John Thynne, steward to the Lord Protector Somerset, the virtual ruler of England for the first couple of years after Henry VIII's death. Another, Burghley House, Northamptonshire, was built in the 1550s by Somerset's Secretary William Cecil, who became Lord Burleigh and Lord Treasurer under Queen Elizabeth.

Somerset's own London house on the bank of the Thames, begun in 1547, is the only building of the time that can be called Renaissance in its general design and its influence was widespread, which requires its mention here although it was demolished in the eighteenth century to make way for the existing Somerset House designed by Sir William Chambers. It had recognizably Classical pilasters and cornices and pedimented windows, employed however in a somewhat hesitant way. Its architecture was French in origin rather than Italian.

At Longleat, at Burghley and at the other palatial houses of the time, Renaissance influence is seen only as a flavour given to certain details and in features like porches and colonnades which were displayed as adjuncts without much relationship to the rest of the design. An even earlier example is Layer Marney, Essex, an ambitious house begun in 1520 of which only the tall gateway was completed.

It has terracotta ornament in Italian style but its form and fenestration as well as its brickwork are orthodox Tudor.

Such Renaissance embellishments were for the most part the work of foreign craftsmen who were imported in great numbers. They grafted exotic details on to many buildings and enriched the interiors with ceilings and fireplaces. In spite of the general failure to understand the new language of the Renaissance, there was, even in England, a developing sense – itself a consequence of the Renaissance – of the need for the total form and layout of the building to be consciously designed rather than simply allowed to grow. The master-mason in charge of the work was acquiring a role much nearer to that of the professional architect as we know it today. John Shute, the author of the first book on architecture to be published in England, *The Firste and Chief Groundes of Archytecture* (1563), described himself on the title-page as 'Paynter and Archytecte'. The book was the fruit of a visit to Italy sponsored by the Duke of Northumberland, the Protector Somerset's successor, and its illustrations include the five Orders of architecture as set out by the Italian architect and author Sebastiano Serlio.

When the Renaissance features incorporated as ornaments into the facades, skylines and interiors of so many Tudor and Elizabethan mansions – and indeed into the Jacobean mansions that followed them – were not the work of foreign craftsmen, they were by English craftsmen guided by the newly popular pattern-books, like *Architecture* by De Vries, published in Antwerp in 1577. These however were often ill-informed about the correct use of the Classical columns, entablatures and suchlike that they introduced and helped to disseminate.

Following John Shute (none of whose buildings has been identified) the most prolific of the newly emerging professional-style architects were Robert Smythson (1536–1614) and John Thorpe (1563–1655). Smythson, of whom most is known,

Blickling Hall, Norfolk, by Robert Lyminge; 1616: the long gallery. Such galleries were a feature of Elizabethan and Jacobean mansions. Blickling is a major Jacobean house, of brick with stone dressings. Begun in 1616, it is quite uninfluenced by the pure Renaissance of Inigo Jones although his Queen's House at Greenwich was begun the same year. The long gallery at Blickling is on the first floor. It is 127 feet long and has a banded plaster ceiling typical of the period.

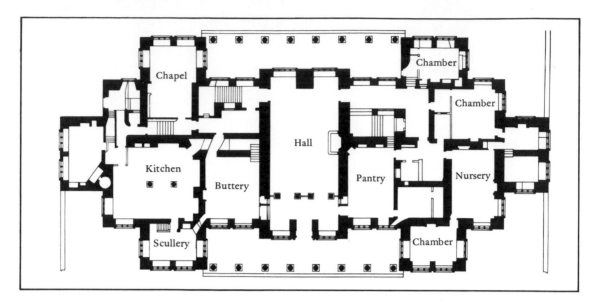

Plan of Hardwick Hall, Derbyshire; the medieval-type hall turned at right angles.

designed Longleat. Its relative simplicity in spite of its great size, its symmetry emphasized by identical projecting bays and its large expanse of windows – Hardwick, Derbyshire, begun in 1590 and also by Smythson, has larger windows still – provide a remarkable contrast to the rambling picturesqueness of the castle residences that preceded it. All four elevations are the same, yet the plan is far from

Plan of Wollaton Hall, Nottinghamshire; symmetrical, with the hall in the centre.

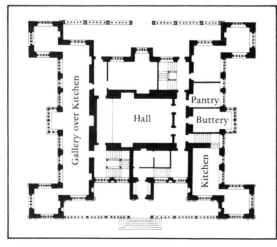

symmetrical, an enclosed courtyard occupying the centre of one half of the building and a hall, unchanged from the medieval pattern (that is, still with a screened passage at one end and a dais and bay window at the other) forming part of the other half. The window of the hall is made to conform to one of the external bays.

At Hardwick the apparent symmetry is made more real by the hall being turned at right angles to occupy the centre of the plan. Wollaton Hall too, another Smythson house of 1580 near Nottingham, has a symmetrical plan with the hall in the centre. But it is more remarkable for its profusion of applied Renaissance ornament and its exuberant outline, a composition of towers, domed turrets and pinnacled gables that aptly reflects the extravagant spirit in which these show-piece country houses were conceived. It is another sign of the times that the owner of Wollaton was not a nobleman or courtier but a newly rich coal-owner, Sir Francis Willoughby.

Other representative great houses of this time include Montacute, Somerset (1580–1600), again

Wollaton, Nottinghamshire, by Robert Smythson; 1580. A symmetrical composition but still, even at this date, more Gothic than Renaissance in conception though with a wealth of ornament of Renaissance derivation applied to the facades. The great hall is in the centre of the building, lighted only through the tall windows in the tower.

Kirby Hall, Northamptonshire: porch facing into courtyard; 1572. The Classical orders are here used in a recognizably Renaissance way, though still for decoration rather than construction. The large window over the arch is an addition of 1638.

symmetrical but fairly restrained compared with Wollaton in spite of its restlessly gabled roofline. It is still, like Longleat, basically Perpendicular Gothic in its array of mullioned windows. Another is Kirby Hall, Northamptonshire (1572), where the mullioned windows are surprisingly set off by near-Classical pilasters and, within the interior court, by a Renaissance-style porch composed of tiers and clusters of unfunctional Classical columns.

In addition to the vestigial plan-features of the medieval castle – the hall, the great chamber and the ranges of lodgings – an innovation during the sixteenth century was the long gallery on an upper floor, incorporated in many big, and a few fairly modest, houses and used for promenading and entertaining. It may, too, have been used as a dormitory, for some of these mansions housed a vast population. At Cowdray, referred to above, two hundred people are recorded as sleeping in the house – all male except for a few ladies in attendance on the owner's (Lord Montagu's) wife. Long galleries continue to appear in the early Jacobean houses. Of these Audley End, Essex (1603), built by Bernard Johnson for the then Lord Treasurer, the Earl of Suffolk, was one of the greatest but only a fraction of it now remains. Another, more complete, is Knole Park, Sevenoaks, Kent (1605), and typical in its mixture of the naive and the sophisticated is Hatfield House, Hertfordshire. Hatfield was begun in 1607 for Robert Cecil, Earl of Salisbury, the second son of Queen Elizabeth's minister Lord Burleigh. It still retains the great hall, but no longer

as a dominant element in the plan, and it spreads its two projecting wings widely to provide a more luxurious variety of rooms. It is the work of a number of designers, including Robert Lyminge, previously recorded as a carpenter and, it is believed, Cecil himself.

Early in the seventeenth century houses appear that have more thoroughly absorbed the new language of the Renaissance, although still the Netherlands version of it. One such is Raynham Hall, Norfolk (1622). It has a fairly correct columned and pedimented central feature and Dutch-style gables. It was designed by the owner, Sir Roger Townshend, an amateur of architecture – a type we shall meet again in the next century. Among other houses of a similar type is the Dutch House at Kew (later Kew Palace), built in 1631 by a London merchant and again crowned by Dutch-style gables. Both houses are of brick, in the case of

Kew Palace, near London; 1631: the garden front. Built by a London merchant of Dutch descent. Similar houses were built in the Home Counties by other prosperous merchants who were forward-looking enough to reject the Tudor style as old fashioned but were not attracted by the Renaissance of Inigo Jones so much admired at Court. They chose instead this Dutch-influenced style with facades elaborately modelled in brick. Their houses include Swakeleys, Middlesex (1630), Broome Park, Kent (1635), Raynham Hall, Norfolk (1635) and Cromwell House, Highgate, London (1637). At Kew the brick pilasters have brick capitals carved *in situ*. Sash windows have replaced the original mullioned casement windows.

Raynham with stone trimmings. Before any of these were finished, however, the Italian Renaissance at last reached England in the shape of the first buildings by Inigo Jones, the hero of the next chapter.

99

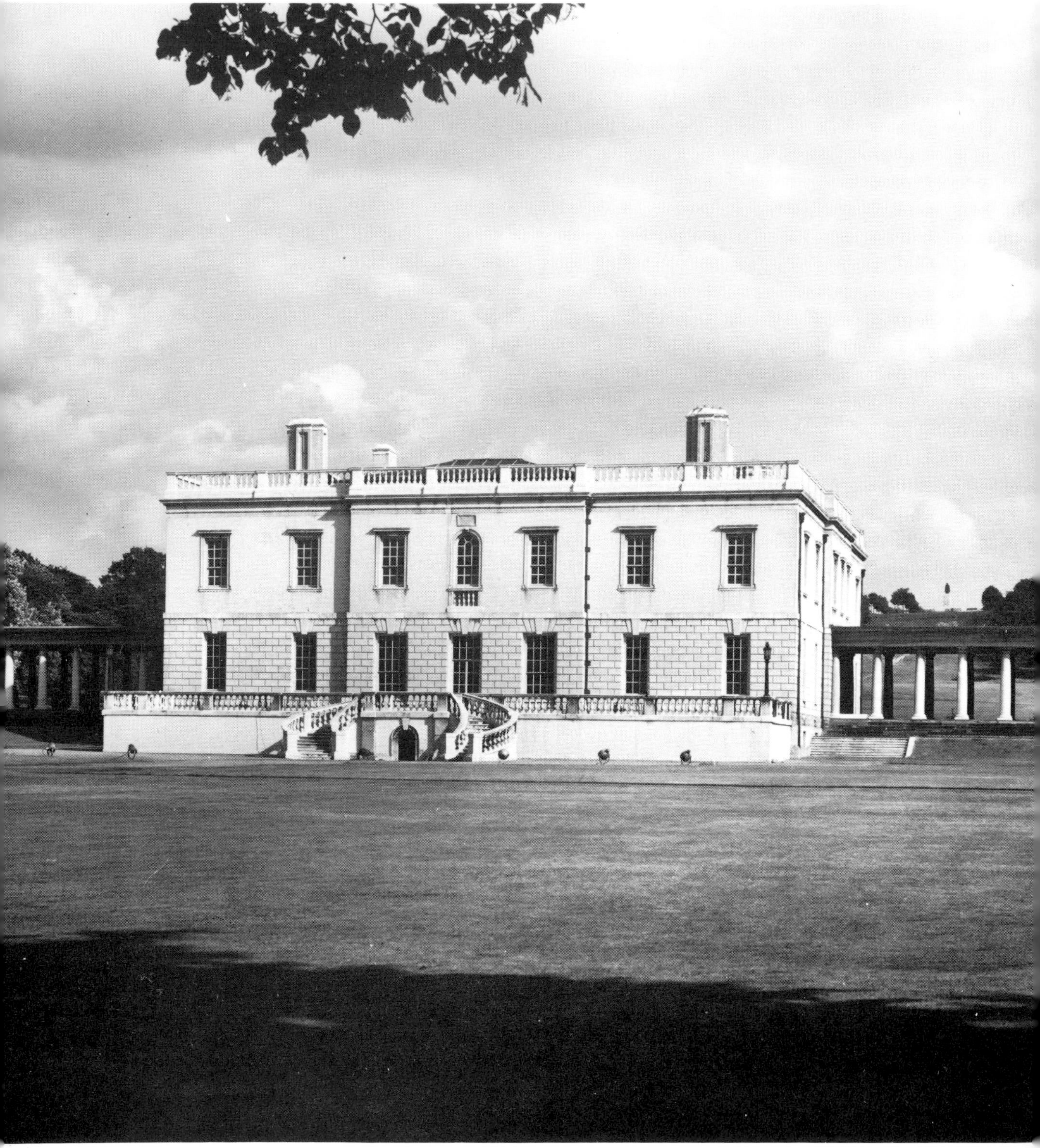

Chapter 8

Court Patronage and Inigo Jones

The Queen's House, Greenwich, by Inigo Jones; 1616–35. The first correctly Renaissance building in England, designed by Jones for James I's queen the year after he returned from Italy in 1615 and completed for Charles I's queen in 1635. This view shows the north block facing the Thames. The three centre windows light a large square hall at first-floor level. Beyond it a bridge crosses a public road which divides the north block from the south – a peculiar arrangement for which the reason is unknown.

IT is an over-simplification of history to say that Inigo Jones transformed English architecture by introducing the Renaissance style of design directly from Italy. His ultimate influence was very great but it was by no means immediate. We know of only four buildings undoubtedly by him and a couple of country houses in which he had a hand, and for some years after these were built English architects continued to regard the Renaissance – see the preceding chapter – as a source of applied enrichments rather than as a new way, inspired by what was being rediscovered of the ancient world, of conceiving a design with the parts and the whole in a planned relationship.

Inigo Jones stands apart from most of the men who had been establishing themselves in the comparatively recent profession of architect. He was dependent on the patronage of the Stuart Court rather than on that of the newly powerful and rich who were still exhibiting their importance and their wealth in prodigious country palaces in many parts of England while Jones was at work in London. Hatfield House was not completed until 1612 and the eccentric, consciously backward-looking Bolsover Castle, Derbyshire, by John Smythson, not until 1617. Jones began to work in London in 1605 when he was already thirty-two, though at first as a designer not of buildings but of masques – stylized dramatic entertainments – for James I's queen, Anne of Denmark. Their scenery, already at that time, was in a fully Renaissance style, as were his early architectural designs – not executed – for London buildings.

These designs, for masques and for buildings, were made immediately after his return from some years spent in Italy, which gave him a first-hand knowledge, unique in England, of the Italian Renaissance. The Earl of Arundel, an influential figure at the Court of James I, took Jones again to Italy in 1613. Himself a connoisseur and collector of

Banqueting House, Whitehall, London, by Inigo Jones;
1619–22. Jones's most important work, confirming his
skill in handling the new Renaissance style from Italy.
His knowledgeable use of the orders – Ionic columns and
pilasters on the lower part of the facade and Corinthian
above – was unprecedented in England. The strong line
of the cornice between them suggests a two-storey
building but the inside is one clear space. The
Banqueting House was an addition to James I's Tudor
Whitehall Palace.

pictures and sculpture, Arundel was one of the
instigators of the practice, shared thereafter by
architects and their aristocratic patrons, of making
the Grand Tour of Europe, with Italy as the
principal goal, an essential part of their education.
On Inigo Jones's return in 1615 he was made
Surveyor-General of the King's Works but, oddly,
the Renaissance idiom he thereupon introduced into
England was not the idiom current in Italy at the

time but that of fifty years before. His achievement
therefore was not to bring England back into step
with European architecture, which early in the
seventeenth century had already begun to move
towards the Baroque, but personally to revive in
England a recently past episode of European
architectural history whose products he had seen
and admired: the strictly disciplined episode
represented by the work of Andrea Palladio
(1508–80), who was himself inspired by the Roman
architect and writer Vitruvius, active around 40 BC
and the composer of the only treatise on architecture
surviving from antiquity. Few at first followed
Jones's precepts in England but nearly a century
after his death Palladianism was re-discovered
and became the predominant English style.

That is the negative side of Inigo Jones's role in
English architecture. The positive side is that his
buildings were the first to be conceived in true
Renaissance fashion as a totality, composed of

elements each with its proper proportions and making its designed contribution to the whole. He was the first for whom architecture was an intellectual discipline and in spite of his humble family background, (his father was a clothworker and he himself began by being apprenticed to a joiner), he was the first to endow the architect with the status of a professional man entitled to make judgements on the basis of his own expertise rather than that of a tradesman accepting orders. His designs appeal to the mind as well as to the eye, and for that reason require some understanding of the rules of Classical architecture before they can be fully appreciated – an understanding that patrons of architecture from Jones's time onwards increasingly possessed.

His first Palladio-inspired buildings are externally cool and well-disciplined. Inside, in contrast, they are exuberantly decorated; but this is not because his style demanded it, only because they were royal. His first building commissioned by James I was externally the plainest of all: a house at Greenwich for the use of James's queen, Anne of Denmark, begun in 1616. She however died before it was finished; the work was held up for more than ten years and not completed until 1635 for Henrietta Maria, wife of Charles I. Meanwhile Inigo Jones created his outstanding work, the Banqueting House in Whitehall. It was built in 1619 as an addition to Whitehall Palace with whose rambling red-brick Tudor buildings it must have made a more striking contrast than it does today with the taller stone buildings – mostly nineteenth-century – alongside which it stands. Jones later made designs for a totally new palace on the site, of which the Banqueting House would have been a part, but this was not built.

The Banqueting House – like the Queen's House at Greenwich quite different from anything hitherto seen in England – shows Jones's complete mastery of the Orders and his assured handling of intricate Classical detail. From outside it appears to be a two-storey building but in fact the inside is one great space, divided horizontally only by a narrow balcony supported on columns – a space that has been compared to a Roman basilica. The rather overpowering ceiling has allegorical paintings by Rubens. Jones's other two authenticated buildings are churches: a chapel added to St James's Palace in 1623 for Charles I's Roman Catholic wife Henrietta Maria and the church of St Paul, Covent Garden

Marlborough House, London, by Inigo Jones; 1623: interior of chapel. Also known as the Queen's Chapel, this was built to serve the existing St James's Palace and for the use of Charles I's Roman Catholic queen. The coffered ceiling and the triple ('Venetian') window are based on current Italian models. This type of window was frequently used in country houses in the next century.

(1631). The latter faces into the huge new piazza that Jones himself had designed as part of a programme of equipping London, still in his time a medieval city of irregular growth, with formally laid-out streets and squares. It now only exists in outline. All that is seen of the church from the piazza is the east end with its simple, somewhat rustic, portico, a telling townscape feature but misleadingly related to the church itself which is entered from the opposite end. The chapel at St James's Palace (now the chapel of Marlborough House) is a more academic and, inside, a more sumptuous building. Its east end has a large Venetian window, that is, a three-light window with

Eltham Lodge, Woolwich, Kent, by Hugh May; 1664. May was one of Inigo Jones's immediate followers. He served Charles II during his exile on the Continent and the Dutch influence on this house is evident. (It now belongs to a golf club.) The windows are Georgian replacements of the original mullioned casement windows. After the Restoration May was put in charge of the royal gardens at Whitehall, St James's, Hampton Court and Greenwich, and of the remodelling of Windsor Castle.

the centre light arched – the first of this kind in England and a pattern much copied by the eighteenth-century Palladian architects.

Of several country houses partly by Inigo Jones the most important is Wilton House, Wiltshire, built in 1636 for the Earl of Pembroke by a little-known architect called Isaac de Caux with help and advice from Jones – quite how much is not clear. Once again it included features, notably the pedimented corner pavilions on the south front, that we frequently find echoed in the eighteenth century. It also contains a famous and highly ornate room, in dimensions precisely a double cube.

Jones, who died in 1652, had a small number of followers among country-house builders but little of their work survives. Outstanding was Coleshill, Berkshire, begun in 1650 and destroyed by fire in 1952, but it must nevertheless be mentioned here because of the influence its easy mixture of dignity and domesticity had on subsequent medium-sized country houses. Its architect was Sir Roger Pratt (1620–84), an amateur who had travelled in France and Italy. His Clarendon House in Piccadilly, London (1664), demolished less than twenty years after completion, must be mentioned too, because it was the first great Classical town mansion. It was also widely imitated, for example at Belton House, Lincolnshire, built by a master-mason, William Stanton, in 1685. Pratt was one of the three commissioners appointed by Charles II to oversee the initial plans for rebuilding the City of London after the Great Fire of 1666.

The houses of Hugh May (1621–84) – another of the commissioners; Wren was of course the third – are more Dutch than Italian but still closely follow Inigo Jones, especially in their interiors. Eltham Lodge, Woolwich (1663), is May's only complete

The Vyne, Hampshire: garden front with portico. The house itself, built for the first Lord Sandys, is sixteenth-century. Its importance here is that when John Webb, Inigo Jones's pupil and son-in-law, remodelled it in 1650 he added the giant white-painted portico to the centre of the red-brick garden front. It was the first of many such porticos to form the central feature of English country houses, especially during the Palladian revival a century later.

surviving work. His country houses and those of Pratt are important as the forerunners of the relaxed and unpretentious (even when it was luxurious) type of moderate-sized house that became an English speciality and remained so until the time of Lutyens two and a half centuries later. Most of Hugh May's interiors at Windsor Castle, which he designed in 1675 with the sculptor Grinling Gibbons for Charles II, have also been destroyed. They included the King's Chapel and were remarkable for being the most elaborate fully Baroque interiors to have been produced at that time in the whole of northern Europe.

Of Inigo Jones's closest (and from his point of view most important) follower, again few works survive. He was Jones's pupil and assistant, John Webb (1611–72). Webb's experience working on the drawings for Jones's never-executed Whitehall Palace shows in his King Charles Building (1664) at Greenwich. This was intended to be the first wing of a new palace for Charles II. There were to have been two other wings, enclosing a courtyard open on the fourth side to the river, but no more was built. The palace (now known as Greenwich Hospital) was completed to a different plan later in the century by Wren. Webb's wing is classically correct, massively monumental in style and a little dull when compared with Wren's lively composition.

Webb also built several country houses, and added a wing to Lamport Hall, Northamptonshire, and a portico to The Vyne, Hampshire. This last, built in 1654, is significant as being the first of those temple-style Classical porticos, with free-standing columns and pediment, that the eighteenth-century Palladian architects, and after them Robert Adam, were to use so frequently as the centre-piece of their country-house facades.

Chapter 9

An English Baroque: Wren and his Successors

I T will be seen that in this new age of reason inspired by ancient precedents the history of architecture becomes more and more a history of individual architects, of the styles in which they built and the influence they exerted on each other. We now come to the greatest of them, Sir Christopher Wren (1632–1723), who, far from being an educated master-mason like Robert Smythson or a self-made professional man like Inigo Jones, belonged from the outset to the world of higher learning and experimental philosophy. Before he turned to architecture he was a distinguished scientist – among other things professor of astronomy first at Gresham College, London, and then at Oxford. His uncle was bishop of Ely and a prominent Royalist. It was he who commissioned Wren's first building, a chapel for Pembroke College, Cambridge.

Wren designed this in 1663. It is a simple building, correctly Classical, and the first in either Oxford or Cambridge to show no signs of harking back to Gothic or Tudor styles. That this was so is an indication of how slowly the new Italian style favoured by the Stuart Court had spread further afield. The lapse of half a century since Inigo Jones had introduced that style with the Queen's House at Greenwich is explained however by the upheaval of the Civil War and by the Protectorate that followed it having brought to an end the patronage the Court had exercised. Although a new and excitingly creative phase of the English Renaissance, led by Wren, may be said to have begun with the restoration of Charles II in 1660, the centre of learning and the fount of new ideas was by then not the Court but the universities.

More significant than Wren's conventionally Classical chapel at Cambridge is his second building, the Sheldonian Theatre at Oxford, also commissioned in 1663; for this gave him the opportunity to exploit his scientific training and to exhibit the structural resourcefulness that was to emerge in

Radcliffe Library, Oxford, by James Gibbs. The idea of a circular building for this purpose was Hawksmoor's – a model of his design survives – but Gibbs was appointed architect instead in 1743. The building was completed in 1749. Until 1863 all eight of the arched openings were open to the air and gave access to the staircase leading up to the main library on the first floor. This has a gallery and a coffered domed ceiling. The external dome is of wood, covered with lead.

Wren remained a professor of astronomy for another ten years but gave his attention increasingly to architecture. In 1665–66 he spent several months in Paris, looking at the work of the French Renaissance architects who were then very actively engaged in Paris and its neighbourhood. There he met one of the greatest Italian architects, Gianlorenzo Bernini, who had been invited to Paris by Louis XIV to make a new design for the Louvre – never executed. That was Wren's nearest contact with the original source of the Renaissance. He never visited Italy; in fact as far as is known he never left England again.

This to some extent explains the peculiarly local nature of English Renaissance architecture during the next half-century, that is, until architects and their patrons began to be more influenced by what they saw in Italy while making the Grand Tour and until their rediscovery of Palladio. Wren's in-

Pembroke College, Cambridge, by Sir Christopher Wren: the chapel. Wren's first building, designed in 1663 two years before the visit to Paris which finally persuaded him to transfer his energies from astronomy to architecture. It was the first purely Classical building in Cambridge. This is the west end, forming part of the college frontage to Trumpington Street.

many of his later buildings. The Sheldonian Theatre is an auditorium for academic ceremonies, requiring a large interior space uninterrupted by columns. Wren spanned the distance across it of eighty feet – a large one for that time – by means of triangular timber trusses (that is, arrangements of timbers none of which is long enough to span the distance individually), concealed by a flat ceiling. The plan of the building resembles that of an ancient Roman theatre. Its exterior, an empirical design owing nothing to Inigo Jones, reveals Wren's inexperience of relating the new architectural language to unfamiliar spatial and technical requirements, a necessity he was later to master with remarkable fluency and ingenuity.

108

OPPOSITE
Royal Naval Hospital, Greenwich, by Sir Christopher Wren: the great hall. Completed in 1714, the hall, which balances the chapel on either side of the formal axis around which Wren planned Greenwich Hospital, has the most splendid Baroque interior in England. The decorations are by Wren's pupil and assistant, Nicholas Hawksmoor, and the painting by Sir James Thornhill.

OVERLEAF LEFT
St Anne's Church, Limehouse, London, by Nicholas Hawksmoor; 1714–30. One of six London churches, four of them in the East End, built by Hawksmoor after his appointment as Surveyor for the Fifty New Churches Act of 1711. They are outstanding for their vigour and geometrical invention. St Anne's was damaged by fire in 1850 and restored by Philip Hardwick.

OVERLEAF RIGHT
Blenheim Palace, Woodstock, Oxfordshire, by Sir John Vanbrugh; 1705–25. Blenheim stands in a large landscaped park and was the nation's gift to the victorious Duke of Marlborough. A monument, according to Vanbrugh's own words, rather than a private habitation, it illustrates in its modelling and skyline the architect's vigorous sense of the Baroque. Hawksmoor assisted Vanbrugh over the detail. Work began in 1705 and was brought to a halt in 1712 when £220,000 had been spent and another £45,000 was owed to the masons (the estimate was £100,000). It was resumed in 1716 at the Marlboroughs' expense and completed in 1725.

clination towards the Baroque inventiveness of Bernini and Guarini (whom he also met in Paris) rather than towards Classical orthodoxy, and the idiom he developed based on the Dutch version of the Renaissance that had already penetrated into England rather than the pure Italian, dominated the English architectural scene. His supremacy was confirmed first by his prestige as an individual and then by the great quantity of building he was able to undertake in London following the Great Fire, which destroyed almost the whole of what we now call the City in 1666 – the same year in which Wren returned from Paris.

In an extraordinarily short time he put forward a scheme for laying out the City afresh on the formal geometrical lines fashionable in Italy and France, with piazzas occupied by public buildings (including a rebuilt St Paul's Cathedral) linked by wide avenues – a plan characterized by monuments and vistas. It proved impracticable in terms of land ownership and could not have been achieved quickly enough to allow the City of London, on which much of the country's economy depended, to resume its activities as soon as was desirable. It was perhaps too utopian: a rigid Classical exercise that might not have suited the organic growth of an expanding national – already becoming an imperial – capital. But it led, or is thought partly to have led, Charles II to appoint Sir Christopher Wren, in 1669, to the post of Surveyor-General of the King's Works and thus to give him responsibility, after the passing of a Rebuilding Act in 1670, for the design of fifty-two churches to replace those destroyed in the Great Fire and ultimately of a cathedral to replace St Paul's.

These are the buildings on which Wren's reputation mainly rests. He designed practically nothing outside London and the older universities, and only a few buildings other than churches until nearly the end of his career. These last (the Royal

OPPOSITE
Guildhall, Guildford, Surrey; 1682. Overhanging the steeply rising High Street, the guildhall makes a bold contribution to the townscape. Its architecture is a mixture of early Renaissance and local vernacular styles: timber-framed structure with over-sailing upper storey and balcony with carved brackets; pedimented windows flanked by pilasters. The cornices and cupola are also of wood. The clock, supported on a gilded beam, is of 1683. The architect – if there was one – is not known. (See page 127.)

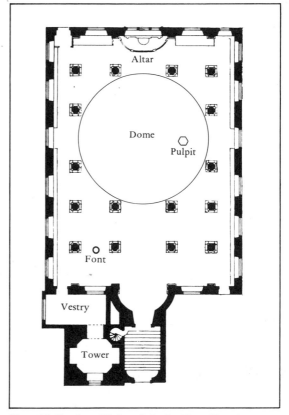

Plan of St Stephen, Walbrook, in the City of London.

Hospital, Chelsea, a new wing at Hampton Court, Greenwich Hospital) were all designed in his capacity as Surveyor-General first to Charles II, then to James II and at the very end to William III. He never worked for private clients, although the best of the younger architects who built houses for these were his pupils and their work was largely founded on the architectural idiom he had evolved and on the geometrical inventiveness that was characteristically his.

The last quality comes out strongly in his City churches. Although the language was Classical, Wren's use of it was original, especially in the way he created satisfactory interior spaces out of the confined and awkwardly shaped sites on which he had to build – every one different: St Stephen, Walbrook (1672), which with its dome resting on a complex arrangement of arches and columns seems to create infinite space out of nothing; St Anne and St Agnes, Gresham Street (1676); St Mary Abchurch (1681). Some of the sites were so hemmed

in by buildings that the churches had practically no facades. Wren's originality comes out also in the variety of the towers which, rising above the surrounding roofs of the closely built-up city, marked the presence of the new churches – an effect now largely lost because of subsequent high building. The invention shown in some of the delicately sculptured towers and spires, some of which were added by Wren several years after the completion of the rest of the church, is remarkable: at St Mary-le-Bow (1670–83) for example – the first of the towers to be built – at Christ Church, Newgate Street (1704), at St Magnus Martyr (1705) – now almost completely hidden behind Adelaide House at the head of London Bridge.

The history of Wren's rebuilding of St Paul's Cathedral is well known; how after various preliminary attempts, all including a great dome, he produced, in 1673, a design with a highly centralized plan, having no separate nave and choir. A handsome wooden model of this design nearly twenty feet long – a beautiful work of architecture in itself – can be seen today in the Trophy Room above the chapel in the north-west corner of the cathedral. It is believed always to have been Wren's favourite,

OPPOSITE
Church of St Stephen, Walbrook, London, by Sir Christopher Wren; 1672–79: the interior. One of Wren's achievements in his City churches was to create an interesting sense of space out of awkward and restricted sites, some almost enclosed by other buildings. St Stephen's, alongside the Mansion House, is an example. Its plan is a plain rectangle containing sixteen Corinthian columns of which eight, arranged in a circle, support a dome.

RIGHT
Church of St Mary-le-Bow, London by Sir Christopher Wren; 1670–80. One of fifty-two churches in the City of London designed by Wren between 1670 and 1711 following the Great Fire. Twenty-five of these were destroyed before 1939 and another nineteen wholly or partly in the 1939–45 War; some were subsequently restored. Until thirty years ago their towers and spires, with the dome of St Paul's, dominated the skyline of the City. The variety of their design, their sculptural invention and their ingenious combination of architectural elements are notable. St Mary-le-Bow, in Cheapside, was the first to be designed, in 1670. It was completed in 1680, gutted in an air raid in 1941 and restored in 1964.

St Paul's Cathedral, London, by Sir Christopher Wren; 1675–1710: from the south-east. This view shows, from left to right, the twin western towers (clock-tower and bell-tower), the south transept with its semicircular porch, the colonnaded dome over the crossing and the choir and apsidal east end; also the marked subdivision into two storeys of which only the lower has windows lighting the interior. The upper storey is a screen-wall concealing the aisle roofs.

but was rejected partly because it would have been difficult to build in stages as the money was made available, but chiefly because its plan departed too far from the familiar cathedral layout with nave and screened-off choir and would have required changes in the form of the services and in its liturgical use generally.

116

Two years later (in 1675) Wren produced a very different design, except in a few details the design that was built. It still had its dome, resting on eight piers surrounding a central space, but its plan was a reversion to that of the medieval cathedral to whose layout the English clergy were accustomed: a long nave, a somewhat less long choir, both with aisles; transepts either side of the crossing. Its interior is grand and spacious but has been criticized because the arches supporting the dome appear to bring down the latter's weight not on the centres but on the edges of the piers. A noteworthy feature of the exterior is the firm horizontal division into two apparent storeys – very like Inigo Jones's Banqueting House. Only the lower range of windows is real and lights the interior. The upper range adorns what is nothing more than a screen wall, concealing the aisle roofs and the flying buttresses that help to support the upper walls of the nave and choir. One reason for this treatment is said to have been to reveal an architecturally self-sufficient facade in the distant view when the lower half of the building was hidden by surrounding houses, whose roofs at that time only reached the height of the intermediate cornice.

The main entrance at the west end is marked by twin towers designed in the Baroque spirit of the towers of the City churches. The prolongation of the nave in this direction to give the building its traditional cathedral plan has the disadvantage of cutting off the view of the dome as the visitor approaches. From further away, and from all other viewpoints, the dome is magnificent – still the focal point of the City's skyline – and at the same time it provides yet another instance of Wren's technical inventiveness. Desiring to raise it to so commanding a height on a drum of giant columns and crown it with a stone lantern, he not only (as several Continental architects had already done) created a lower dome – the one seen from the inside – to preserve the internal proportion, but in between he built an enormous cone of brick, invisible from inside or out, which supports the weight of the dome itself, a timber structure covered with lead, and that of the lantern. To prevent spreading he bound the base of the cone with a heavy iron chain. Such ingenuities furnish a perfect illustration of the difference between Renaissance architecture and the Gothic architecture of the preceding age: in the former, structure has to be contrived to achieve the desired effect; in the latter the effect grows out of the structure.

Wren's important secular buildings are only four in number. First comes his library at Trinity College, Cambridge (1676), open at ground level, above which is one of the most splendid library interiors in Europe. Then comes the Royal Hospital at Chelsea (1682), answering the new need for a refuge for old soldiers – new at this time because England had never had a regular standing army until the Civil War. Its plan continued the tradition of the charitable homes of several centuries before (see Chapter 6) and of many university colleges: a courtyard surrounded by lodgings with a hall balancing a chapel. It is an unpretentious but supremely elegant building, designed for Charles II and completed under James II, in red brick with a stone portico. Next comes a new wing at Hampton

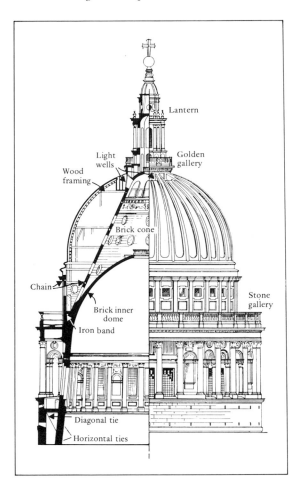

Section through dome of St Paul's Cathedral showing its construction.

Court (1689) for William and Mary. This is in a more florid style; also in brick and stone. Finally comes Wren's last great work, the Royal Hospital for Seamen at Greenwich (1696–1716).

This is a more palatial, and inevitably more Baroque, conception than the palace on the same site begun by Webb for Charles II (see preceding chapter) but has Webb's one completed wing incorporated in it. It is splendidly monumental, designed to be reached by river and planned on either side of an open vista terminating distantly in Inigo Jones's Queen's House (which it somewhat overpowers). Flanking this vista are twin colonnaded and domed pavilions. Again the chapel is balanced by the hall. The former was damaged by fire in the eighteenth century and refurnished in neo-Greek style. The

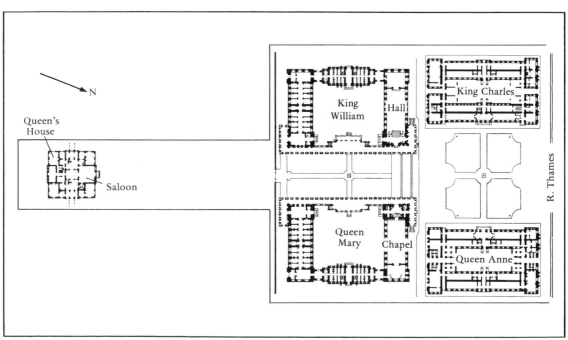

Royal Naval Hospital, Greenwich, by Sir Christopher Wren. Designed in 1695 for William and Mary on the Thames-side site where Charles II had begun a new royal palace in 1664. Wren's symmetrical layout, seen here from the river, incorporates the wing Webb had built for the palace. The twin domes on either side of the colonnaded central avenue mark the position of the great hall and the chapel. Between them can be seen, in the distance, the Queen's House designed by Inigo Jones eighty years earlier (see Chapter 8).

OPPOSITE
Plan of Royal Naval Hospital, Greenwich. The eastern part of the north-west block was built first as part of a projected royal palace. At the far left is the Queen's House.

latter survives intact, a suite of three chambers on slightly different levels, richly decorated by Nicholas Hawksmoor and with a ceiling painted by Sir James Thornhill.

Mention of Hawksmoor brings us to the generation of architects who succeeded Wren and continued the Baroque tradition he initiated. Hawksmoor was in fact his pupil and for many years his highly valued assistant. Just how much Hawksmoor contributed, especially to the detail of the buildings by Wren on which he worked, is not known. They included Greenwich Hospital on which Vanbrugh also worked, completing in fact one wing after Wren's death.

Nicholas Hawksmoor (1661–1736) spent much of his career serving as assistant first to Wren and then to Vanbrugh. In his origin he was humbler than either and his temperament was more diffident, with the result that he was late in establishing himself as an architect in his own right. When he did so he emerged as a brilliant original, his masterpieces being the six churches he built in London after being appointed Surveyor for the Fifty New Churches Act, passed in 1711. They are at the same time spectacular and severe and in places eccentric, using Classical elements in an almost Gothic way with emphasis on their basic geometry. The most impressive are St George's-in-the-East (1715) and Christ Church, Spitalfields (1723), and the most orthodox St George's, Bloomsbury (1720), in spite of its unusual stepped spire topped by a statue of George I. Hawksmoor's interest in Gothic effects is underlined by his use of actual – or near – Gothic styles at All Soul's College, Oxford (1716–35) and at Westminster Abbey, to which he added the present western towers in 1734.

If Hawksmoor designed in a style of his own but in a Baroque spirit, Sir John Vanbrugh (1664–1726) created buildings that are more like the Baroque currently understood in Europe. Like Wren he came to architecture after pursuing other careers; in his case first that of a soldier and then that of a successful playwright. He acquired influential social connections and in 1669 was invited by the Earl of Carlisle, in spite of his very limited architectural experience, to design for him a large country mansion in Yorkshire, Castle Howard. He completed it with Hawksmoor's assistance, and showed himself a master of country-house building in the grand manner. Vanbrugh's work echoes Hawksmoor's feeling for the use of simple masses and combines it with a sense of Classical architecture as a theatrical backcloth. At Castle Howard the house is spread across the landscape either side of a higher central block faced with giant pilasters and containing a hall that rises into the roof. The hall is lit through the drum of a dome that forms the climax of the composition. At his next house, Blenheim Palace, Oxfordshire, given by the nation to the victorious Duke of Marlborough and begun in 1705, for which Vanbrugh also had Hawksmoor's assistance over the detail, the masses are bolder and more varied, the scale still more monumental and there is still more excitement in the skyline.

After Blenheim Vanbrugh no longer had Hawksmoor's assistance, but his two other great houses, King's Weston, near Bristol, begun in 1710, and Seaton Delaval, Northumberland, begun in 1720 but gutted by fire a century later, show the same sense of the dramatic, exemplified by the giant columns flanking the entrance to Seaton Delaval, and the same boldness of modelling.

Neither Hawksmoor nor Vanbrugh ever went to Italy but another of the small group of English architects that can be classed as Baroque, Thomas Archer (1668–1743), did, and to other European countries as well. Some of his work suggests the direct influence of Bernini but his best-known building, the church of St John, Smith Square, London (1714), derives more from Borromini with its broken pediments and elaborately composed turrets at each corner. It is nevertheless personal and original. Its interior was destroyed by fire in a 1941 air raid but this was not a severe loss as the church had been refurnished in the nineteenth century. It has been restored for use as a concert-hall.

William Talman (1650–1719) was another country-house architect of talent and imagination, again a follower of Wren, but he achieved relatively little owing, it is said, to his quarrelsome temperament. He must be mentioned here because of his one highly distinguished design: the south front of Chatsworth House, Derbyshire, which he rebuilt in 1686 for the Duke of Devonshire. Unlike the houses

Plan of Blenheim Palace, Oxfordshire (see pages 110–11).

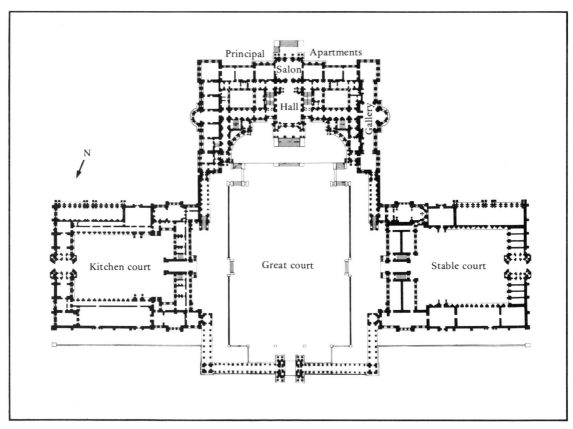

Seaton Delaval, near Blyth, Northumberland, by Sir John Vanbrugh; 1718–29. Built for an admiral, Seaton Delaval illustrates Vanbrugh's powerful, even aggressive, use of the Classical architectural language. The compactly planned central block, containing a hall 30 feet high, is linked by curved arcades to pavilions enclosing an entrance court. A fire burnt out one wing in 1752 and another gutted the main block in 1822.

of his near contemporary (and rival) Vanbrugh, it is calm with a level skyline. It is given presence and dignity by projecting end pavilions bearing giant fluted pilasters. Talman also designed the east front, again with giant pilasters. Other parts of the present house are later and by various architects including, it is thought, Sir James Thornhill who is better known as the leading ceiling painter of his day.

There remains the considerable figure of James Gibbs (1682–1754), who not only visited Italy but studied there, in the office of Carlo Fontana in Rome. His Italian training combined with his natural talents should have earned him a more successful career but he was handicapped by being a Roman Catholic and a Tory. When he returned from Italy and set up in London in 1709 the Whigs were in power and the Hanoverian succession made his

Catholic – it has even been suggested his Jacobite – allegiances suspect. He did however build two important churches in London: St Mary-le-Strand (begun 1714) and St Martin-in-the-Fields (begun 1721). The second of these is of outstanding significance not only because of its handsome, beautifully balanced design but because it became the model on which eighteenth-century churches all over the world were based. Its tower, unlike any of Wren's, grows out of the main roof at its western end, with its base concealed by a pedimented portico. This precise pattern – rectangular nave and choir under a single roof, tower at the west end with spire or turret, temple-like portico – can be found repeated wherever in the world the English settled during the coming century and more, in North America, the West Indies and the Far East. This was largely the outcome of the widespread influence of Gibbs's own *Book of Architecture*, published in 1728, which became a popular source book for builders. Another of its illustrations is thought to have suggested the design of the White House at Washington.

Debarred from official employment, Gibbs worked chiefly for the universities and for country

gentlemen. His university buildings include, at Cambridge, the Senate House (1722) and the Fellows' Building at Kings College (1723), the latter a simple but subtly proportioned rectangular block that makes a splendid foil to the Tudor chapel, and at Oxford his masterpiece, the Radcliffe Library (1737–49). This circular domed building is one of the triumphs of the several efforts made at this time to exploit those sculptural qualities in Italian styles which do not easily emerge under grey English skies. It fuses a variety of architectural elements into a bold and rhythmic composition involving some unexpected relationships of parts that are not so much Baroque as Mannerist – something rare in England.

Church of St Mary-le-Strand, London, by James Gibbs; 1714–17. This and St Martin-in-the-Fields are Gibbs's outstanding London churches, both (especially the tower of this one) influenced by Wren's City churches. It was begun in 1714 under the Fifty New Churches Act. Its facade is divided horizontally like the Whitehall Banqueting House and St Paul's Cathedral but with more logic since the two tiers of windows light the aisles and the galleries over them.

Ditchley Park, Oxfordshire, by James Gibbs; 1720–22. This house has a central block linked by curved corridors to smaller pavilions, enclosing a railed-in forecourt. The relatively severe facades anticipate many of the changes that were to come in with the Palladians. The square blocks on the door surround are, however, typically Gibbs. The Ditchley facades are additionally enlivened by urns and lead statuary on the skyline. The house has highly ornamental interiors by William Kent and Henry Flitcroft.

Gibbs's country houses are much simpler in style. Typical is Ditchley, Oxfordshire, built in 1720 and sumptuously decorated inside by William Kent. The house has several features that were later to be the favourites of the Palladian architects who came very soon after Gibbs – though not the most fashionable feature of all, the temple portico. So although the Palladians turned their backs on the work of Gibbs's generation and although Palladianism was promoted especially by the Whigs, a house like Ditchley can be regarded as an introduction to the coming Palladian age.

Chapter 10

Town Building: Terrace, Square and Crescent

Bedford Square, London; 1775 onwards. The best preserved of the sequence of squares, connected by built-up streets and with gardens in the centre, laid out in the late eighteenth century on his Bloomsbury Estate by the Duke of Bedford. The square's architect is uncertain: possibly Thomas Leverton (1743–1824) who is known to have designed the interior of at least one of the houses. They are of brick, with the central feature on each side of the square stuccoed and the front doors emphasized by rusticated surrounds in artificial stone.

WHEN in 1713 the Treaty of Utrecht ended the War of the Spanish Succession it did more than usher in a period of peaceful reconstruction in Europe, free from the threat of French hegemony. For Marlborough's victories on land were accompanied by the establishment of England's command of the sea, which was to be sustained for a couple of centuries, and by the eclipse of the Dutch as the chief beneficiaries of the growing ocean trade. England became the world's principal trading nation, and as a consequence first commerce and then industry developed at home, resulting in the growth of towns and the acceleration of the process of transforming the English from the primarily agricultural people they had been since the beginning of the Middle Ages to the most highly urbanized people in Europe or America.

Although the eighteenth century was in many ways an age of personal, rather than corporate, initiative, its characteristic building activities were, because of this steady conversion to an urban life, no longer isolated architectural monuments but the streets and squares of England's expanding market towns, of her ports like Bristol and Falmouth, busy with the new ocean trade, and of London, which became, as Venice and Amsterdam had been earlier, the world's financial and mercantile capital, a position that subsequent wars and even the loss of the American colonies did not alter.

The existence of the architectural idiom already popularized in Sir Christopher Wren's generation – a simple idiom requiring only a limited range of materials and permitting the near standardization of house-plans and the rationalization of elements like windows, doors and staircases – meant that all over England builders with little sophisticated architectural knowledge could create streets of sensible, economical houses with the help of the pattern-books that were published for their benefit; notably those by Batty Langley (1696–1751) and William

125

Halfpenny (died 1755). With the guidance these books provided, masons, carpenters and the like were able, even in remote parts of the country, to elevate their status to that of professional architects.

These changes were of course gradual. Except in certain rapidly expanding towns the urban picture at the beginning of the eighteenth century was still largely composed of medieval-style houses, mainly of timber, arranged on no regular plan. But among them were now beginning to rise a few larger buildings other than the churches that for centuries had provided almost the only architectural landmarks. For the growth of trade and commerce, besides leading to an increase in town dwelling, led to a higher degree of urban administration and to a variety of buildings to house it. The medieval guildhalls gave way to town halls and to often quite ambitious accommodation for dealing in commodities like cloth. The colonnaded Piece Hall at Halifax (1775, by Thomas Bradley) is a splendid though fairly late example. In the growing seaports were built commercial buildings like the Cooper Hall at Bristol, handsomely designed in 1743 by the William Halfpenny referred to above. In the City of London and elsewhere new types of building facilitated the conduct of business – the early forerunners of the modern office building.

The architectural quality of the many buildings of this kind that still survive offers evidence of increasing civic pride in the late seventeenth and early eighteenth centuries, and also of the degree to which knowledge of the Classical language of architecture and the ability to adapt it to English needs was spreading far beyond London and the old university towns where it had first emerged. Such elegant and expertly designed buildings as the custom-house of 1683 at King's Lynn, Norfolk, by Henry Bell (1647–1711), the dramatically sited Guildford town hall in full-blooded Restoration style (1682), the town hall at Abingdon, Berkshire

Custom-house, King's Lynn, Norfolk, by Henry Bell; 1683. Originally designed as the Exchange, this elegant early Renaissance composition was by a local architect who was twice mayor of the town. He was also a prosperous merchant, a connoisseur of art, a practising engraver, an amateur scientist and had made the Grand Tour of Europe. The building was paid for by John Turner, a merchant of the town and patron of the arts, like many of his kind in East Anglia at this time.

Piece Hall, Halifax, West Yorkshire, by Thomas Bradley; 1775. Built as a cloth market, the Piece Hall indicates the prosperity the textile trade was beginning to bring to the northern manufacturing towns. A large enclosed square, reached through a pedimented archway, is surrounded by a three-storey building, arcaded on the ground floor, with a colonnade of square rusticated piers above and another colonnade of Tuscan columns above that. The Piece Hall has over 300 rooms.

(1677), thought to be by Christopher Kempster (1627–1715), the guildhall at Worcester (1723, by Thomas White – better known as a sculptor) and the corn exchange at Rochester (1766) were all the work of local, rather than metropolitan, architects. As the eighteenth century progressed, architectural skill and knowledge progressed also, and local architects earned the patronage of the nobility and the civic authorities, who no longer felt impelled to seek the latest architectural guidance in London.

John Carr (1723–1807), to take just one example, the son of a Yorkshire mason and quarry-owner, set up in the city of York and acquired a flourishing practice there and in neighbouring counties. He built the County Assize Courts in York itself and the town hall at Newark, Nottinghamshire, both in 1773 and both displaying a confident mastery of the Classical idiom. He also built a number of country houses, all (except the very distinguished Basildon, Berkshire, 1766) in the north of England. Local architects – and some families of architects – less well known than Carr and, like him, originating as masons, created respectable, educated buildings in all parts of the country; the Billings of Reading, the Hiorns of Warwickshire, the Lumbys of Lincoln, the Trubshaws of Staffordshire, the Patys of Bristol. James Paty built the Theatre Royal at Bristol, one of the oldest theatres still in use, in 1764 (the street frontage was rebuilt later) and Thomas Paty and his son (1713–89) laid out a whole sequence of Bristol streets and designed their facades in the new sober and regular style.   Sometimes there were architectural opportunities of an even more comprehensive kind, for example the rebuilding of the small town of Blandford, Dorset, after a fire had destroyed its whole centre in 1731. Here once again the work was given to a local family, the Bastards. Besides numerous houses and the Red Lion inn, modestly composed out of the same range of Classical elements, their buildings include a church and a town hall, the latter with a fine pedimented facade with embellishments derived, it is believed, from the work of Thomas Archer under whom one of the younger Bastards had studied in London.

From the activities of many such local architects and builders, adopting at several removes the innovations brought in by the travelled architects of the metropolis and their gentlemen-patrons, there emerged a recognizable vernacular style – the style we now call Georgian. Unmistakably English, its origin can be traced partly to the influence of Wren but also to the overseas contacts resulting from foreign trade and from the accession of William of Orange to the English throne. It derives more, therefore, from the Dutch than from the Italian or French Renaissance. It furnished the whole country with a language flexible enough for everyone to use – the socially ambitious classes grandly, the country

builder simply. The town expansion of these years spread it widely and many an English market town transformed itself from a medieval huddle of buildings round a market-place into a spacious arrangement of streets, using this new Georgian idiom to present a degree of uniformity unknown before. Only the medieval church, and perhaps the remains of a castle, a guildhall or a group of almshouses, furnished a reminder of the past.

In the centre too – in the rebuilt market-square – there would probably now be a handsome coaching inn, or at least a reconstruction in the new style of the principal medieval inn, indicating the influence of the new turnpike roads (the first turnpike trust was set up in 1706) on the life of the town and on the rapid distribution of ideas – and of people – from the centre of the country to all parts of the periphery. The first official service of mail-coaches, connecting Bristol and London, did not begin until 1784, but stage-coaches, carrying parcels and passengers, had been running for many years. The great days of the stage-coach were, however, in the early nineteenth century, after road surfaces had further improved. There are good examples of a Georgian coaching inn at Market Harborough (The Three Swans), at Marlborough (The Castle and Ball) and at Saffron Walden (The Rose and Crown).

In this new town architecture brick superseded the timber frame as the main domestic building material because of the danger of fire and because of the shortage of strong timbers that had been increasing since the forests were cut down in the late Middle Ages. At the same time, as a matter of fashion, many timber-framed buildings were given street facades in brick with the new-style Georgian windows, doors and balconies.

An important influence on the ubiquitous use of brick was the increase at this time of water transport, by which bricks could be carried far more cheaply

Town hall, Abingdon, Berkshire; 1677–80. A handsome example of the new type of civic building that from the seventeenth century onwards was taking the place of the medieval guildhall. The lower storey is an open market; the upper one a town assembly-room. It was built in an ambitious early Renaissance style, probably under the influence of Wren, for the designer is thought to have been Christopher Kempster, a mason from nearby Burford who worked for Wren on several of the City churches, including St Stephen's, Walbrook.

and in far greater bulk; a horse-drawn wagon, even on the new hard-surfaced roads, could carry a load of only two tons for every horse employed whereas a river barge could carry thirty tons and a canal barge fifty. As we have already seen, the stone for the great cathedrals was brought from the quarries almost wholly by sea and river, and from the sixteenth century onwards the navigation of the English rivers was being steadily improved by the construction first of weirs and sluices and then of locks. The first lock on the Thames was built in 1632, and the works that made the River Wey navigable the whole distance from the Thames to Guildford completed in 1653.

In the eighteenth century there was a new incentive for improving water transport: the increasing use of coal for iron-making and the need to carry it from the coal-mining areas to other parts of the country. So the improvement of rivers was followed by the construction of canals, the first being the Bridgewater Canal linking the Duke of Bridgewater's Worsley pits with the River Mersey and built by James Brindley for the third Duke in 1760. From then onwards canal building was continuous, especially in the north of England and the Midlands, and there was no longer any problem transporting heavy building materials – roof-tiles and slates as well as bricks and stone – over long distances. As a result the appearance of towns was no longer almost exclusively determined by the colours and textures of the locally produced materials, although these of course, being the cheapest, remained the commonest.

Stone was still regarded as the handsomest material, but for the more modest houses and streets brick altogether superseded both it and timber except in regions where stone lay immediately beneath the ground. One of Britain's greatest architectural achievements was created in one of these regions: in the hills where Gloucestershire and Somerset meet. Here at Bath the Roman garrisons of

Rose and Crown Inn, Saffron Walden, Essex. The coaching inns were the main social centres of market towns from the seventeenth century until at least the coming of the railways. The front of the Rose and Crown dates from about 1700 but the building itself is a century earlier. The lower part is of brick; the upper part was pargetted in traditional East Anglian style in 1874 by the 'Queen Anne' architect Eden Nesfield (see Chapter 16). The opening on the left leads into the stable-yard.

nearly two thousand years before had valued the medicinal waters, and the city they founded had flourished throughout the Middle Ages chiefly as a centre of the cloth trade. However it had not altogether lost its reputation as a health resort; for example when Robert Cecil, Earl of Salisbury and Lord Treasurer to James I, became seriously ill in 1612 (in fact he died the same summer), the best hope was for him to travel to Bath and take the waters there. Then in 1702 and 1703 Queen Anne visited Bath for her health and soon after this, promoted by Beau Nash, it again became a successful spa and soon a highly fashionable place of resort. It grew in a few years into a handsome city which was given architectural distinction and variety by a sequence of geometrical spaces and finely proportioned terraces of houses for letting to its visitors. As in other places, the architects were local and self-made, first John Wood (1705–54), the son of a builder, and then his son, John Wood the younger (1728–81).

The principal contribution of the elder Wood, who had had experience in London before returning to Bath and starting work in that city, was also one of his first: Queen Square (begun 1729). He financed it himself as a speculation when the Bath Corporation found his plans for developing the city too ambitious. Queen Square was not only a financial success, leading to the further rapid growth of the city on the same lines, but is of unusual significance architecturally. Each side of the square is treated as a self-contained architectural composition as though it was the facade of a palace rather than a row of identical houses. This practice of designing residential squares with their sides resembling complete buildings soon became the pattern employed all over the country.

The elder Wood also designed the Circus at Bath. It was still uncompleted at his death and was finished by his son, who went on to surround these two isolated show-pieces, Queen Square and the Circus, by the famous sequence of streets, terraces and crescents which is the most distinguished of its kind in Europe. Imaginatively disposed along the shelving sites that Bath provided, his layout can be regarded as an urban example of the Picturesque movement which became England's special contribution to landscape architecture. The climax of the younger Wood's contribution to Bath was the Royal Crescent (1775).

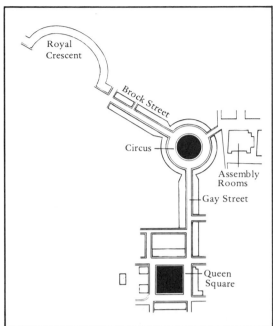

Bath: layout of central residential area.

Bath of course was exceptional, but many other English towns and cities were furnished at this time with new residential areas and their streets enlivened by formal squares and crescents, mostly by local builders or builders turned architects. The houses were of two or, more usually, three storeys – sometimes four – plus an attic in the roof, and in the more densely built cities where space was precious in London especially – with a basement also, lighted from a railinged area. The houses were never higher, for everywhere in England the spread of towns was

Queen Square, Bath, by John Wood the elder; 1729 onwards. Wood was one of the promoters, as well as being the first notable architect, of the eighteenth-century resurgence of Bath as a spa. He laid out a large part of the sequence of residential streets that was to be built up in due course by his son, and himself designed Queen Square and the Circus (begun 1754 and finished by his son after his death in that year). The north front of Queen Square was one of the first instances, along with Thomas Archer's Cavendish Square, London (on which Wood had worked a few years before), of a group of individual houses being treated as a single architectural composition, with in this case a pedimented centre and columned projections at either end.

133

Royal Crescent, Bath, by John Wood the younger;
1767–75. Wood carried on his father's enterprises,
equipping the newly fashionable city of Bath with
residential streets and public buildings, all in the
beautiful local limestone and imaginatively laid out to
exploit the contours of the ground. Royal Crescent was
the first of its kind and was frequently imitated in other
towns. It is a semi-ellipse and consists of thirty houses
behind a continuous facade of giant Ionic columns.

outwards, not upwards. Even London spread
outwards, engulfing country villages on the way. It
provided an absolute contrast to, say, Paris (and
Edinburgh) where high tenements became the
urban way of living. The Continental conception of
apartments, where instead of each family occupying
one plot of land, several families spread themselves
horizontally in layers, did not become socially
acceptable in England until near the end of the
nineteenth century.

The high cost of land required frontages to be as
narrow as possible, and there emerged in the late
seventeenth and early eighteenth centuries an almost

completely standardized pattern of town house,
forming the unit out of which the Georgian streets
and squares were largely composed. This standard
house was three windows wide, the windows of the
first floor, where the main living rooms were placed,
being taller than the others and one of the windows
on the ground floor being replaced by the front door.
This floor was raised above the pavement to admit
more light into the basement, and the door was
approached by a flight of steps. The doorway was
usually arched, with a fanlight to let light into the
hallway inside, and was the only part of the exterior
to be given any degree of architectural elaboration –
sometimes simply flanking pilasters and a crowning
pediment; sometimes a projecting porch with
columns and entablature – so that it was the
succession of front doors or porches that marked the
rhythm along the street.

The windows were unadorned except perhaps by
wrought-iron balconies on the first floor. The roofs
and attic windows were almost hidden behind a
parapet, the regular use of which followed a legal
statute of 1707, forbidding wooden eaves or cornices

because of the danger of fire. Other variations, too, on the general pattern enable one to distinguish the earlier houses from the later. For example window-bars became progressively more slender. Sash windows were the rule after their introduction from Holland around 1710; few casement windows, with their characteristic mullions and transoms, are to be found after this date. The window glass began by being almost flush with the wall-surface but afterwards had by law to be set back at least four inches. The window reveal, when thus exposed, gives an appearance of greater solidity to the brickwork, and in later terraces of houses it became the custom to plaster the reveals and paint them white, which emphasizes the regularity of the facade pattern when it is viewed obliquely, as it normally is, along the street.

In spite of such minor variations the general design changed little; nor did the interior layout of the houses, of which this facade pattern was the direct expression: a narrow hallway leading to the foot of the stairs; alongside it two main rooms on each floor (linked by folding doors in the case of the first-floor rooms) and a smaller room over the front door. Until well into the nineteenth century this design was being repeated on every scale from that of the great mansions of Belgravia to that of the two-storey artisans' dwellings built in innumerable terraces in the expanding industrial towns.

It was not only the growth of commerce and industry, nor only the sudden increase in England's population, that caused this nation-wide construction of new residential streets. The prospering middle classes no longer wished to live, as they had done for centuries, over their shops or workshops. This was a move they could afford because the eighteenth century, although it brought some overcrowding – the beginning in fact of the industrial slums of the nineteenth century – was for most of its course a period of improving living standards, at least for the townsmen. Only in the countryside was there more poverty instead of more prosperity as the enclosure of fields, necessary in order to increase grain production, turned the peasantry into landless labourers. This change in the social nature of the countryside is something we shall have to return to when we come to look, in Chapter 13, at the architecture of the Industrial Revolution.

The rapid development of towns accelerated especially after the Peace of Paris of 1763, which

Clifton, Bristol. Unity combined with variety was achieved in the modest but fashionable accommodation provided at the beginning of the nineteenth century in the many new streets and squares of middle-class houses: vertical development because of the price of land; stucco the favourite material; plentiful bay windows delicately subdivided; ornament restricted to ironwork and pillared porches.

ended the Seven Years War. The internal expansion that had somewhat slackened in wartime was renewed. Streets and squares and crescents were laid out in many places on a large enough scale to endow the residential quarters even of small towns with a sense of unity quite different from the unplanned though often picturesque arrangement of their ancient centres. But in the new manufacturing towns unity often became monotony. In fashionable places, such as Clifton (a suburb of Bristol), Cheltenham and Leamington, a new vernacular of bay-windowed terrace houses, adorned with delicate ironwork, set standards of domestic elegance that have never been surpassed.

Another phenomenon typical of this period is that the efforts of the speculative builders who had

135

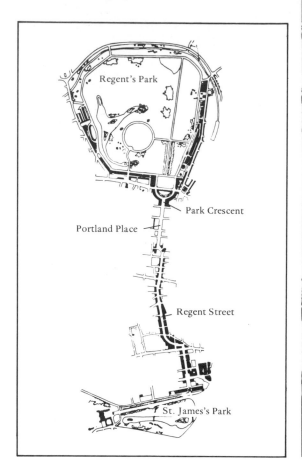

Nash's layout of Regent's Park and the streets to the south of it for the Prince Regent.

hitherto dominated the town-development business were supplemented, notably in north-west London, by those of big landlords who saw the profit to be made from converting their estates into housing. They made ambitious plans commensurate with their own status and their purpose of providing residences not only for the expanding middle classes but for the gentry and the newly rich; for example for the new generation of businessmen that the prestige of the City was attracting to London and the new provincial aristocracy of finance and industry who wanted London houses in which to spend part of the year. Typical of the latter were northern land-owners with coal beneath their estates which was now being profitably mined.

Among these redeveloped London properties

were the Grosvenor, Portman, Portland and Bedford Estates. As well as experienced builders, some of the better-known architects (such men as Adam, Cockerell and Nash, whose individual works we shall be noting in the next two chapters) were called in to provide more attractive layouts and more elegant facades than in the usual speculative builder's identically repeated streets. Bloomsbury, part of the Bedford Estate, was planned as a sequence of tree-planted squares which introduced a surprising impression of greenery into an area densely filled with bricks and mortar and perfected a type of urban layout, full of spatial variety, that was a peculiarly English achievement.

These late-eighteenth-century London estates have for the most part now been mutilated although from some an impression can still be obtained of the dignified layout and the consistent architectural character with which they furnished considerable parts of a London that was still on the whole

The process of laying out large areas of London in formal sequences of residential squares, terraces and crescents reached its climax when the Prince Regent commissioned Nash to redesign parts of the royal estates in St Marylebone. Cumberland Terrace on the east side of the park treats a block of houses like one exuberant stucco palace, using Nash's favourite repertoire of Classical ornaments. The executive architect for this particular terrace was James Thomson.

operating – as it is operating to this day – within the restrictions of its medieval street plan. One example of this formally designed residential architecture must suffice. Of the sequence of squares laid out by the Duke of Bedford on his Bloomsbury Estate, the best, Bedford Square, survives almost intact. Begun in 1775, it has the typical repetition of plain windows enlivened by wrought-iron balconies and emphatically embellished doorways, and a pediment over the centre of each side of the square, giving it the appearance of one architectural unit.

The climax of this phase of the replanning of London by aristocratic landlords came in the year 1811 when the most aristocratic of them all, the Prince Regent, commissioned John Nash to design Regent's Park and connect it by a series of streets to his residence at Carlton House, taking in on the way Portland Place, a wide new street that had been created in 1774 as part of the redevelopment of the Portland Estate. The Prince Regent's enterprise gave London its most impressive display of planned urban architecture. It, too, has been mutilated in parts, but Park Crescent and the terraces facing into Regent's Park which the crescent introduces still stand as the most spectacular exposition of the English art of Picturesque planning, in which the elements of domestic architecture are skilfully manipulated to produce at the same time dignified habitations and dramatic urban scenery.

Chapter 11

The Palladian Age

THE last chapter described the architectural outcome of the accelerating move from the countryside into the towns and took us up to, and into, the nineteenth century. Now we must go back to the eighteenth, for simultaneously with the establishment of the Georgian urban vernacular, and its rural equivalent in the shape of small farmhouses and cottages, another phenomenon, peculiar to England, came at this time to dominate nearly the whole of the architectural profession and leave its mark also on the vernacular itself. This was an obsession with the example set and the rules laid down by the Italian architect Andrea Palladio (1508–80).

It was far from being the first time his influence had been felt in England. It will be remembered from Chapter 8 that when Inigo Jones introduced fully fledged Italian Renaissance architecture to the Stuart Court he took Palladio's work as his model. But the fashions he set were soon superseded by the less restrained – and less Italian – styles of Wren, Hawksmoor and Vanbrugh (see Chapter 9), styles that had more in common with those of their own near-contemporaries on the Continent. Then in the eighteenth century England took a step back; not in the quality of her architecture but back in time, looking instead to the sixteenth-century Palladio for guidance.

Just as in the fourteenth century England had turned her back on the late – generally flamboyant – tendencies of Continental Gothic and evolved her own more austere and geometrically disciplined form of Gothic in the shape of the Perpendicular style, so in the eighteenth century she turned away from the Baroque (the only term one can use in this context although in England Baroque meant something far less extreme than elsewhere) and adopted a very different discipline. The leading English architects, and the men of taste and wealth for whom they worked (in the Hanoverian age the Court no longer set the fashion), dedicated them-

Houghton Hall, Norfolk, by Colen Campbell; 1722.
Houghton was designed for Sir Robert Walpole and begun the year after he became Prime Minister, although not finished until 1735 (after Campbell's death). Campbell's design was executed by Thomas Ripley (1683–1758), another protégé of Walpole's; there were then minor modifications by James Gibbs and, inside the house, by Kent. Houghton has more robustness than the classic Palladian house – a lingering flavour of the Baroque of a century before. The main block shown here has curved colonnades connecting it to service wings. The end pavilions were intended by Campbell to have pediments, following the precedent of Inigo Jones's Wilton House (pages 90–91). The stone domes on each corner were added by Gibbs.

Chiswick House, London, by Lord Burlington; 1725.
Designed for entertaining his friends and displaying his collections, this was the house with which Richard Boyle, Earl of Burlington, set the fashion for the style of Andrea Palladio which was to dominate English architecture for most of the century. It is closely modelled on Palladio's Villa Capra near Vicenza. Inside it has richly decorated rooms by Burlington's protégé William Kent.

selves not to the excitements of the Baroque but to obedience to a strictly regulated Classical style based on that of Palladio.

The ground had been prepared by a growing interest in Classical learning and by the practice on the part of the wealthy and well-educated English of making the Grand Tour of Europe at least once in their lives, culminating in a spell in Italy. But in architectural terms the beginning of the Palladian age in England can be precisely dated: 1715, the year in which two influential books were published. One was a translation (by Nicholas Dubois) of Palladio's *I Quattro Libri dell' Architettura*. This was edited and brought out in England by the Venetian-born architect Giacomo Leoni (1686–1746) who redrew Palladio's woodcut illustrations in the form of large

engravings. Leoni settled in England and designed, among other houses, Clandon Park, Surrey (1713–29), and Argyll House, Chelsea (1723).

The other book was *Vitruvius Britannicus* by the English architect Colen Campbell (1676–1729). This was a survey of the preceding hundred years of English architecture with special stress on the attributes it had derived from Palladio and that he had himself derived from his Roman master Vitruvius. It illustrated some unbuilt projects by Campbell in the style of Palladio and the climax of the book was the presentation of a vast country house that Campbell had designed in this style. The house, Wanstead House, Essex (just east of London), was completed in 1720 and demolished a hundred years later. Its most striking feature, besides its restraint generally, was the temple-style portico in the centre of its long flat facade, reached by a double flight of steps – a feature that was to be incorporated in innumerable Palladian mansions from then onwards. Wanstead House was coolly Classical in contrast to the restive romanticism of houses like Blenheim and Castle Howard.

Colen Campbell built some smaller houses also, even more closely modelled on Palladio's buildings, but the movement towards a new style and away from Baroque extravagance took its biggest step forward when Richard Boyle, third Earl of Burlington (1694–1753), a cultivated patron of the arts who had made the Grand Tour and who had been a subscriber to *Vitruvius Britannicus*, took up the cause of Palladian architecture with dedication and enthusiasm. In 1719 he commissioned Colen Campbell to remodel his London House in Piccadilly in the new fashion (Burlington House has, however, since been altered again more than once) and in the same year he himself went to Italy on a second visit, spending some months in Vicenza, Palladio's home town in or near which some of his principal works are situated, and bringing back a collection of Palladio's own drawings.

Lord Burlington also brought back with him from Italy the English painter William Kent (1685–1748), who was studying in Rome and whom Burlington was to employ later on as a decorator and then as an architect. First of all, however, in 1727, he employed Kent on the publication of a collection he had made of the designs of Inigo Jones, an architect he admired almost as much as Palladio. Those two, and the antiquities of ancient Rome which he had also

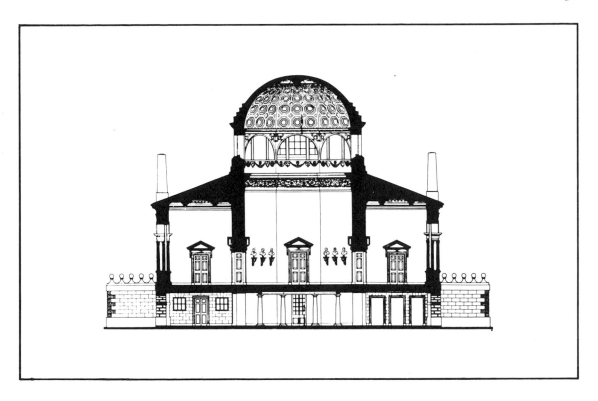

Section through Chiswick House (to larger scale than plan below).

Plan of Chiswick House, London.

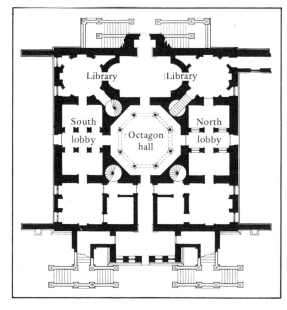

spent time studying, are the main constituents of the new style that Lord Burlington played the largest part in establishing. His part was more than that of a patron, for he was himself an amateur architect of great talent. His first substantial buildings were a country house, Tottenham Park, Wiltshire (1721), now demolished, which had corner towers like Inigo Jones's Wilton House, adorned with the three-light 'Venetian' windows also used by Jones (see Chapter 8) and soon to become one of the hallmarks of Palladian architecture, and a dormitory for Westminster School (1722), the acceptance of which in place of a Wren-type design was an indication of the way taste was changing.

Burlington's most remarkable building soon followed: the villa he embarked on in 1725 at Chiswick, London, for his own use – not primarily as a residence but for entertaining and exhibiting collections of art. Its design is approximately modelled on that of one of Palladio's country villas in the Vicenza region, the Villa Capra (1566), also known as La Rotonda. It has the same external form – a domed central block rising out of the roof of a square building entered through temple-style

porticos – but the original has porticos on all four sides whereas Lord Burlington's has them on only two and there are many differences of detail like the shape of the clerestory window in the Chiswick villa, which Lord Burlington took from Roman baths. It is, especially in its garden setting, English rather than Italian, yet it is essentially Palladian in spirit. Its influence was very great, including that of its interior, a sequence of differently shaped rooms which became the basis of many of the more palatial domestic interiors of later architects, notably of Robert Adam.

Burlington's protégé, Colen Campbell, also built Houghton Hall, Norfolk (1722) and Mereworth Castle, Kent (1723), the latter being even more closely modelled on Palladio's Villa Capra than Burlington's Chiswick villa although Campbell had never seen the original. Campbell died not long after Mereworth was finished and Burlington, after himself designing, among several minor buildings, the Assembly Rooms at York (1731) with a handsome ballroom lined with giant columns, again very Roman, made William Kent his professional associate. Kent had already been responsible for the rich interiors at Chiswick House. They now jointly (and it is thought with the help also of their client William Coke, later the Earl of Leicester) designed Holkham Hall, Norfolk (1734), the first of the great Palladian country houses, partly as a setting for Coke's collection of antique sculpture. Holkham has the horizontal lines, the simple massing and the expanses of plain walling (in this case, however, of brick) of the typical Palladian mansion. By contrast its interiors are brilliantly rich and palatial, suggesting that Kent, who was responsible for the interiors, had not been completely weaned away from the influence of his immediate seniors such as Vanbrugh.

The Assembly Rooms, York, by Lord Burlington; 1730. These reveal the influence of the buildings of ancient Rome, especially of the baths which Burlington had studied during his travels in Italy in 1720. He brought back drawings by Palladio, interpreting the work of his master, the Roman architect Vitruvius, and Burlington described his York interior as a reconstruction of what Vitruvius had called an Egyptian hall. It is 112 feet long and 40 feet wide. The close-set Corinthian columns are painted brownish-yellow and marbled. The present facade of the building, by Pritchett and Watson, dates only from 1828.

Kent's flair for handling Baroque interior spaces is shown again by a house he designed in Berkeley Square, London, in 1724 and his versatility by the important role he played as one of the first of the new school of informal landscapists. He pioneered a style of landscaping that Lancelot ('Capability') Brown (1716–83) elaborated in due course, in conscious opposition to the French tradition of geometrical formality, into the internationally admired and imitated landscaped park, the setting of many eighteenth-century country houses.

In one of the first of these parks at Stowe, Buckinghamshire, Kent designed (1730–36) a number of small Classical buildings as landscape ornaments. They were modelled on ancient Roman temples and were similar to those buildings that appear in the backgrounds of paintings by Poussin and Claude which themselves strongly influenced the work of the Picturesque landscapists. The patronage of Lord Burlington also obtained for William Kent the post of Deputy Surveyor of the Board of Works, for which he then built the Horseguards in Whitehall, London (1748). That he was given such a post was another indication that the new Palladian style was becoming recognized as ripe to replace the style of Wren and his colleagues in official as well as private circles.

Lord Burlington extended his patronage also to Henry Flitcroft (1697–1769). Flitcroft was first a carpenter, then a draughtsman (he drew many of the illustrations for Burlington's *Designs of Inigo Jones* on which Kent worked also) and finally an architect. He built the church of St Giles-in-the-Fields, London (1731), which was influenced by Gibbs but had not the superimposed orders that the strict Palladians disliked in Gibbs's St Mary-le-Strand, nor the latter church's liveliness. He also built several country houses including the vast and rather dull Wentworth Woodhouse, South Yorkshire (begun 1733), like a stretched-out version of Colen Campbell's Wanstead which itself had something in common with Gibbs's Ditchley (see Chapter 9), Gibbs being in a sense the link between the generation of Vanbrugh and Hawksmoor and that of the Palladians. Flitcroft in fact designed several of the interiors at Ditchley. As in the case of Kent, Lord Burlington obtained for Flitcroft a position in the Board of Works, thus promoting further his own ambition to establish the Palladian as the official style.

It did in fact, for a hundred years, dominate English architecture both for public and privately commissioned buildings. Church building was no longer a significant influence as it had been in the centuries before. Among successful London architects who conformed to its rules and followed its precedents, outstanding were Sir Robert Taylor (1714–88) who began as a sculptor (Heveningham, Suffolk, 1778–88, and a now totally vanished rebuilding of the Bank of England) and James Paine (1717–89) who shows more pronounced Roman influence (the Mansion House, Doncaster, 1745, and Wardour Castle, Wiltshire, 1769, although the former has a beautiful example of the Palladian 'Venetian' window). Taylor and Paine were among the first English architects to take articled pupils in their offices, a system that continued to dominate the training of architects until architectural schools gradually took over in the twentieth century.

Among architects who took Palladian principles to the provinces were those already referred to (Chapter 10) as establishing there a degree of sophistication that had previously been restricted to men continuously in touch with the capital and the Court; men like John Carr of York and the Woods of Bath. The elder Wood built a house for Ralph Allen, one of the men behind the revitalization of Bath as a fashionable resort, not far from that city. This was Prior Park (1735–48), which is a model of the symmetrical Palladian country house with a central portico reached by flights of steps and spreading wings linked to it by arcades, all set in a landscaped park itself adorned with elegant minor works of architecture.

As in the case of the Georgian town vernacular described in the last chapter, the Palladian style became widely accepted. Its relatively simple idiom

Holkham Hall, Norfolk, by Lord Burlington and William Kent; 1734: the south front. Its abrupt subdivision into geometrical compartments makes a significant contrast to the flowing lines of the Baroque of a generation earlier. The house, designed for the Earl of Leicester, displays most of the features that were to be associated with English Palladian architecture: the pedimented end pavilions; the triple ('Venetian') windows; the temple portico (which was not however in this case the entrance, this being on the opposite side of the house). The two wings contain a chapel and a suite of libraries. Unusually for such a palatial house, the walling material is yellow brick, not stone.

Constable Burton Hall, North Yorkshire, by John Carr; 1762–68. A model of the Georgian country house of the middle size. Although it is somewhat formal and its stonework all ashlar, it is given a rural flavour by, for example, the overhanging eaves finished with a modest cornice instead of a parapet or balustrade. The main rooms are on the upper floor, reached by a typical Palladian external staircase. The lower-floor windows, lighting the kitchens, etc., have surrounds with projecting square blocks made fashionable by Gibbs (see Ditchley, page 123).

was easily mastered with the help of the many books published for the guidance of architects and builders. All over England Palladian and near Palladian country houses were put up, by modest country squires for family habitation as well as by rich magnates and land-owners for display and entertainment. Frequently they replaced existing houses, so much eagerness was there at this time to use architecture to show that one was in the fashion. The Palladian architectural language could be readily adapted to whatever scale of residence was required; so one of the virtues of the eighteenth-century English country house, apart from its sensitive integration into the landscape of enclosed fields of which its surrounding park is only a kind of idealization, is that the smaller examples are suited

architecturally to their modest size and do not look – as do many of the smaller French and central European country houses – like miniature versions of larger palaces and châteaux.

Prior Park, Bath, by John Wood the elder; 1735. Built for Ralph Allen, a patron of Wood's, who began as the local assistant postmaster, married General Wade's only daughter, prospered and, in 1727, bought the Combe Down limestone quarries with the idea of exporting the stone down the River Avon, which had lately been made navigable as far up as Bath. He commissioned Wood to build Prior Park as an advertisement of the qualities of Combe Down stone for building. He was also one of Wood's principal backers in the development of Bath itself. Prior Park follows the pattern of the classic Palladian house: central block (seen here) with temple portico, flanked by wings linked to it by curved arcades. As a result of being converted into a school (1829) and of other changes, little of the house except the outside of the central block remains exactly as Wood designed it, but it still has the informal landscaped setting of many of the houses of this period, complete with architectural embellishments like the covered 'Palladian' bridge by the lake (1755). This is thought also to be John Wood's work, although Ralph Allen's clerk of works, Richard Jones, claimed that it was his. It is a copy of the bridge at Wilton, designed in 1736 by Colen Campbell and Roger Morris. There is a similar bridge at Stowe.

146

Chapter 12

Discovery of the Ancient World: Adam and the Neo-Classicists

WE saw in the last chapter how Palladio's echoes of his master Vitruvius and Lord Burlington's interest in the ruins of ancient Rome were the principal new themes that the early eighteenth century introduced into English architecture; also how curiosity about the buildings of all parts of the ancient world was being fostered by noblemen and gentlemen returning from the Grand Tour. Increasingly as the century progressed an exotic colouring was given in this way to the work of most of the leading architects, especially those who made their name as young men by measuring and drawing the antiquities of places outside Rome and Vicenza – indeed outside Italy, for soon the whole Mediterranean basin was the hunting-ground of those for whom antiquity had a growing fascination.

The many books published by subscription among gentlemen connoisseurs, and especially by the members of the Society of Dilettanti which had been founded in 1733, indicate the source of the new influences and the names of the architects who established reputations in this manner. Among them were *The Ruins of Palmyra* by Robert Wood (1753), *The Antiquities of Athens* by James Stuart and Nicholas Revett (1762) and *The Ruins of the Palace of the Emperor Diocletian at Spalatro* by Robert Adam (1764). Adam's great rival, Chambers, went even further afield than the Mediterranean. His *Designs of Chinese Buildings, Furniture, Dresses etc.* was published in 1757. The oriental, however, remained a minority taste, for a time influencing Chippendale's furniture but not architecture except on one isolated occasion when Chambers himself indulged in a few oriental fantasies. In that same year, 1757, he laid out the grounds of her house at Kew for the dowager Princess of Wales and incorporated a Chinese pagoda among other embellishments. The Hindu fashion that showed itself occasionally in the Regency period came through trade with India, not through scholarly research.

Heveningham Hall, Suffolk: the saloon, by James Wyatt; 1780–84. Designed after the architect of the house, Sir Robert Taylor, had quarrelled with his client and Wyatt had been called in to complete it and design the interiors. These are after the manner of Robert Adam but on the whole less elaborate, and there is no precedent in Adam's work for the brilliantly inventive ceiling shown here.

149

*Somerset House, London, by Sir William Chambers;
1776–98.* The first major English building in the Neo-
Classical style long practised on the Continent and
introduced by Chambers on his return from five years of
study (1750–55) in France and Italy. It stands beside the
Thames on the site of the Protector Somerset's house of
1547, the first truly Renaissance mansion in England (see
Chapter 7). On the river front the main facade, 800 feet
long, is set back behind a terrace (in Chambers's time
open to the public on Sundays) carried on rusticated
arches which originally rose straight from the water. The
present roadway was built in front of them in 1872.

Classical antiquities were the main source of
changing architectural taste; Greek, Etruscan,
Pompeian as well as Imperial Roman. All these were
being studied on the spot by scholars and anti-
quarians. The influence of ancient Greece was the
strongest, if only because of the leading place held by
Greek literature and history in the upper-class
Englishman's education, but the direct imitation of
Classical Greek architecture did not come about for
a little while in spite of the attention given to Stuart
and Revett's publications. Its purity and restraint
were not what the increasingly self-indulgent
patrons of architecture were looking for. Ancient
Rome furnished the models they were initially more
ready to respond to and provided most of the
inspiration for the two men – intense rivals – who
dominated English architecture in the late eighteenth century: Sir William Chambers (1723–96)
and Robert Adam (1728–92).

The Neo-Classical style with archaeological
overtones that these two did most to establish in
England represented, unlike the Palladian style, a
Continental as well as an English trend. French
Neo-Classical architecture was already being promoted by Germain Soufflot (1713–80), afterwards
architect of the Panthéon in Paris, and by others less
known, and it was in Paris that Chambers, after
serving in the Merchant Navy (and seeing while
doing so the Chinese buildings whose style he
imitated at Kew), studied architecture under the
leading French theoretician, Jacques-François
Blondel, before going on to Rome. He stayed in
Rome for five years and there came under the
influence of the engraver Giambattista Piranesi
(1720–78), whose picturesque interpretations of
Roman ruins did much to popularize them as a
source of style, and of another Frenchman Jacques-

Louis Clérisseau (1721–1820), a decorative designer
and draughtsman whose vision of the antique
coloured both Chambers's and Robert Adam's
employment of Roman motifs.

When Chambers returned to England in 1755 he
was appointed tutor to the Prince of Wales
(afterwards George III), and in 1758 he designed the
so-called Casino, a beautifully proportioned
pleasure-pavilion in the grounds of Marino House,
the Earl of Charlemont's residence outside Dublin,
which confirmed his mastery of the language of
Classical architecture. Chambers went on to publish
a *Treatise on Civil Architecture* which became in its
later editions the standard guide to the proper use of

the Orders. He had much success as a country-house architect although most of his work took the form of extensions and reconstructions of existing houses, since by the time he returned from Italy nearly all the Whig aristocracy, who now dominated English life politically and financially, had already built their new country mansions. These were in the Palladian taste, which continued to prevail in England, compelling Chambers to compromise with the strict Neo-Classical taste he had absorbed overseas.

Chambers's talents were soon recognized officially. In 1761 he joined the Office of Works as one of the two Crown architects and in 1769 he succeeded Flitcroft as Comptroller. When the office was reorganized in 1782 Chambers became the head of it with the title of Surveyor-General. These appointments brought into his hands the building to which he devoted all the later part of his life: Somerset House, London (1776–98), designed for government offices and to house the Royal Academy and a number of learned societies – the largest official building since Greenwich Hospital. It has lost some of its dignity since the Embankment roadway separated its main facade from the River Thames, but it has a sober monumentality that none of Chambers's contemporaries could have achieved. Chambers was one of the founders of the Royal Academy, its first treasurer and, it is said, more

Kedleston Hall, Derbyshire: the south front, by the brothers Adam; 1760–70. A house in which several architects had a hand; first Matthew Brettingham (1699–1769) who designed a house for Sir Nathaniel Curzon, later Lord Scarsdale, of which only one wing was built, in 1758; then James Paine who built the other wing and began the central block and the curved linking colonnades. Paine was succeeded by Robert and James Adam who completed the central block as well as a number of architectural ornaments in the park. The south front shown here is wholly theirs. The high-domed portion with the giant Corinthian columns contains the saloon, which has one of the grandest of all Adam interiors, and the great hall behind it.

influential in its councils than its president Sir Joshua Reynolds.

Robert Adam was an even more energetically ambitious character than Chambers. He was a Scot, one of the ten children of William Adam, the most successful building contractor and architect of his time in Scotland, who designed public buildings (mostly since demolished) in several Scottish cities and houses for many of the Scottish gentry. These showed, however, no great convictions as to style. His eldest son, John, continued his business. Two other sons, Robert and James, came south after the father died to make their fortunes as architects.

Renaissance and antique, which he had acquired on his travels, ousted the more restricted Palladian repertoire. Elegant and inventive, it was not this time a revival of an earlier style but Adam's own, ripe to be adopted by anyone eager to be in the fashion. With the success Robert Adam achieved with it, English architecture can be said to have launched itself into the habit of assembling in the same building ideas and details drawn from a variety of sources, a habit that was maintained throughout the nineteenth century except during the purist phases (see Chapter 14) of the Greek and Gothic Revivals.

One reason for the widespread influence of Robert Adam's personal style was that he did not restrict his attention to the building itself but designed or controlled every detail of its interior: the plaster-work, the fireplaces, the furniture and carpets, even the doorknobs and escutcheons. The whole was thus given a consistent character. The style, moreover, that he made fashionable could be used relatively simply to give an air of elegance and up-to-dateness to a modest interior or it could be used to decorate a grand interior with the most sumptuous effect. On such occasions Adam devised room-sequences of contrasting geometrical shape in the manner first used by William Kent at Chiswick and Holkham, but decorated with the new vocabulary of ornament, drawn from Pompeian, Etruscan, Roman and other sources – fragile and somewhat attenuated when compared with the preceding styles – that Adam quickly made famous with the assistance of a number of craftsmen with whom he worked closely on one interior after another.

Although Robert Adam became one of the busiest architects in England, much of his domestic work, like that of Chambers and for the same reason, consisted of remodelling existing houses and inserting handsome new apartments into them. Among the showiest of Adam's elaborately dec-orated and furnished interiors are those at Osterley Park, Middlesex, a Jacobean house that Adam remodelled in 1763–80 for Robert Child the banker, at Syon House, Middlesex (1762), another remodel-ling for the Duke of Northumberland, and at Kedleston Hall, Derbyshire (1760), where Adam completed for Lord Scarsdale a house begun by Matthew Brettingham and James Paine in 1759. The highly monumental garden front of Kedleston is Adam's.

Robert was the more dynamic, embarking (1754) on the Grand Tour in the company of a young Scottish aristocrat Charles Hope. In Italy, as with Chambers a few years earlier, his chief mentors were Piranesi and Clérisseau. He took the latter with him to the Dalmatian coast to make drawings for the book on Diocletian's palace at Spalatro already referred to.

By the time the book was published Robert Adam was back from Italy, had settled in London, where he was joined by his brother James, and was already on his way towards changing the whole face of English domestic architecture. The new repertoire of ornament, drawn from many sources,

153

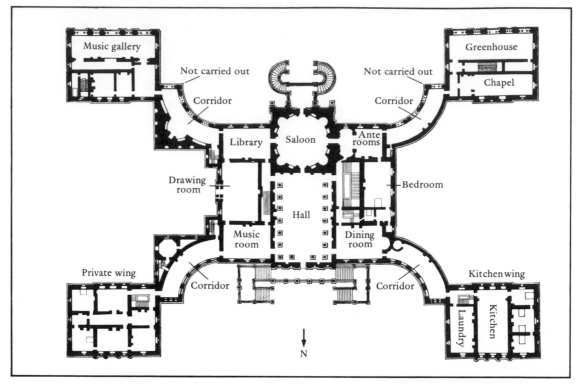

Plan of Kedleston Hall, Derbyshire.

In spite of their ambition to design great public buildings, and in spite of their highly effective exercise in self-advertisement in the shape of a book, *Works in Architecture of Robert and James Adam*, of which they published the first volume in 1773, the brothers had few opportunities of this kind except at Edinburgh, where Robert built the Register House (1774–92) and the University (1789). The latter, now known as the Old College, was only completed in 1817, long after the Adam brothers' death, by W. H. Playfair, but Adam was able to give the arched entrance front something of the grandeur he had admired in Rome. On a more modest scale he also built the theatre and town hall at Bury St Edmunds, Suffolk, in 1775.

An important contribution made by the Adam brothers to the external appearance of English buildings was their widespread use of stucco, which they first introduced in 1773 in the facades of some houses, designed in fact by James Adam, in Portland Place, London. After they had made the material fashionable it became common all over the country

both as a covering for brickwork and in combination with it. Gentlemen's houses could now display the elegance of white or cream-painted walls and porticos and the precise modelling of classical cornices and pediments even in areas where there was no local building stone. Towards the end of his career Robert Adam became fascinated by medieval castle architecture and embellished the exteriors of several country houses in Scotland (Culzean Castle, Strathclyde, 1777, is an example) with battlements,

Edinburgh University (Old College): the entrance, by Robert Adam; 1789. Adam's most ambitious public building, it was still unfinished when he died in 1792. All that had been completed was the frontage to South Bridge Street, including the main entrance shown here, and the Anatomy School in a corner of the further of the two courtyards he had planned. The building was finished, but with the two courtyards merged into one, by W. H. Playfair in 1817–26. Adam's entrance achieves a truly Roman grandeur. The dome is an addition of 1887 by Sir Rowand Anderson.

bartizans and corner turrets. There was no source from which he was not prepared to borrow notions that attracted his fancy.

Robert Adam's successor as the busiest and most fashionable architect of his day was James Wyatt (1747–1813). He was one of a large and confusing family of architects. It includes his elder brother Samuel, one of his sons, Benjamin Dean Wyatt, and two cousins of the next generation, Thomas Henry Wyatt, who built up a large practice in Wales, and Sir Matthew Digby Wyatt. The latter was a typical Victorian and is best known as the designer of the architectural ornament for Brunel's Paddington Station (1854) and of the various courts illustrating different styles of architecture in the 1851 Crystal Palace. Other cousins were Lewis and Jeffry, but the latter, after remodelling Windsor Castle for George IV in 1824 at a cost of over half a million pounds and being awarded a knighthood for doing so, changed his name to Wyatville as being more in keeping with the recreation of romantic scenery that had inspired the work at Windsor.

James Wyatt is the only one of this family who requires a place in a short account of English architecture. He carried on the country-house tradition of Robert Adam with almost equal elegance (Dodington House, Avon, 1798; the interior of Heveningham Hall, Suffolk, 1780–84), he worked closely with Lancelot Brown on the landscaped parks that surrounded his country houses and he continued further Adam's interest in the castellated exterior, building a number of houses (for example Ashridge Park, Hertfordshire, 1808) in the increasingly fashionable Gothic style. The culmination of this romantic fashion was the ambitious and much publicized Fonthill Abbey, Wiltshire (1796–1812), that Wyatt built for the wealthy dilettante William Beckford. Its soaring tower collapsed in 1825 and the rest of the house, except for one wing, was demolished later.

Wyatt had a reputation for carelessness and dilatoriness. He was nevertheless a brilliantly

Culzean Castle, Strathclyde, Scotland, by Robert Adam; 1777. An example of the romantic castellated style that Adam indulged in towards the end of his career, Culzean achieves a medieval silhouette with the aid of bartizans and battlements, in spite of the Georgian sash-windows regularly spaced out between the towers.

inventive, though rather superficial, designer. His Pantheon exhibition hall in Oxford Street, London, begun in 1769 when he was only twenty-two (much altered afterwards by him and others and demolished in 1937), was considered one of the finest interiors of its time. He succeeded Chambers as Surveyor-General of the Office of Works, but little official building was undertaken during his regime because it coincided with the Napoleonic Wars.

The extravagant excess and the eager pursuit of novelty prevailing in Wyatt's day brought their own reaction. Some of the leading architects of his and the following generation reverted to a stricter Neo-Classicism. Among them was Henry Holland (1745-1806), who built Carlton House, London, in 1783 for the Prince of Wales (later the Prince Regent and then King George IV and the first monarch to be a knowledgeable patron of architecture since the Stuarts). He also worked closely with the landscapist Lancelot Brown, whose daughter he married, and although he was in many ways a follower of Adam he put more emphasis on correct than on lavish decoration. In this respect Holland's work looks forward to that of Soane who in fact was an assistant in his office.

Another architect who preferred a sober and more correct Neo-Classicism was the younger George Dance, the son of another architect of the same name (1695-1768) who built the Mansion House in London (1739-53), notable for its so-called Egyptian Hall lined with enormous close-set columns. George Dance the younger (1741-1825) spent some years in Italy. Directly on his return he built the church of All Hallows, London Wall (1765), but his masterpiece was Newgate Prison in the City of London (built 1768; demolished 1902), one of the most severely powerful compositions of its time, in which the influence of the Roman Renaissance, and of Piranesi in particular, was

strikingly evident. Dance was one of the first four architect Royal Academicians.

Even more of an original was his contemporary Sir John Soane (1753-1837) who likewise mastered the Classical language of architecture but used it in an individual way to create spatial, rather than ornamental, effects. Soane was a pupil of the elder Dance as well as of Holland, travelled in Italy and in his early work – mostly additions to country houses – showed promise without making much impact. In 1788, however, he was appointed architect to the Bank of England, which he rebuilt piece by piece during the next twenty years, creating a series of geometrically inventive and gracefully decorated interiors almost none of which unfortunately remains. The Bank's single-storey exterior, blank-walled but enriched by rustication and groups of Corinthian columns, still stands but is difficult to appreciate beneath the pretentious and unsympathetic superstructure added by Sir Herbert Baker in 1921.

Apart from the Bank of England Soane's most prominent works were Dulwich Art Gallery and his own house in Lincoln's Inn Fields, London, both of which survive. The gallery at Dulwich (1811) is an austere brick building with the Classical elements pared down to a token of their fully elaborated selves. The house (1812-24) was as much a museum (which it still is) as a residence, being designed to contain the architect's collection of antiquities, some of which he made an integral part of a complex series of rooms and vistas. At the same time he created highly original spatial effects in spite of the house being of relatively small size. Soane was influential as a teacher as well as a practitioner, and with his death the first phase of the Classical Revival came to an end.

The other great figure of this period was very different although he and Soane were born and died within a year of one another. This was John Nash (1752-1835), as much an entrepreneur as a creative artist and yet a man who has left an enduring mark on London especially. We have already noticed him in Chapter 10 as one of the most effective practitioners, through his work for the Prince Regent, of the new art of laying out the residential quarters of towns. But Nash aimed to please a far wider public than the scholars and the aristocratic patrons. His architecture was more that of a scene-painter. He had an extrovert personality which

Dulwich Art Gallery, by Sir John Soane; 1811. Soane's very individual style is Classical in inspiration but with a flavour as much Greek as Roman, with everything simplified down to its basic geometry. This gallery at Dulwich, a south London suburb, was designed to include a mausoleum for its founder Sir Francis Bourgeois and a couple of his friends. The top-lit mausoleum is shown in this picture; the galleries are behind.

sometimes involved him in rash speculations but caused him to infect his clients with his own enthusiasm.

John Nash began as the architectural partner of the landscapist Humphry Repton (1752–1818), Lancelot Brown's successor, but soon after they parted Nash became instead his rival; for in 1815 the Prince Regent chose Nash's design for the rebuilding of his house at Brighton – the Royal Pavilion – instead of Repton's. By this time Nash was already a favourite with the Prince (and his wife, so it was said, was something more), and he prospered with the Prince as patron until the latter's death (as George IV) in 1830. The Royal Pavilion at Brighton (1815–21) was something of a freak: a pleasure-house enlivened by Hindu and other oriental motifs appealing to the Prince's, and Nash's, enjoyment of the exotic.

Elsewhere Nash drew on other past styles including – when he sought romantic and Picturesque effects – the Gothic. But he is chiefly associated with a somewhat free, late Georgian style often known as Regency, in which he used the Classical language effectively, although rather inaccurately from the point of view of academic correctness. Covered in his favourite cream-painted stucco, Nash's country houses and urban terraces, the latter ranging in scale from the modest residential parts of Leamington, Warwickshire, to the magnificence of Carlton House Terrace, London (1827), represent a prodigious quantity of work. The list of his buildings runs to seventy-five houses in London or the country, including those he only altered or added to but not those forming part of his many town-planning schemes, and nearly forty buildings in other categories.

These include several besides Carlton House Terrace that are still well-known London landmarks: the Royal Opera Arcade (1816), the Haymarket Theatre (1820), Clarence House (1825), the United Services Club (1826 – still a landmark although no longer a club) and All Souls Church, Langham Place (1822). The latter illustrates Nash's talent for townscape as well as architecture by the way its spire marks from a distance the point where Portland Place swings to the west at the top of Regent Street.

Although many of Nash's country houses are straightforward Neo-Classical buildings, Regency versions of the eighteenth-century Palladian

formula, others reflect Nash's own, and his generation's, fascination with the antique and interest in the exotic. He had shown evidence of the last long before introducing the Hindu style into his Brighton Pavilion. At East Cowes in the Isle of Wight he had built a Gothic mansion for his own occupation as early as 1798 (it was demolished in 1950) and he designed houses and cottages to accord with the Picturesque fashions favoured by his associates among landscape architects: Blaise Hamlet, Gloucestershire (1811), and the villas along

OPPOSITE
Holkham Hall, Norfolk; 1734: the entrance hall, by William Kent. The interiors at Holkham, for which Kent was mainly responsible, are spectacular rather than domestic. In this colonnaded hall he combines into an original composition elements derived from a number of the Italian buildings – Roman and Palladian – that he had studied with Lord Burlington. The hall is at entrance level and from it the stairs lead up to the rooms on the main floor. The lower walls are faced with pink Derbyshire marble. (See page 143.)

OVERLEAF
The Royal Pavilion, Brighton, Sussex, by John Nash. The celebrated extravaganza of the Prince Regent (later George IV), designed in approximately the present form in 1815–21. The Prince's building adventures at Brighton began in 1786, when he was still Prince of Wales, with a house in elegant but conventional Georgian style designed for him by Henry Holland. In 1803 William Porden (1755–1822) added stables and a rotunda, the latter already with some oriental details which may have been inspired by Sezincote, the country house in Gloucestershire that S.P. Cockerell (1753–1827) was in the process of building for his nabob brother in the so-called Hindoo style – in fact Muslim Indian rather than Hindu. Porden had been a pupil of Cockerell. In 1805 the Prince asked the advice of Humphry Repton (best known today as a landscape architect) who recommended the transformation of the house into a pavilion in the Hindoo style. The Prince, who had already introduced chinoiserie into some of its rooms, welcomed the proposal, but nothing was done to implement it until 1815 when he commissioned Nash, then Surveyor-General, to begin the work. Nash built on to the main walls of Holland's original house and created, at vast expense, not only the fantastic exterior with its skyline of domes and minarets but suites of rooms inside with equally exotic decorations. Porden's rotunda, later known as the Dome, was converted into a concert-hall in 1935.

OPPOSITE

Syon House, Middlesex: the ante-room, by Robert Adam; 1762. Like many of Adam's best interiors, those at Syon House, which he designed for the Duke of Northumberland, had to be adapted to an existing building. They consist of a sequence of apartments surrounding a square enclosure, within which Adam planned a great circular saloon never carried out. The ante-room, occupying the south-west corner of the house, is characteristic of Adam at his most elaborate and colourful. The greenish-grey marble columns were found in Rome in the bed of the Tiber. Adam added their Ionic capitals and bases in gold and white and used them to support gilded figures. The plasterwork in the frieze and ceiling is unusually delicate. The floor is scagliola (a kind of artificial marble) in a pattern echoing that of the ceiling.

Cottages at Blaise, near Bristol, by John Nash; 1811. Two of a group of nine cottages built in a field on the estate of a banker client whose house Nash had been altering. He was already engaged by then on the vast enterprises in and around Regent's Park, London, for the Prince of Wales, so these exercises in the Romantic and the Picturesque demonstrate his versatility.

the canal east of Regent's Park. The last, embarked on at the very end of his life, were completed by his pupil (and son-in-law) Sir James Pennethorne (1801–71).

In some of his buildings Nash showed a more sober judgement and much skill in adapting new influences, especially from Italy, to the needs of the

House at Cronkhill, Shropshire, by John Nash; 1802. Nash was prepared to turn his hand to any style or combination of styles. This country house, designed before he had become socially and commercially successful, shows Italian vernacular as well as Neo-Classical influences. Responding to the picturesque site, looking across country to the Wrekin, the composition is picturesquely irregular. The circular tower is only for external effect; except at the very top, there are no circular rooms inside it.

country house and its position in the landscape (Cronkhill, Shropshire, 1802; Rockingham House, County Roscommon, Ireland, 1810 – destroyed by fire, 1957). He may therefore be regarded as a link between the masters of the Renaissance idiom and those of the later nineteenth century to whom all the world's and all the centuries' styles were at architecture's disposal. Unfortunately the extravagance of his principal patron, George IV, was financial as well as architectural. Nash's conversion of Buckingham House into a new palace for the king was much criticized and became the subject of a succession of official inquiries into its structural deficiencies and its cost. Nash, who had achieved status as well as success, since he had shared with Soane and Sir Robert Smirke the position of architect to the Office of Works, finished his career by sharing also the disrepute in which the reign of George IV was held by the Victorians.

Part Three

The Age of Confusion

Chapter 13

The Industrial Revolution: the Rise of the Engineer

Bristol Temple Meads Station, by I.K.Brunel; 1839: the train-shed. This illustrates the early engineers' romantic attachment to the styles of the past in spite of the newness of the structures they were pioneering. The Tudor-style hammer-beam roof, spanning 72 feet, is of timber. The exterior of the station, also by Brunel, is of Bath stone in a castellated Tudor style. The train-shed is now disused.

IN the same way that Chapter 7, describing the Prodigy Houses built in the sixteenth century by the wealthy and ambitious men who guided the fortunes of Elizabethan and Jacobean England, belongs partly to Part One of this book because their architecture was not yet disciplined by Renaissance rationalism, and partly to Part Two because it was no longer the product of religious aspirations, so does this chapter belong partly to the Age of Reason and partly to the Age of Confusion that followed it. Nothing could be more reasonable than the part engineers began to play in the latter half of the eighteenth century in providing England with new types of structure to meet new needs, and yet nothing could have caused more confusion, or done more to bring about the eventual divergence of architectural styles from their functional origins, than the evolution of a separate engineering profession.

It will be recalled that in the Middle Ages most of the steps forward on which Gothic architecture throve came about through the master-masons – the forerunners of the architects – discovering ways of doing things they had been unable to do before, such as carrying vaults over great distances or reducing the extent of load-bearing walls so that far larger windows could flood interiors with light. In the eighteenth and nineteenth centuries, after architects had been content for the previous two hundred and fifty years with the static rather than the dynamic structural methods used by the Romans (that is, with no other elements but the wall, the column, the beam and the arch), there arose once more a desire to explore new possibilities. A mood took over that encouraged experiment, not unlike the mood that had set the Gothic masons venturing along unknown paths. This time however the experiments were not made by architects, whose minds were focussed on style and scholarship, but first by a new breed of scientist and then by engineers who created whole new categories of building, new in conception, use and structure, with which the profession of architecture had very little to do.

The separation of the two professions was perhaps inevitable following the proliferation of new techniques and materials; for there is a limit to what one man, unless he is a genius, can encompass. The reason why Sir Christopher Wren is to be so revered is that he provides a rare example of the scientific and the aesthetic approach to building combined in a single individual. Yet much of the confusion after which Part Three of this book is titled came about through the functional and the artistic initiatives becoming increasingly separated, not only in different people but in different professions.

It is difficult to determine whether, in the new age of creative engineering that began in the late eighteenth century, the new types of building which changed the appearance of town and countryside emerged from the demand for structures to serve new purposes, or whether the demand itself was stimulated by the invention of the means of satisfying them. The answer is, no doubt, that it was a combination of both: trade and industry, for example, required better transport, and the existence for the first time of a nation-wide transport network and the buildings that went with it encouraged trade and industry to expand further.

The manufacture of cloth, which had been the basis of England's export trade for centuries, demanded huge new buildings when it became industrialized – first the spinning process, then the weaving, which remained a cottage industry until the power-loom was introduced in the 1820s. But industrialization would not have been economic without large buildings with floors strong enough to carry heavy machinery and reasonably undivided so that the machines could be conveniently laid out. The need produced the means: iron beams and columns.

These multi-storey textile mills were the first of the many types of building created by the Industrial Revolution to make an impact on the English countryside. Hitherto castles and abbey churches had been the only structures with such an overwhelming presence. The new giants were misnamed 'mills' (a word that came from the Latin verb to grind) because, like the water-mills employed to grind corn which had long been common in all country districts (see Chapter 6), they were sited on fast-flowing streams and rivers which furnished the power for their machinery. Although industry is associated with the growth of towns, the first industrial buildings were thus constructed in remote rural areas and only moved to the towns when steam-power replaced water-power and they could be established more conveniently near the supplies of labour and near the ports from which their products were distributed.

In the steep valleys of the Derbyshire and Lancashire dales, where the damp air was suitable for spinning cotton, and in the Stroud Valley in Gloucestershire, close to a prosperous wool-growing area, there still stand examples of these impressive multi-storey textile mills, now used – if used at all – for other purposes. Their walls were solid stone and their floors at first of wood, supported on wooden posts. The latter however not only obstructed the internal space but were liable to catch fire, a risk increased by friction in their primitive machinery. The search for fireproof building methods was stimulated by the destruction by fire in 1791 of the power-driven Albion flour mills in Southwark, London, built only seven years before (by the great engineer John Rennie, 1761–1821, designer also, in 1817, of the old Waterloo Bridge) with machinery by Boulton and Watt. It was reputed to be the most up-to-date industrial building in Europe.

By this time iron floor-beams and columns were already being experimented with in some of the northern textile mills. Cotton mills that employed iron construction at an early date include those at Belper, Derbyshire, where the original mill was founded in 1776 by Jedediah Strutt, partner of William Arkwright, the inventor, after Hargreaves, of some of the first spinning machinery, and at Calver Mill, Curban, Derbyshire (1785). In such as these, and in several of the many woollen mills in the Stroud Valley, for example Stanley Mill, Stonehouse, Gloucestershire, the main support of the iron floor-beams was the outside walls of stone (or brick and stone in the case of Stanley Mill), which continued to be used in any case because of their fire-protection qualities. But before long the whole structural frame was being made of iron. The first building so made was a flax mill at Shrewsbury, designed by Charles Bage and begun in 1796. It had iron beams and iron columns and was therefore the ancestor of all the iron, and eventually the steel-framed, structures which in the years that followed

Stanley Mill, Stonehouse, Gloucestershire; 1813. One of the woollen mills built in the Stroud Valley to exploit its water-power, conveniently near the sheep-raising regions. They were plain and functional with rows of identical windows, and of a bulk unknown in the English countryside since the medieval abbeys and castles. Stanley Mill is brick and stone with an internal structure of iron with traceried arches.

transformed the very nature of commercial and industrial architecture.

The simple rectangular outlines of these early mills and factories piled themselves up into the impressive townscapes of northern cities like Halifax and were repeated in warehouses round the dock basins of England's expanding harbours: Bristol, London and especially Liverpool. The last grew most rapidly as a base for ocean-going merchant shipping and as the port at which the thriving cotton trade brought in its raw material from America and dispatched its finished products to every country in the world. Similar buildings had been rising also during a somewhat longer period in the naval dockyards. The earliest, the Royal Dockyard at Portsmouth, was founded as far back as 1540 on a site where Henry VII had built the first permanent dry dock in 1496. Invisible behind high walls along the waterfronts of Portsmouth, Chatham, Sheerness and Plymouth there still exist some of the most handsome brick buildings of their kind with floors of timber and iron: storehouses, workshops, roperies and boat-sheds. Sparse embellishments in the Georgian vernacular, such as cornices, string-courses and clock-turrets on their roofs, lend them official dignity and an appropriate formality.

At Portsmouth and Chatham the main ranges of dockyard buildings are eighteenth-century. At

Sheerness they are nineteenth-century, notably the exceptionally fine Quadrangle of 1824, the centre of a group of buildings laid out by Sir John Rennie (1794–1874), the son of the Rennie referred to above, and designed individually by Edward Holl (died 1824), the Admiralty architect who was in charge of all naval works from 1804 onwards. The younger Rennie was responsible also for the Royal William Victualling Yard (1832) at Stonehouse, near Plymouth, perhaps the finest of all these massive groups of naval buildings.

The warehouses surrounding the civil harbours too, although boldly functional, nearly always aimed at some degree of architectural refinement. That their design as well as their structure was regarded seriously is shown by the fact that for the great range of dock warehouses constructed in 1802 on the Isle of Dogs, London, for the West India merchants,

Sheerness Dockyard, Kent: the Quadrangle; 1824. A yellow brick building, originally a storehouse in the form of an open square but later covered in, the Quadrangle was the central building of Sheerness naval dockyard, laid out by Sir John Rennie. It was begun by Edward Holl, civil architect to the Admiralty, and completed by his successor in the post, G.L. Taylor (1788–1873). Inside it has cast-iron columns and floor-beams; outside it has a sufficiently Georgian flavour to give it the formality suited to its naval status.

designs were received from architects of the standing of Soane, Nash, the two Wyatts and George Dance. The commission went however to George Gwilt (1746–1807), not an architect but first a mason and then a surveyor, though his two sons George and Joseph, the first of whom helped him at the West India Dock, became architects. These were the first civil docks to be surrounded by an impregnable wall with guardhouses at intervals, the consequence of an epidemic of pilfering which had become alarming by the end of the eighteenth century. There were six blocks of buildings, each five storeys high. All but one were destroyed by bombing in 1940. Their fate in any case had become uncertain as the increasing size of ships during the present century has required deeper water, and more modern docks have been built further down the Thames, a process that has continued with the growth of container traffic.

At St Katharine's Dock a little further up the river alongside Tower Bridge a distinguished academic architect *was* employed: Philip Hardwick (1792–1870), architect also of the monumental Doric gateway to Euston Station, London, built in 1836 as London's gateway to the North but destroyed in 1962, and of the ornately Classical – in fact almost Baroque – Goldsmiths' Hall in the City of London (1829). At St Katharine's Dock he had an equally distinguished engineer associated with him, Thomas Telford (1757–1834), who is best known as a builder of bridges but was perhaps the greatest of

Albert Dock, Liverpool, by Jesse Hartley; 1845. The most splendid range of dock buildings in England, now disused and under threat. The warehouses are red brick, with cast-iron Doric columns along the open lower floor, which is given greater height at intervals by elliptical arches. Hartley was Dock Surveyor of Liverpool 1824–60.

the pioneer engineers to whom the Industrial Revolution owed so much. Hardwick's warehouses at St Katharine's Dock (1827–29), most of which have been demolished, have the minimum of architectural embellishment but fine proportions. The heaviness of their yellow brick walling is relieved by recessed panels into which tiers of segmental arched windows are set. On the side facing the basin the walls are brought forward to the water-line for easier loading into ships and the

ground floors set back behind rows of cast-iron Doric columns.

Similar columns support the upper storeys of what is perhaps the finest range of dock warehouses in England, those enclosing the basin at the Albert Dock, Liverpool, built in 1845 by the dock surveyor Jesse Hartley (1780–1860), but now likewise obsolete and threatened. Here the walls are red brick and the cast-iron columns unevenly spaced with the wider intervals between them bridged by an elliptical arch. The national pride taken in such buildings is shown by the fact that a model of these Liverpool docks was one of the exhibits at the Great Exhibition of 1851.

Although manufacture in nearly all its aspects began to demand new types of building and to form an increasingly conspicuous part of the urban scene (beginning with brewing, the first process to be

King's Cross Station, London, by Lewis Cubitt; 1851. A cathedral-like scale was introduced into city streets in mid-century by the construction of the great railway termini. The two huge arches of the yellow-brick frontage of King's Cross echo the form of the double-arched iron and glass (originally timber) train-shed behind.

transferred from home to factory), the most spectacular of all the opportunities offered to the new breed of civil engineers came with the growth of internal transport, which at the same time arose from, and contributed to, the Industrial Revolution. Canals required docks and warehouses besides bridges and aqueducts and many similar structures which have no place in a book on architecture. Railways required the same, but also station buildings, which are indubitably architecture and yet made stimulating new demands on their designers in the way of space to be enclosed and structures that could do this economically.

The larger railway stations, including the London termini, were first of all feats of engineering, but they were also the places where the railways confronted their public, and such was the pride taken in them, and their creators' sense of a challenge triumphantly met, that these and similar edifices were consciously endowed with an architectural presence over and above their functional roles. They acquired the status and dignity of civic monuments. The nineteenth century became itself aware of this. In 1875 the *Building News* wrote: 'Railway termini and hotels are to the nineteenth century what monasteries and cathedrals were to the thirteenth century. They are truly the only real representative building we possess. . . . Our metropolitan termini have been leaders of the art-spirit of our time.'

The engineers were inspired by the same sense of adventure as the builders of the prodigy houses of the sixteenth century, and in addition by the knowledge that they were serving a purpose and employing a structural technique which were both altogether new. Their sense of obligation to the cities the railways linked together was made evident at Euston Station, London, where Philip Hardwick was called in to provide the massive gateway already referred to, and his son P.C.Hardwick (1822–92) to add a Great Hall, magnificently Roman, to the wholly functional train-sheds of Robert Stephenson (1803–59). Impressive in a different way is the exterior of King's Cross (1851) in spite of the whole structure being engineering unadorned. Here Lewis Cubitt vigorously expressed the train-shed behind the station by the size and strength of his pair of deep brick arches.

Again at Paddington (begun 1850) the engineer Isambard Kingdom Brunel (1805–59) had the assistance of two highly regarded architects, Matthew Digby Wyatt for the architectural trimmings and Owen Jones for the decorations. Brunel, however, besides being one of the greatest engineers of this age of heroic engineering, was, with the confidence of his kind, fully prepared to be his own architect also. At Bristol, Temple Meads (1839), he not only designed a castellated Elizabethan station building (which he is said to have modelled on Rickman's recent addition to St John's College, Cambridge), but somewhat eccentrically built the train-shed of wood in the same period style some years before it became fashionable to revive Tudor and Elizabethan styles among his architect colleagues. The Temple Meads train-shed – disused but still standing – has a hammer-beam roof with a span four feet greater than that of Westminster Hall.

One distinguished architect succeeded in combining in his own practice mastery of the engineer's spectacular new vocabulary with mastery of the traditional Neo-Classical language. This was John Dobson of Newcastle-upon-Tyne (1787–1865). He

Great Malvern Station, Hereford and Worcester, by E.W.Elmslie; 1863. The new structural material, iron, was widely used in the expansion of the railways around the middle of the nineteenth century. The platform roofs at Malvern, a romantic spa station, are supported on cast-iron columns and have iron beams and cantilevers carrying the verandah, all characteristically ornamented in a style resembling Gothic tracery; the columns have wrought-iron foliage. The station building is also Gothic, with a steep roof and tall, moulded chimneys. There was a wooden tower over the entrance, now demolished. Elmslie built the Gothic-style Imperial Hotel at Malvern (1861) and was also a church architect (St Thomas's, Winchester, 1845).

was a pupil of Sir Robert Smirke (see next chapter) and worked on the restoration of Vanbrugh's Seaton Delaval after a fire – an experience which may have given him his feeling for monumental effects. Then, having designed for his native city a series of handsome streets comparable in some ways with those John Nash had built a few years before in London, but all in stone instead of stucco, Dobson

went on, in 1845, to create his masterpiece, Newcastle Central Station. This has a long, well-balanced Classical facade behind which is a train-shed with a high vaulted iron and glass roof composed of arched ribs – the first roof of its kind. It influenced station building for many years, in Britain and then all over the world. Stations with similar vaulted roofs were built at Birmingham New Street (1854), Liverpool Central (1874), York (1877) – the roof at York, by Thomas Prosser, is particularly beautiful – and Manchester Central (1880), and, in London, at Charing Cross (1863), Cannon Street (1866) and Liverpool Street (1874). The most daring arched roof of all is at St Pancras Station, London, where in 1868 W.H.Barlow threw a single span no less than 243 feet across the whole width of the station. It is, however, almost totally concealed from outside by Sir Gilbert Scott's towering Gothic hotel, a London landmark that belongs to a later chapter.

The smaller railway stations were different. Here there were no constructional challenges to be met but an earnest desire, perhaps only unconscious, to

The Higher Market, Exeter, Devonshire; by Charles Fowler; 1838. An example of the use, frequent at that time, of conventional street facades, in this case Greek Revival, to buildings for which the same architect provided strictly functional iron and glass structures. Fowler specialized in markets, being also responsible for Covent Garden and Hungerford markets in London (the latter demolished to make way for Charing Cross Station) and the Lower Market, Exeter (destroyed by bombing in 1942). The Higher Market is based on a design by George Dymond who died before it was built.

ameliorate the shock of the sudden intrusion of the railways into familiar scenes and places. In country stations especially the impact was softened by clothing the buildings, and their various appurtenances, like signal-boxes and station-masters' houses, in the manner of the architectural ornaments of the

rural landscape – of the Tudor or Italianate gate lodge and the cottage *ornée*. These stations are domestic in scale but are given their own distinctive form by the horizontal spread of the verandahs (as they are called by railwaymen) which shelter the platforms. In supporting the latter the new material, iron, on which the railways so much depended, was ingeniously used, and often decoratively also, as for example (to mention only a couple of instances out of many) at Kettering, Northamptonshire (1857), and Great Malvern, Hereford and Worcester (1863). Country and small town stations, however, called far less on the inventive resources of the engineer and belong, with their characteristic mixtures of styles, in the Victorian period and therefore in a later chapter.

Mention must be made here of architects who, while learning from the engineers the potentialities of iron as a structural material, combined the roofing in of the large spaces required by many of the new types of building arising from the growth of trade and industry with the Classical styles and proportions of more orthodox structures, and thus added ornaments of a new kind to English cities. One of these was Charles Fowler (1792–1867), a specialist in covered markets who made his reputation by building a huge glass and iron conservatory for the Duke of Northumberland at Syon House (1827) and went on to build markets at Covent Garden, London (1828), and in his native Exeter. Another was James Bunning (1802–63), the designer of several highly original London buildings that made daring use of glass and iron, including the Coal Exchange in the City (1847), recently demolished.

The need for large unobstructed spaces was the origin of the most spectacular glass and iron building of all, the Crystal Palace, designed by Sir Joseph Paxton (1803–65) to stand temporarily in Hyde Park and house the Great Exhibition of 1851 when other types of structure had proved unsuitable. Like others who had the imagination to use the new materials to answer new needs, Paxton was not a professionally trained architect although later in his career he became the architect of several rather stodgy and conventional country houses, mostly for members of the Rothschild family (Mentmore, Buckinghamshire, 1852). He was the superintendent of the Duke of Devonshire's gardens at Chatsworth, where he built a lily-house and a conservatory in

which he made experiments in iron and glass construction that he was able to follow up at the Crystal Palace.

The latter's chief significance, especially now that it can no longer be seen and studied (it was destroyed by fire in 1936 at Sydenham, to which south London suburb it had been removed after the Hyde Park exhibition closed), is not its vast size – although in 1851 it was the largest building ever erected in any material, 1800 feet long and enclosing an area of 770,000 square feet – but the astonishing rapidity with which it was completed due to its being constructed wholly from standardized prefabricated parts, designed for mass production. It thus forecast another and much later influence that the Industrial Revolution was to exert on architecture.

The Palm House, Kew Gardens, near London, by Decimus Burton; 1844. Industry made a new addition to architecture's vocabulary when iron and glass were combined to roof in unprecedented spaces. The Palm House was an early example of this, designed for the Royal Botanic Gardens at Kew by one of the most distinguished Greek Revival architects. At Kew Burton collaborated with the engineer Richard Turner of Dublin. The Palm House is 362 feet long and 62 feet high. Similar structures had already been employed for botanical purposes at Chatsworth, Derbyshire, where Paxton had erected a 65-foot-high conservatory in 1836–40. This was in many ways the prototype for the most famous of all iron and glass buildings, Paxton's Crystal Palace in Hyde Park, London, of 1851.

Chapter 14

The Battle of the Styles: the Greeks and the Goths

THE last chapter but one referred to the rediscovery of the antiquities of ancient Greece as the principal source of the pure Neo-Classicism that established itself in Europe in the second half of the eighteenth century, following the researches and writings of many scholars, most notably the German Winckelmann. Carefully designed buildings in the strictest Greek mode sprang up in every part of Europe from Copenhagen to Athens. In England, however, in spite of Stuart and Revett having been the first to publish the results of investigations undertaken in Greece itself, the Greek Revival did not make such headway to begin with. It was opposed by the Roman loyalties of Sir William Chambers and confused by the multiple sources on which Robert Adam based his widely popular eclecticism. Its purity and restraint, in addition, were inconsistent with the fascination with the Picturesque that had overtaken Englishmen of taste and with the rather slapdash exuberance of the Regency as exemplified in the work of Nash.

Of the eminent English architects of this period only Soane, as already described, maintained in his buildings the discipline and simplicity that Europe was relearning from the Greeks. However by the time of the deaths of Nash and Soane (in 1835 and 1837) a reaction was setting in, encouraged by the unpopularity of George IV's extravagance, by the example of men like Gilly and Schinkel on the Continent and by English sentiment in support of the Greek efforts to gain her independence from the Turks. Already, ahead of this time, one or two English architects had advanced from the un-scholarly handling of the Classical idiom by such as John Nash to a quite strict reinterpretation of ancient Greek precedents in line with international fashion. They included Thomas Harrison of Chester (1744–1829) who between 1788 and 1822 built a group of county buildings on the site of the little that remained of Chester castle – law courts, a gaol, a

Taylorian Institute, Oxford, by C.R.Cockerell; 1839. The Greek Revival at its most vivacious. The Ionic Order is that used in the Temple of Apollo at Bassae. The Institute is part of the Ashmolean Museum (the main entrance to which is on the left of the picture). The Taylorian was paid for with money left in his will by Sir Robert Taylor, the eighteenth-century architect, to establish a foundation for the teaching of European languages.

179

*County buildings, Chester, by Thomas Harrison;
1788–1822.* This portico to the shire hall is the central
feature of a group of buildings erected on the site of
Chester Castle, founded by William the Conqueror.
They are among the earliest examples of scholarly neo-
Greek architecture and might have had a profound
influence had they not been so far removed from London,
where most architectural fashions were then being set.

shire hall and military barracks arranged on three
sides of a large courtyard – and in 1802 the Lyceum
at Liverpool; also William Wilkins (1778–1839)
who, although belonging to the generation after
Harrison's, built when he was only thirty Grange
Park, Northington, Hampshire (1804). a monumental country mansion with temple porticos,
the grandest Greek Revival house in Europe.
Wilkins, who published several books on Greek
architecture, went on to build Downing College,
Cambridge (1806–20), and the National Gallery,
London (1832), a generally Greek-style composition
although Wilkins was required to incorporate in its
portico a number of Corinthian columns from

Henry Holland's Carlton House, lately demolished.

By Wilkins's generation many other English
architects had adopted the Greek mode with
enthusiasm. The most influential was C.R. Cockerell
(1788–1863). He had studied in Greece and
approached the use of Greek elements with

OPPOSITE ABOVE
*Newcastle Central Station, by John Dobson; 1845: the
train-shed.* The first iron and glass train-shed with arched
ribs forming a high vaulted roof, it influenced station
design all over the world. The roof is supported on
slender iron columns with ornamental capitals. The
station buildings are in Dobson's handsome Neo-
Classical style, with a long arcaded portico added by
Thomas Prosser, who was architect to the North-Eastern
Railway Company, 1854–74. (See pages 174–5.)

OPPOSITE BELOW
Bridges at Conway, Gwynedd, North Wales. With the
development of transport there arose some outstanding
engineers, whose structural achievements however were
often disguised under period styling, perhaps from a
sense of the romance of the work they were engaged on
(see Brunel's Temple Meads Station, Bristol), perhaps
simply from contemporary custom, perhaps in the case of
these Conway bridges from a desire to keep in harmony
with the medieval castle close by. The castle (one of those
built by Edward I after his campaign in Wales of 1294–95
– see Chapter 2) can be seen in the background of the
picture. In the foreground are two parallel river bridges.
On the right is the road bridge by Thomas Telford, built
in 1815 to carry the London-Holyhead stage-coach
highway which he constructed. It is a suspension bridge
and preceded by only four years Telford's most famous
bridge – the first long-span iron suspension bridge –
which carried the same highway across the Menai Strait.
On the left of the picture is one of the castellated towers
of the railway bridge, built in 1846 by the engineer
Robert Stephenson and the architect Francis Thompson.
The trains run inside a continuous rectangular tube. (See
Chapter 13.)

OVERLEAF
*Houses of Parliament, Westminster: the Queen's robing
room, by A.W.N.Pugin.* The interiors Pugin designed for
Barry's building are richly coloured with hardly a square
foot not encrusted with ornament. He was responsible
for even the smallest details, which he trained craftsmen
to execute. The walls of the robing room, above the
panelling and between the sculptured figures, are covered
with patterned flock-wallpaper. The flat ceiling has
Tudor-style geometrical panelling.

archaeological exactitude. The Taylorian Institute at Oxford (1839) is his most distinguished work. It is livelier than many of the Greek Revival buildings, not being so strictly confined within flat facades, and is handsomely enriched with sculpture. Cockerell's influence was strengthened by his position as Professor of Architecture at the Royal Academy.

Other architects prominent for their Greek Revival buildings were Sir Robert Smirke (1780–1867), who fronted the whole width of his British Museum, London (1821–47) with an impressive Ionic colonnade, George Basevi (1794–1845), a pupil of Soane, who built the Fitzwilliam Museum, Cambridge (1834), and Decimus Burton (1800–81), who built the Athenaeum Club, London (1828), giving it a stately interior enriched with pure Greek ornament. Burton also built the Ionic screen (1825) that forms the

OPPOSITE
Grange Park, Northington, Hampshire, by William Wilkins; 1804. The finest Greek Revival house in Europe, now partly ruined. The temple portico is based on the Thesion at Athens. The house began as a transformation of a seventeenth-century mansion for the banker Henry Drummond. It was further remodelled in 1823 by S.P. Cockerell and again in 1852 by his son C.R. Cockerell.

St George's Hall, Liverpool, by H.L.Elmes; 1841–54. A grandly sited civic monument, unusual in being seen from all four sides. It is Greek in detail but modelled as regards its plan on the Baths of Caracalla in Rome. The design was the outcome of a competition held in 1839. Work began in 1841 but Elmes died in 1847 aged only thirty-four, leaving the building to be completed externally (in 1851) under the supervision of the engineer in charge, Robert Rawlinson, and internally (in 1854) by C.R.Cockerell, who designed much of the interior himself.

south-eastern entrance to Hyde Park and the Constitution Arch nearby. He also provides a link with the early nineteenth-century architects who were beginning to take an interest in new structures and materials, for in 1844–48 he built, in conjunction with the engineer Richard Turner, the huge and gracefully shaped iron and glass Palm House at Kew Gardens.

As the nineteenth century progressed the Greek Revival became less archaeological and at the same time absorbed many other influences from the Mediterranean. The most monumental of all the Greek buildings in England, St George's Hall, Liverpool (1839), by Harvey Lonsdale Elmes (1814–47), which Cockerell completed after Elmes's early death, has for example a Roman plan based on

185

the Baths of Caracalla. Several other cities to which the textile trade had brought sudden prosperity employed Greek architecture when adorning themselves with new civic buildings. One of the best and purest of these, the museum and library in the Market Place at Preston, Lancashire, by the otherwise unknown James Hibbert (1833–1903) is an impressively correct exercise in the manner of Schinkel and shows how long the enthusiasm for the Greek persisted in some places, for it was designed as late as 1882.

The city that pursued these scholarly standards most closely was however Edinburgh, notable for the work of two Greek Revival architects of great distinction: Thomas Hamilton (1784–1858) and William H. Playfair (1789–1857). Both were Scots, although Playfair worked for a time in London under Sir Robert Smirke and James Wyatt. He won a competition for the completion of Robert Adam's university buildings in Edinburgh and afterwards designed streets and terraces of houses in the neighbourhood of Calton Hill (1819), the Royal Institution (1833) – later the Royal Scottish Academy – and the National Gallery (1850). Hamilton designed the George IV Bridge (1827), the Royal High School (1825) and the Burns Monument (1830), both the latter on Calton Hill. It is the prominent siting of these two architects' buildings that gives parts of Edinburgh their strikingly Athenian silhouette.

Ancient Greece seems to have had a special appeal to the Scots, for a generation later Glasgow produced an architect whose highly original work, though far removed in spirit from the anti-

LEFT ABOVE
The Harris Library, Preston, Lancashire, by James Hibbert; 1882. A surprisingly pure and correct example of Greek Revival architecture for so late as this, since by the 1880s civic building generally had long been overtaken by the Gothic Revival or by the picturesque amalgam of styles favoured after the middle of the century by architects like Waterhouse and Colcutt.

LEFT
St Vincent Street Church, Glasgow, by Alexander Thomson; 1857. One of several Presbyterian churches by this Glasgow architect who evolved his own personal style: severe, with sparsely used but very correct Greek ornament and an occasional outbreak of less orthodox ornament with an Egyptian or Assyrian flavour – as at the top of this tower.

The Royal High School, Edinburgh, by Thomas Hamilton; 1825. One of a number of distinguished, somewhat academic, public buildings that give a Greek flavour to the upper town at Edinburgh. The Thesion at Athens was the model for the centre portion.

quarianism of the true Greek Revival, was based on a devotion to the Greek ideal. This was Alexander Thomson (1817–75), who built several Presbyterian churches in Glasgow (the only one to have survived intact is St Vincent Street of 1857) and many

terraces of houses (Moray Place, 1859, is particularly powerful) influenced by Greek models and embellished with delicately positioned Greek ornaments.

Well before this a London architect, Sir Charles Barry (1795–1860), was introducing an alternative fashion to the Greek, based not on antique styles but on those of the Renaissance. After spending his early years travelling about the Mediterranean after the manner of his eighteenth-century predecessors, Barry set up in London in 1820 and surprised the West End with a couple of buildings in a totally new

style: the Travellers' Club (1829) and the Reform Club (1837), both in Pall Mall and both adaptations of Renaissance town palaces. These were followed by Bridgewater House, St James's (1847), a grander version of the Reform Club, and several country houses including Cliveden House, Buckinghamshire (1850), all of which reinforced the new tendency to look no further back than the Italian Renaissance instead of right back to antiquity.

Barry was at the same time responsible for a very different achievement which illustrates his versa-

Reform Club, Pall Mall, London, by Sir Charles Barry; 1837. In the Renaissance style introduced by Barry (first at the Travellers' Club, next door to this, in 1829) as an alternative to the Greek. The Reform has a Portland stone facade modelled on that of an Italian palazzo and a central courtyard covered by a glass dome.

Houses of Parliament, Westminster, by Sir Charles Barry; 1837–60. The symmetrical river front, revealing the Classical regularity of a large part of Barry's plan, which achieved its Gothic character with the help of Pugin's detail. The competition that Barry won was in 1835 and building began in 1837; St Stephen's Tower (right in picture) was finished in 1858 and the Victoria Tower (left) in 1860, when Barry died and his son completed the work.

tility and which constitutes one of the outstanding landmarks in nineteenth-century architectural history. In 1836 he won first prize in what was undoubtedly the most important architectural competition of the century for a new Houses of Parliament to replace the conglomeration of medieval buildings that had been almost totally destroyed by fire two years before – the eleventh-

189

St Michael's Mount, Cornwall: the drawing-room and boudoir; about 1740. Very early Gothic Revival: plaster ornament and, in the inner room, plaster vaulting installed in the early eighteenth century when a disused chapel was converted into living rooms. The chapel was part of a group of medieval monastic buildings the remains of which are incorporated in the present house. The precise date of these Gothicized interiors is not known, but Sir John St Aubyn who installed them died in 1744, so they must be earlier even than Walpole's more famous interiors at Strawberry Hill.

especially in the Middle Ages, revealed for example by the popularity of Sir Walter Scott's 'Waverley novels'. But the more particular reasons for the choice of Gothic for the Houses of Parliament were the traditions attaching to the site (the surviving medieval fragments could not easily have been incorporated in a Classical building) and a feeling that a building with this purpose required a style as essentially English as Gothic was thought to be. That Gothic had originated in France was ignored even if it was known.

Those who claimed that revived Gothic would appear typically English at least showed foresight; it quickly became a far more powerful rival to the Greek than Barry's neo-Renaissance, but the Gothic Revival was never, like the Greek Revival, a Europe-wide movement. With some exceptions, and those much later in the century, it remained an English phenomenon. The Houses of Parliament was thus the first major public building of modern times to be specifically commissioned in the Gothic style. Yet in a small way versions of Gothic had been employed for many years before. In fact the earlier phases of the Gothic Revival might more truthfully be named Gothic *Sur*vivals, since building in the Gothic style had never really stopped.

Until the eighteenth century it was not however called 'Gothic', a term which did not exist in the Middle Ages, for then it needed no name, being just the customary way of building. Palladio was the first to apply the word to medieval architecture and it became popular in eighteenth-century England, at first as an expression of scorn for – or at best superiority to – the primitiveness and barbarity that were all people saw in medieval buildings and their manner of embellishment, and which they contrasted with the rational and educated style of the Renaissance. Nevertheless, so slow was the rate of

century Westminster Hall was the only substantial part of the Palace of Westminster to survive the fire.

It was a condition of the competition that the new building should be in a 'Gothic or Elizabethan' style, a perhaps surprising requirement in view of the fact that Greek or Renaissance was at that time the normal style for public buildings of every kind – the British Museum and Goldsmiths' Hall, to mention two London buildings already referred to, were both under construction in 1836 – and that most of the parliamentary commissioners who selected a Gothic style must have been brought up in Georgian houses. But to set against these considerations there was a growing interest in English history and change outside sophisticated circles that long after the Renaissance had been established in England by Inigo Jones, country masons still employed no other than Gothic ways of building. As late as the eighteenth century they were fashioning humble village buildings in a style that makes them difficult to distinguish from those of two or three hundred years before.

Traditional-style Gothic churches, too, were still being erected by local builders in the seventeenth century and the universities were persisting with their customary collegiate Gothic. This suited both their needs and their conservative outlook (Wadham College, Oxford, 1613; the central parts of University College, 1634). The remarkable hall staircase at Christ Church, Oxford, with a Perpendicular central column and a fan-vaulted ceiling, built as late as 1640 and referred to at the end of Chapter 3, illustrates not only the continuing taste for Gothic but the survival of medieval masonry skills.

In more self-conscious circles too, those of the architects who followed after Inigo Jones and became the leading figures of the English Renaissance, there was always willingness to turn to Gothic on occasion. Sir Christopher Wren used it for several of his City churches, for example St Mary Aldermary (1702). Before this, in 1681, he had built Tom Tower for Christ Church, Oxford. His pupil Hawksmoor showed knowledge of Gothic when he designed the north quad of All Souls College, Oxford, in 1716 and the western towers of Westminster Abbey in 1734. Vanbrugh reacted to the romance of Gothic and wrote of his intention that Kimbolton should have 'a castle air'.

Attitudes like his mark the beginning of anti-quarianism, of an intellectual curiosity about anything old which was one aspect of eighteenth-century Romanticism and kept an awareness of Gothic architecture alive even when the Palladians were most in the ascendancy. Parallel to this was an interest in ruins, which fitted well with the importance accorded to the art of landscape gardening. The fashionable Picturesque landscapes were based on the work of painters like Claude who incorporated Classical ruins in their compositions, and it was an easy adjustment to include Gothic ruins instead and an obvious one also, because that was the style of the genuine ruins which, since the dissolution of the monasteries, had littered the

English countryside. Even that dedicated Palladian William Kent built Gothic ruins in his landscape gardens.

At first the Gothic Revival was as much a literary as an architectural movement. It expressed itself through historical romances and Gothic novels like Horace Walpole's *Castle of Otranto* (1764) long before the widespread popularity of Sir Walter Scott. Walpole's contribution is important because his enthusiasm for Gothic took an architectural form also. He began to Gothicize his own house at Strawberry Hill, Twickenham, in 1750 with the help of an otherwise obscure architect Richard Bentley (1708–82), who like Walpole came to architecture by way of literature, having previously illustrated the poems of Thomas Gray, one of the pioneers of romantic medievalism.

With Walpole setting a much-publicized example and with the help of books on Gothic ornament (at this time often distinguished from the genuinely medieval by being spelt Gothick) by writers like Batty Langley (*Architecture Improved*, 1742), the style became widely familiar. This phase of the Gothic Revival limited itself almost wholly to private houses, except for the imitation ruins in landscaped parks and gardens referred to above and except for its use in the ambitious remodelling of some old castles that the fashion for Gothic inspired some while afterwards – Arundel, Sussex, was rebuilt between 1791 and 1815 and Windsor in 1824. Although Walpole had a more genuine understanding of Gothic principles than most of his contemporaries, he and his fellow enthusiasts, being interested in the ornamental, not the structural aspect of Gothic, made no use of the country craftsmen still building by medieval methods. Such men were kept in business only by the need to keep old churches in repair.

With the next phase of Gothic we have reached the beginning of the nineteenth century when the Greek had become something near to an official style. Yet even at this time many of the leading architects, who had made their reputation with Classical buildings and whose training was wholly Classical, enjoyed, like Wren and Hawksmoor before them, an occasional excursion into Gothic. We have already seen how Robert Adam built houses in Scotland with medieval features, how James Wyatt's Fonthill was a serious and highly imaginative creation and how John Nash built his own house in the Isle of Wight in a Gothic style. J.M.Gandy (1771–1843), a protégé of Soane famous for his paintings and drawings of architectural fantasies, designed in 1802 the Shire Hall at Lancaster in the Gothic taste as part of his reconstruction of Lancaster Castle. George Dance built in Gothic too, and even Sir Robert Smirke, that most dedicated Greek Revivalist in his important London buildings, was not above building castellated houses in the country.

New Gothic churches were rare, but then very few churches of any kind were built between about 1760 and 1820 in spite of expanding populations (between those years, for example, exactly twelve churches were built in London, although the population nearly doubled – from three-quarters of a million to about a million and a half). Then in 1818 a Church Building Act was passed, resulting in the construction of 214 new churches. By then Gothic was becoming fashionable and 174 of them were in an attempt at a Gothic style – a cheap 'Carpenters' Gothic' for the most part, plain brick with stone ornaments. Perhaps the most satisfactory was St Luke's, Chelsea (1820), by James Savage (1779–1852), where the style is correct although somewhat thin and where there is a groined vault in stone – the first groined vault of the Gothic Revival. It was this Act also that led to Sir Charles Barry, by instinct a Classicist, building several Gothic churches at the beginning of his career. One was St Peter's, Brighton (1824), which was unusual, anticipating later developments, in being in a Decorated style whereas most of the churches built under the new Act were in a version of Perpendicular.

There was every reason why this residual enthusiasm for Gothic should now spread from houses to churches and take over church building programmes from the 1830s onwards. Although genuine medieval country mansions were rare, the English landscape was peopled with medieval churches still in everyday use. Religious worship was associated with the Gothic style. One major problem arose however when it came to modelling new churches on medieval prototypes: that the latter were all pre-Reformation and therefore designed to serve a liturgy that had long been discarded. Their elaborate arrangement of chancel and chapels, from which the geometry of their plans was inseparable, had no contemporary role. Churches had become

preaching halls, which is the nature of all those by Wren and his successors.

It was not until a new religious movement revived an interest in ritual that Gothic Revival church architecture was able to reestablish a logical relationship between the traditional church plan and what took place in it. This occurred after the passing of the Catholic Emancipation Act of 1829 permitted once again the building of Roman Catholic churches, and with far greater effect after the High Church (Oxford or Tractarian) Movement, which introduced into the Anglican Church a new emphasis on ritual observances, was launched in the 1830s. Had the existing type of church service, with its emphasis on preaching, been retained – had ritual and symbolism, that is to say, continued to be identified only with Popery – the Gothic Revival might not have become the force it did. But under the influence of the Oxford Movement churches again required chancels and chapels and ambulatories. Fresh attention was paid to the whole of their interior arrangement as part of the process of recreating the mystery and colour of the old forms of worship.

There were in fact two events that established Gothic as a rival, and as far as church architecture was concerned as an overwhelmingly successful rival, to the Greek and Roman and Renaissance. One was the Oxford Movement; the other was the passionate dedication to medievalism of one architect, Augustus Welby Pugin (1812–52). The two were not in active alliance, for Pugin was a Catholic convert and his work as an architect was all for Catholic purposes, whereas Tractarianism was a movement within the Anglican Church.

The significance of Pugin's belief in the necessity of Gothic is that he regarded it not only as the preferable architectural style but as the only one appropriate to a Christian country. His aim was not aesthetic appreciation of the architecture of the Middle Ages but the recapture of the style of life he associated with that time, and especially its attitude to building and the crafts. The impassioned advocacy of medieval styles on doctrinal, and even moral, grounds in Pugin's publications marks the beginning of the first serious – as distinct from the decorative or dilettante – phase of the Gothic Revival.

Before describing the architectural outcome of this we must introduce Pugin in another role. When

Barry entered for the Houses of Parliament competition and was obliged by its conditions to employ a style in which he was not particularly at home, he brought in the young Pugin as his associate. All the Gothic detail that gives the building its well-known silhouette and its thorough-going neo-Gothic personality – inside and out – is the work of Pugin. It contradicts in many ways the balanced Renaissance nature of Barry's plan, a fact that Pugin acknowledged when he wrote of 'Tudor details on a classic body'. The thoroughness of the building's period embellishment, incidentally, had a long-term effect on the progress of the Gothic Revival because it necessitated training craftsmen in unfamiliar medieval techniques in every conceivable material, and they were available afterwards to furnish high standards of craftsmanship for other neo-Gothic enterprises.

Pugin's own buildings are relatively few in number. They include St George's Roman Catholic Cathedral at Southwark, London (1841), and St Augustine's Church, Ramsgate, Kent (1845), but fail generally to meet the expectations aroused by his writings, being meagre and unconvincing. He was a thinker rather than a builder. But as the former he was far ahead of his time. In his most influential book, *The True Principles of Pointed or Christian Architecture* (1841), he wrote that 'every building that is treated naturally, without disguise or concealment cannot fail to look well'. It is not surprising that the prophets of modernism nearly a century later classed him as one of their movement's progenitors (see Chapter 19).

1839 was a crucial year. It saw the formation of what was to become an all-powerful body, the Cambridge Camden Society, whose aim was the reform of church architecture in the light of the new interest in ritual and its architectural setting. On its removal from Cambridge to London in 1846 it changed its name to the Ecclesiological Society. It demanded that new churches should conform with its beliefs and it went so far as to put forward rules in its periodical *The Ecclesiologist*, not only concerning the plan arrangements of new churches but the style they should follow, and to attack architects who designed otherwise. In 1844 it considered the question which period of Gothic should be preferred and decided on the Decorated of the fourteenth century (which it called 'Middle Pointed'), a somewhat perverse choice since Early English would

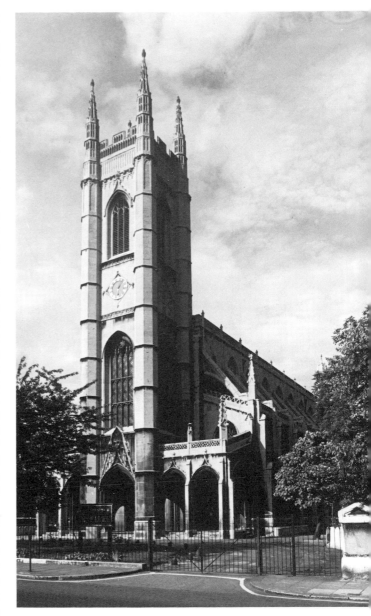

St Luke's Church, Chelsea, London, by James Savage; 1820. This was a product of the Church Building Act of 1818. More than three quarters of the churches built under this Act were Gothic; yet at this date the Gothic Revival was far from superseding the Greek, even for churches. St Luke's, in rather spindly Perpendicular, is exactly contemporary with the most conscientiously Greek (and the most expensive) church of its day, St Pancras New Church, London, by H.W. Inwood (1794–1843).

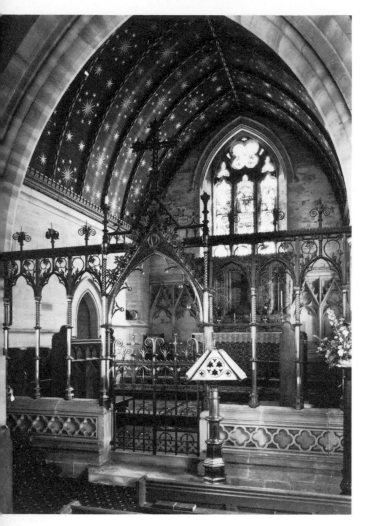

St Mary's Church, Fimber, North Yorkshire, by G.E.Street; 1871. One of Street's later churches, with an ornate interior wholly by the architect. The chancel has a pointed wagon roof with painted stars; the reredos is alabaster and marble, and the chancel screen iron and brass.

have been less dependent on a supply of skilled and knowledgeable carvers and craftsmen and Perpendicular would have been far more adaptable. Nevertheless *The Ecclesiologist*'s rulings and its judgements about church designs were widely accepted even among those who were not devotees of Tractarianism.

A large programme of church buildings, especially in the new manufacturing towns and

suburbs, was thus channelled in one architectural direction. The new churches did not all conform to the Middle Pointed style and their quality naturally varied with the talents of the architects responsible, but there were several among the latter who were master architects and could speak the new language of Gothic confidently, creating buildings equal to those of any period of English architecture. Three were outstanding. The first was George Edmund Street (1824–81), a loyal member of the Ecclesiological Society whose most distinguished church, nevertheless, is not of the approved period or even characteristically English: St James-the-Less, off Vauxhall Bridge Road, London (1860), which makes a splendid group with its adjacent parish-hall and school. The second was William Butterfield (1814–1900), a dedicated Tractarian whose approach to architecture was functional rather than decorative but who was notable nevertheless for introducing contrasting and multi-coloured materials into such churches as All Saints, Margaret Street (1849–59), and St Alban's, Holborn (1863) – both in London – and the chapel at Keble College, Oxford (1867). The third was John Loughborough Pearson (1817–97), who based his style as much on French as on English Gothic and whose work belongs more typically to the High Victorian age which we shall come to in the next chapter.

Before we do so an account must be given of the most successful and prolific of all the Gothic Revival architects, whose practice included many churches: Sir George Gilbert Scott (1811–78). His knowledge was extensive and he had the merit, like the three architects just mentioned, of being a constructor rather than a mere decorator. Though he had not their original genius, his career is outstandingly important because he was the first (after Barry's sole effort at the Houses of Parliament, which had no

All Saints Church, Margaret Street, London, by William Butterfield: 1849–59: the entrance courtyard. This is flanked by houses belonging to the church, striped with the same multi-coloured brickwork that Butterfield used so insistently here and elsewhere. In spite of its harshness and vigour, and the multiplicity of patterns everywhere, the church conscientiously follows the rules of the Ecclesiological Society. In the distant view the dominant feature is the slender tower with a broach spire, slate covered.

St Pancras Station Hotel, London, by Sir George Gilbert Scott; 1868. One of the most dramatic London silhouettes and a building that epitomizes the later phase of the Gothic Revival when faithful adherence to one style or period had given way to an amalgam of borrowings from many. The building draws on North Italian Gothic and on various English and French medieval sources. The materials were chosen to advertise the products of the Midland region of England which St Pancras served: hard red bricks from Nottingham, terracotta and iron. In addition there are stone dressings and red and grey granite. The building has not been used as a hotel since 1935 but as railway offices. Nevertheless many of the best interior features, including the splendid cast-iron staircase, survive.

196

immediate influence) to address himself to the question of how Gothic could be used for other buildings than churches.

Scott in fact began his career by designing workhouses, which were required in some numbers after the passing of the Poor Law Act in 1834. His first church, at Lincoln, was built in 1838 in a rather unconvincing Gothic, but after 1840, when he had been infected by Pugin's idealism and converted to the beliefs of the Camden Society, his churches became more coherent and assured. In the late 1850s there were still relatively few neo-Gothic buildings other than churches and a limited number of castellated country houses, but Scott set about changing this, first by means of his writings, especially his *Remarks on Secular and Domestic Architecture, Present and Future*, published in 1857, and then most effectively by the example of the many opportunities his enormous practice gave him of building town halls, libraries, schools and colleges in various Gothic styles, a programme facilitated by the passing of the Municipal Corporations Act of 1835, which gave a degree of self-government to the expanding towns and cities and therefore required them to equip themselves with all kinds of civic buildings. Scott and the other architects involved were able to work unrestricted by the rules laid down for churches by the Ecclesiological Society since for other types of building there were no precedents for the medievalists to refer back to.

Scott had one set-back, which is worth our attention because it illustrates the passions that were aroused by the conflict between Greek and Gothic from which this chapter takes its title. In 1857 a competition was held for the design of government offices in Whitehall. Sir George Gilbert Scott's entry, which he was confident would win, was Gothic with a French flavour. It failed to win, but Lord Palmerston, then Prime Minister, gave Scott an opportunity to launch a protest when he nominated an architect who had not entered for the competition. There was an outcry in the profession, led by Scott, and such was his influence and prestige that as a result he himself obtained the commission after all. His original design, however, was not accepted, a Classical style for such a building and in such a setting having been demanded by many, most vocally by Sir William Tite (1798–1873), a prominent architect (the Royal Exchange, London, 1841; the Caledonian Station, Edinburgh, 1847) who was also a member of parliament. Scott then put forward a Byzantine design, but Palmerston, while acknowledging in parliament that 'men above sixty still love Palladian, men below sixty hate it', was firm against Gothic and Scott was compelled, rather than lose the commission, to design a Classical building.

A legend has grown up that for the St Pancras Station Hotel, the masterly brick and terracotta pile with a Flemish flavour and one of the most dramatic silhouettes in London, which Scott built in 1868, he used the design he had prepared for Whitehall. This is not so, but St Pancras certainly owes its emphatically Gothic character to Scott's de-

termination, after his rebuff over Whitehall, to add a major Gothic building to the London landscape. The climax of his career was the Albert Memorial, completed in 1872, six years before his death, but this too belongs to a period when the Battle of the Styles was over and new attitudes to style were overtaking English architecture.

One other aspect of the Gothic Revival, however, in which Scott played a central part, must be given a place here. The mid-nineteenth century was an active time of church restoration. The great medieval cathedrals and abbey churches (those which had not fallen into ruin after the dissolution of the monasteries) were of course still in use as well as the medieval parish churches; they were still the setting of the people's Sunday worship and of ceremonies like weddings, baptisms and funerals. But two hundred years after the disappearance of the medieval system of caring for them they were badly decayed. The late eighteenth-century enthusiasm for Gothic had inspired some measures to restore them, handicapped however by lack of knowledge and skill, and the comprehensive restorations undertaken by James Wyatt aroused controversy even at that time. But this was nothing compared with that which arose when the nineteenth century's new devotion to Gothic architecture and its theories about correctness of style led to a programme of drastically thorough restoration.

Sir Gilbert Scott was a central figure in this, and after his death J. L. Pearson. In 1844 Scott had won a competition for the design of a new cathedral at Hamburg, thereby introducing the Gothic Revival, hitherto a wholly English phenomenon, into Germany. As a consequence he was the architect chosen to restore a number of English medieval cathedrals. He has been severely criticized for his unnecessary destruction of old work in order to rebuild it in the approved Middle Pointed style and for his policy of removing later additions and replacing them by new with the purpose of achieving consistency of style (at Oxford Cathedral he dismantled most of the east end and rebuilt it in the Norman style on the grounds that it had been Norman in the first place). It was Scott's work more than anyone's that created the almost continuous arguments as to the relative merits of restoration and conservation that were the basis of William Morris's campaigns a generation later – arguments that have lasted to this day.

Chapter 15

High Victorian: the Triumph of the Picturesque

IN the last chapter we left the nineteenth century battling between allegiance to the Classical and to the Gothic styles, with the Gothic claiming a positive victory as regards church architecture and the Renaissance a partial and rather uncertain one in civic and public buildings. But although this battle was a significant as well as a much publicized event, the architecture of the Victorian age had enough in common to outweigh all such differences. The chief quality nearly all Victorian buildings display, especially in the latter part of the century, is a refusal to accept any longer the constraints of academic correctness. Antiquarianism was finished. Architects no longer subscribed to the rules laid down for one particular style, whether it was Middle Pointed Gothic or Classical Greek or Florentine Renaissance; instead they felt free to build up the pictorial effect they fancied by mixing whatever styles they cared to draw on from the profession's growing repertoire.

This is over-generalization; for there were still architects with a partiality for, or a belief in the suitability of, one particular past style and who followed it conscientiously, especially some church architects. Almost up to the end of the century there were individuals who set the kind of value on scholarly accuracy that the Ecclesiological Society had insisted on before. Nevertheless in those years of middle-class prosperity, richness of detail and materials and liveliness of silhouette became the attributes demanded from successful members of the profession, and all past ages – some of course being more fashionable at one moment and some at another – could be drawn on to achieve them. Not only the greater knowledge of past styles but the greater range of available materials was responsible for the extraordinary number of Victorian buildings which, though often wilful and even eccentric, are daringly constructed and richly and colourfully detailed.

The Law Courts, London, by G.E.Street; 1866–82. The outcome of a hotly contested competition in 1866 but not completed until the year following Street's death. It is in a consistent Early English style and so belongs strictly to the more antiquarian phase of the Gothic Revival, but the picturesqueness of this oblique view along the Strand is a quality it has in common with many High Victorian buildings. The great hall inside with its high stone vaulting is one of the finest of its kind.

The general diminution of the old regard for scholarship had one interesting result. Previously the architect without much talent, as long as he followed the rules governing the chosen style, would not go far wrong; now, without their discipline and guidance, his inadequacies were revealed. This explains why the worst Victorian architecture is more noticeable than, say, the worst Georgian, which may be dull but is seldom actively ugly. On the other hand the sense of adventure and the belief in progress characteristic of the Victorian age encouraged its many talented architects to venture outside the academic conventions. It should be added that the romantic, and even the outlandish, quality of many Victorian buildings was at the same time a form of escape from the other and less desirable results of industrial prosperity: urban squalor, environmental monotony, slum housing.

In the High Victorian period the rivalry between Gothic and Classic nevertheless persisted to some degree. Gothic was still accepted as correct for churches; Classic was only one among many styles thought suitable for secular buildings and when chosen seldom appeared in its pure antiquarian form – a Classical building was simply one that incorporated the Orders. Both the use and the form of Gothic were influenced in mid-century by one powerful personality who was not by profession an architect, the writer and critic John Ruskin (1819–1900). Like Pugin's, Ruskin's view of Gothic was not only a stylistic but a moral one. He reinforced Pugin's message (see Chapter 14) with his similar insistence on ethical values, which he set out in his *Seven Lamps of Architecture* (1849), and in his criticisms of society as well as its buildings – it was this as much as his medievalism that inspired his successor as an architectural philosopher, William Morris. But Ruskin was an unyielding Protestant while Pugin was a fanatical Roman Catholic. Ruskin held himself apart from the propagandists of the Gothic Revival which he associated chiefly with the Anglo-Catholic obsession with ritual.

Ruskin's conversion to the modern use of Gothic (though not to the Middle Pointed insisted on by the Ecclesiologists) came after the studies in Italy that led to his second influential architectural book, *The Stones of Venice* (1851). But later he became disillusioned with the architectural outcome of the Gothic Revival as it emerged in the quantities of new churches he saw being built in England, and even

The University Museum, Oxford, by Sir Thomas Deane and Benjamin Woodward; 1854–60. Founded by Dr Henry Acland, Reader in Anatomy and a friend of John Ruskin who was closely involved in the design. A competition was held in 1853, the year of the completion of Ruskin's *The Stones of Venice*. Two entries were shortlisted: an Italian one by E.M.Barry (1830–80, the son of Sir Charles; he completed his father's Houses of Parliament) and this Gothic one – Italian Gothic in a mixture of yellow and red stone with traceried windows. Inside, unexpectedly, it is one large galleried space with a pointed iron and glass roof (described by Acland as 'these railway materials'). The iron columns supporting the roof have wrought-iron foliated capitals and there is much highly original carving throughout.

more so with the destruction of old buildings that occurred as a result; for he showed a rare sensibility in his appreciation of medieval architecture and craftsmanship. When he was at the peak of his fame in 1874 he was nominated by the Royal Institute of British Architects (RIBA) for England's highest architectural award, the Royal Gold Medal, but he refused it – the only man who has ever done so except Norman Shaw who refused it twice – because of the architectural profession's part in the destruction of medieval buildings. The RIBA president at the time was Sir George Gilbert Scott.

The building Ruskin was most closely involved with was the University Museum at Oxford. It was the subject of a competition held in 1853, won by two Irish architects, Sir Thomas Deane (1828–99) and Benjamin Woodward (1815–61), with an Italian Gothic design but a symmetrical one which thus rejected the picturesque irregularity so much admired in the Gothic. Ruskin associated himself with the building's construction and embellishment and is even said to have worked on some of the carving. He seems to have tolerated the glass roof with iron tracery – materials he had scorned when used in combination elsewhere, notably at the Crystal Palace built in Hyde Park only a few years before – but he must have been disillusioned by his whole experience at Oxford because he ceased afterwards to speak for the Gothic Revival; in fact he turned somewhat away from architecture, making the arts generally and their relation to modern life the subject of his preaching, and indeed modern life itself.

The names of some of the most distinguished church builders of the Gothic Revival, and some

representative buildings by them, were mentioned in Chapter 14: Street, Butterfield, Scott, Pearson. There were many others, and increasingly so as the growth of population in the new urban communities led to a boom in church building. Some were capable of the scholarly work such bodies as the Ecclesiologists demanded; some of devising striking new arrangements of the various Gothic elements;

even the designs of the less competent stand out in the newer towns and suburbs as the only prominent architectural gestures amid acres of domestic roofs. A surprising number have something interesting about them: their choice of materials, their geometrical inventiveness, their contribution to the townscape.

There is space here to add the names of only a few

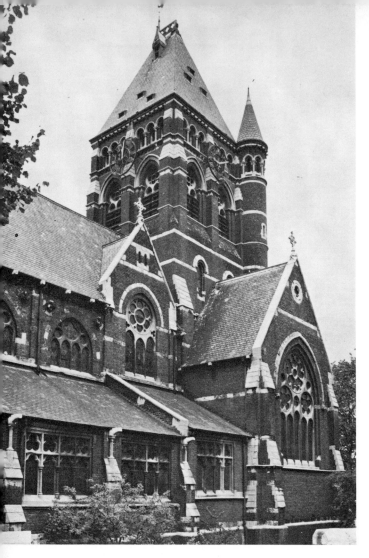

St Stephen's Church, Rosslyn Hill, London, by
S.S. Teulon; 1869. Teulon, an architect of French
descent, made up in vigour and a sense of movement
what he lacked in scholarly refinement, and drew the
elements of his designs from a variety of periods and
places. Note the use of plate tracery here, uncommon in
the Gothic Revival. The material is dark red brick,
trimmed with contrastingly white stone.

of the leading late Gothic Revival architects:
Benjamin Ferrey (1810–80), correct but not always
interesting, highly praised by the Ecclesiologists and
the biographer of Pugin, whose multitudinous
churches include St Stephen's, Rochester Row,
Westminster (1845); R.C. Carpenter (1812–55),
who built the spectacular French-English Lancing
College Chapel, Sussex (begun 1854), enormously
high (only Westminster Abbey and York Minster
among medieval churches are higher) but unfinished

in his lifetime; James Brooks (1825–1901), also fond
of French detail as can be seen in several churches by
him in the East End of London; G.F. Bodley
(1827–1907), a pupil of Sir Gilbert Scott who built a
great number of thoughtful and elaborately ornamented churches of which Hoar Cross, Staffordshire
(1872), is one of the best; S.S. Teulon (1812–73), a
more eccentric designer whose work is despised by
many but when looked at with an unprejudiced eye
is fresh and lively (St Stephen's, Rosslyn Hill,
London, 1869); Bassettt Keeling (1836–86), another
whose churches are scorned by the purists but typify
the energy of much Victorian Gothic; J.D. Sedding
(1838–91), who came to the fore later in the century
– late enough in fact to be influenced by the Arts and
Crafts Movement, as in his uniquely decorated Holy
Trinity, Sloane Street, London (1888).

The most successful of all, after Sir Gilbert Scott,
was J.L. Pearson, who has already been mentioned
as the main target, along with Scott, of the reaction
against the over-restoration of medieval buildings
launched by Ruskin and Morris. In 1879 Pearson
was chosen in a competition, for which many of the
leading Gothic Revival architects entered, to design
the first new cathedral (except for St Paul's which
was on the site of an old one) to be built by the
Church of England since the Middle Ages, at Truro,
Cornwall. It is a mixture of French and English
Gothic, too correct, it has often been said, to be very
inspiring, but with its triple spires making a
dramatic addition to the town's skyline. Pearson's
smaller churches like St Augustine's, Kilburn,
London (1870), are notable for their subtle handling
of internal space, their elegant vaulting and their
graceful, semi-detached towers.

Of the architects who worked in some kind of
Gothic style but not primarily on churches, the most
interesting is William Burges (1827–81). He had
travelled widely and displays a knowledge of the
medieval practices of many countries in his rich,
colourful and often aggressive detail. This is best
seen in the interiors and furnishings of Cardiff Castle
(1867) and Castell Coch, near Cardiff (1875), both of
which he remodelled for the Marquess of Bute –
significantly a coal magnate as well as an aristocrat.
Burges's romantic medievalism and his care for
inventive craftsmanship make him an even more
positive link than Sedding with the Arts and Crafts
Movement that was shortly to become a force in
English architecture and design.

Truro Cathedral, Cornwall, by J.L. Pearson; 1880–1910.
By one of the leading architects of the later Gothic
Revival, Truro is as much French as English in its
derivation although the plan, with its double transepts
and square east end, is not unlike those of Lincoln,
Exeter and Salisbury. It has been criticized as dully
academic but it rides splendidly, as this picture shows,
over the roofs of the city.

Harlaxton, Lincolnshire: the north front, by Anthony Salvin; 1831–38. An early example of the spectacularly picturesque, rather than the pedantic, use of historic styles, although the style here is largely of one period – Elizabethan – not the amalgamation of several styles more associated with the Victorian age. In fact Harlaxton is just pre-Victorian. William Burn completed the building on Salvin's retirement in 1831, himself designing much of the interior.

Another uninhibited romantic – a designer mostly of country houses – provides a link in the opposite direction. This is Anthony Salvin (1799–1881), a pupil of John Nash and an authority on, and restorer of, ancient castles. He built a number of castellated country houses that had much in common with those that followed the same fashion a century before. His masterpiece, Harlaxton, Lincolnshire (1831 onwards), is far less conventional, an astonishing echo of Elizabethan exuberance but with a Baroque staircase hall like those he had seen in Central European palaces. Salvin retired before the house was finished and the remainder of the interior is the work of William Burn (1789–1870), one of the busiest of the Victorian country house architects, but less of an original than Salvin. Burn worked principally in Scotland and most of his houses, whether in Scotland or England, are variations on a

standard Jacobean theme with clustered chimneys, gabled facades and mullioned bay-windows.

Leaving churches and country houses aside, the most typical High Victorian architecture is to be seen in the great number and variety of public buildings erected in the newly prosperous manufacturing towns. As these towns and cities grew and as they developed their own administrations after the passing of the Municipal Corporations Act in 1835, they acquired a civic pride that was expressed in architecturally extrovert and consciously picturesque town halls, museums, law courts, libraries and the like; also in the commercial offices where the businesses that created their prosperity were

housed. The central streets of Manchester and Glasgow were lined with stone palaces in all styles from Florentine Renaissance to Venetian Gothic. The expense of sculptured friezes and carved capitals was never spared.

One of the most imposing of the new civic buildings is the town hall at Leeds (1853). It still displays the bold simplicity that the Greek Revival had introduced into the growing provincial cities during the generation before, but it incorporates elements, such as a dome, that are foreign to the Greeks – elements in this case taken from the Renaissance rather than antiquity – and its vigour is Victorian. Its architect was Cuthbert Brodrick

(1822–1905), who also built the huge Grand Hotel at Scarborough, North Yorkshire (1863), more French in derivation and representing another of the new types of building that changing social customs were requiring from architects from the mid-century onwards.

The most discussed new public building was nevertheless in London: the new Law Courts in the Strand. This was the subject of a competition not embarked on until 1866 although part of its role was to replace some of the accommodation lost when the Palace of Westminster, where trials had been held since the Middle Ages, was burnt in 1834. The competition aroused more interest than any since that which replaced the Palace of Westminster by the Houses of Parliament in 1836. It was won by

Leeds town hall, by Cuthbert Brodrick: 1853. One of the great Victorian civic buildings, it shows the discipline and scholarship of the preceding age of strict Classical revivals but suggests the changes that were coming by incorporating a domed tower, which derives from the Renaissance – even the Baroque – and not from the Greek to which the remainder pays allegiance. The arched windows, too, on either side of the portico of giant Corinthian columns, are a departure from neo-Greek orthodoxy and the influence of Barry is evident in the treatment of other details.

G.E. Street, one of the architects referred to in the preceding chapter as being – along with Butterfield and Pearson – the most distinguished of all the Gothic Revival church architects. Street's Law Courts effectively follow the High Victorian practice of creating picturesque groups when seen obliquely along the surrounding streets, but the thirteenth-century Gothic that Street employed is rather lifeless and the building has been criticized for its practical drawbacks – notably in the acoustics. The lofty central hall, which might be the vaulted nave of a cathedral, is without doubt impressive.

It will have been noted that after the first years of the nineteenth century it was the custom for nearly every major new public building to be the subject of an architectural competition. This reflected the competitive spirit of the age just as the system of aristocratic patronage had reflected the spirit of the eighteenth century, and it indicated also the degree of organization now achieved within the architectural profession. The competition system was relished, for example, by the man who was perhaps the most typical of all the eminent High Victorian architects, both as regards the types of building on which he was engaged and the variety of styles and materials he employed. This was Alfred Waterhouse (1830–1905). It is significant that he was born in Liverpool and practised initially in Manchester, two cities closely identified with Britain's commercial prosperity. Waterhouse migrated to London – still the goal of those seeking reputation as well as success – in 1865 in order to take part in the Law Courts competition, unsuccessfully on this occasion, but much of his work came to him through victories in competitions, including his first important building, the Manchester Assize Courts (1859), which was in a Venetian Gothic that even Ruskin praised. It was recently demolished.

Waterhouse was a skilful planner, an increasingly necessary accomplishment in an age when more and more buildings had to fulfil complex functions involving such problems as internal circulation. He did not hesitate to make use of iron for structural purposes. The picturesqueness of his exteriors was emphasized by his use of hard polychromatic materials like terracotta and variously coloured brick; also by his buildings' dramatic silhouettes. The range of historic styles at his command is illustrated in the sequence of important buildings with which he followed the Manchester Assize Courts: Caius College, Cambridge (1868), in early French Renaissance; the Natural History Museum, London (1868), in North German Romanesque, with a colourful use of terracotta inside and out; Manchester Town Hall (1869), in Early English

Manchester Town Hall, by Alfred Waterhouse; 1869: the staircases. The plan of the town hall is a triangle of offices with a hall in the middle. The building, which was the outcome of a competition, is academically Gothic but makes the most, inside and out, of the opportunities for picturesque composition that the Gothic style offers. The traceried openings in the walls of the main stair allow views of a circular secondary stair beyond.

Gothic; the Prudential building, Holborn, London (1876), in beefy red brick and terracotta with a spiky skyline; the Metropole Hotel, Brighton (1888), again with a dramatic skyline; University College Hospital, London, (1897), whose picturesqueness belies the fact that it grows out of a wholly functional plan.

The stylistic versatility of the Victorian age and its refusal to put neighbourliness before competitiveness are both well illustrated by the South Kensington quarter of London, in which Waterhouse's Natural History Museum stands out prominently. It was developed as a museum and educational area after the Great Exhibition of 1851 and is formally planned about a north-south axis – an axis, however, that is invisible except from the air. It begins at the southern end with the Natural History Museum, passes through the tower (all that survives) of the Imperial Institute, through various London University buildings and the Albert Hall, and terminates in the isolated splendour of the Albert Memorial, which is also sited on the east-west cross-axis created by the Crystal Palace. Each building of the group is by a different architect. Between them they represent an extraordinary range of styles, having only the conspicuousness of their skylines in common. They include Waterhouse's museum, the Imperial Institute by T.E. Colcutt (1840–1924) in a mixture of Flemish and Spanish motifs as well as brick, stone and terracotta, and the more restfully shaped and coloured Albert Hall by two military architects, Captain Francis Fowke (1823–65) and Major-General H.Y.D.Scott (1822–83). A little to one side is the coarser and more confused Victoria and Albert Museum by Sir Aston Webb (1849–1930), a typical Edwardian building although begun in 1899, two years before Queen Victoria's long reign ended.

Typically Victorian, on the other hand, is Sir Gilbert Scott's Albert Memorial which encapsulates many of the qualities of the High Victorian age, and especially its apparent enslavement to imitation of

South Kensington, London: the museums area. A group of buildings, each in a different Victorian style, laid out along a formal axis that is only discernible from the air. The axis is marked, from south to north, by the arched entrance, flanked by twin towers, of Waterhouse's Romanesque Natural History Museum, by the slim tower of Colcutt's highly eclectic Imperial Institute, by the dark brick and spiky outline of Sir Arthur Blomfield's French Baronial Royal College of Music, by the circular bulk of the Albert Hall and finally, set among the greenery of Kensington Gardens, by Sir George Gilbert Scott's richly Gothic Albert Memorial.

Carpet factory, Glasgow, by William Leiper; 1889. The Victorians' enjoyment of fantasy and their liking for architectural embellishment were expressed at times even in their industrial buildings. This factory for Templeton Carpets, in multicoloured brick with Venetian Gothic windows of various shapes and with battlements along the skyline, is on Glasgow Green. The architect, William Leiper (1839–1916), worked in London for J.L.Pearson but most of his own buildings are in the Glasgow area.

the past which it employs nevertheless to create effects peculiar to its own age. The form of the memorial, a canopy sheltering the seated statue of the Prince Consort, is similar to that chosen by G.M.Kemp (1795–1844) for his memorial to Sir Walter Scott at Edinburgh, designed in 1840, more than twenty years earlier. It is modelled on a medieval shrine, a notion appropriately full of symbolism – the Victorians delighted in symbols –

210

but is executed in a greater variety of rich materials than the Middle Ages ever brought together in one place: bronze, enamel inlay and marble; gilding, granite and mosaic. It is recognizably Gothic (the iron girder that supports the canopy and *flèche* is invisible), yet the white marble sculpture around its base makes no pretence to be anything but Victorian, being smooth and realistic, as are the elaborately symbolic supporting groups at the outer corners.

A different view of the triumph of the Picturesque and of nineteenth-century English architecture's stylistic versatility, even more comprehensive than that obtainable in South Kensington, can be gained from the great number of railway stations built during the boom years of the 1850s and 1860s. These take us therefore a little distance back in time as well as on a journey round England. The impact of the new engineering, of which railway building was but a part, has been described in an earlier chapter; so have some of the terminal and big city stations which are among the significant monuments of their age, representing by the vigour of their architectural display the same increasing civic consciousness that we have seen in town halls, law courts and museums. The arrival of the railway was an important event in the history of many towns, and the attention given to the architecture of the station reflected this. Nevertheless the stations in the smaller towns, and in the countryside, were not always conceived in a monumental spirit but to be absorbed into the local scene, and in the case of the latter were wholly domestic in scale. Many indeed were also domestic in purpose, since they incorporated a station-master's residence.

The number of country stations was very great.

RIGHT ABOVE
Bucknell Station, Shropshire; 1860. A village station in romantic cottage *ornée* style; stone-built with ornamental fish-scale tiles on the roof. The platform side has a triple gable similar to the single gable over the entrance. Architect unknown.

RIGHT
Shrewsbury Railway Station, Shropshire, by T.K.Penson; 1848. An early example of a revived Jacobean style, possibly influenced by the old buildings of Shrewsbury School nearby. Penson was a local architect, practising in Oswestry and Wrexham and responsible for other stations on the Chester line. Shrewsbury station was partly rebuilt in 1903 but in the original style.

They were built close together because in the days of horse-traffic anything more than a very few miles was inconveniently far to drive or ride. The sense of isolation felt by those living more than this distance from a station is an indication of how quickly railway travel had become an essential part of everyone's way of life. Its subsequent replacement by motoring caused the loss of many stations – indeed of many of the lines of which they were part – but there still remain a great number of stations which together provide a revealing demonstration of the range, variety and inventiveness of nineteenth-century architectural taste.

They were designed in many different circumstances: by railway engineers and surveyors adapting ideas from pattern-books or directly from neighbouring buildings; by architects practising in the locality; in some larger towns by quite well-known architects (Sir William Tite, already mentioned in this chapter as the designer of the Royal Exchange in the City of London, made a speciality of railway stations, mostly, in contrast to the Exchange, Gothic or Jacobean, including those at Carlisle, Southampton and Edinburgh Caledonian); and by surveyor-architects employed on the staffs of the railway companies. Two of the last category – both belonging to the earlier years of railway development – were outstanding: Francis Thompson of Derby and David Mocatta. Thompson built a number of cultured and elegant stations on the old Midland line (Wingfield, Belper and Ambergate were among the best) and on the line from Chester to Holyhead, including the somewhat florid Jacobean station at Chester itself. Mocatta (1806–82) built many stations in an equally elegant Italianate style on the London-Brighton line; also the terminal station at Brighton (1841), but his work there has been partly obscured by later additions. Mocatta's station style, being both economical and flexible, was widely imitated. His quality is not surprising seeing that he began as a pupil of Sir John Soane.

These two left their personal mark up and down the lines they served. On other lines a great variety of architectural talent was expended on station design. Stations could be conscientiously Gothic, like that at Battle, Sussex (1852), by William Tress, a pupil of Tite, or gabled and half-timbered like Fenny Stratford, Buckinghamshire, or – especially in the case of somewhat larger stations – elaborately Tudor or Jacobean. Good examples of the last type are

Shrewsbury (1848), by an Oswestry architect Thomas Penson (1790–1859) who also designed a number of local churches in the Norman style, and Stoke-on-Trent (1850) by H.A.Hunt, which has features imitated from Jacobean country houses.

Returning to the more famous and more centrally situated nineteenth-century monuments, it is notable that one of the last great Victorian buildings was in a style few architects had previously attempted: the Byzantine. This is the Roman Catholic cathedral at Westminster by John Francis Bentley (1839–1902). Commissioned in 1894, the building is all in red brick striped with stone and has a tall, slender campanile. Its shallow domes are of concrete, but no iron or steel is used – Bentley called iron 'that curse of modern construction'. The domes and their supporting walls were meant to be covered in mosaic and coloured marbles, and thus to be as richly decorative as the Albert Memorial, but the cost necessitated their being left bare initially. A noble interior resulted, which has already lost some of its scale and dignity as the process has gone forward of obscuring its simple geometry with decorations.

Before the bare brick carcase of the cathedral was completed in 1903, architecture in England had undergone another change: two interrelated changes in fact. It had come under the influence of the Arts and Crafts Movement which stemmed from William Morris's efforts to bring back a respect for hand craftsmanship, and a totally new style had been invented, initially for domestic buildings only but soon to become more widely fashionable and even to rival the various Gothic styles for churches.

This new style, rather misleadingly known as 'Queen Anne', represented also a change of mood. This is best examined in the smaller country and suburban houses which looked towards the homely and the vernacular rather than the foreign and exotic.

Westminster Cathedral, London, by J.F.Bentley; 1894: the nave looking east. London's principal Roman Catholic church, and the last great monumental building of the Victorian era. Unusually, it is Byzantine in style. The outside, in striped red brick and stone, is a lively composition of domes and turrets with a slender campanile. The inside is more austere while the brick arches and domes remain bare, but these are being covered gradually with marble and mosaic.

Chapter 16

The New Mobility: Town versus Country

FOR architectural reasons as well as social the country house plays an important part in the story of English architecture from the sixteenth century (the Prodigy Houses, Chapter 7) throughout the seventeenth and eighteenth centuries and into the nineteenth. It still did so in the later nineteenth century but in totally changed conditions. First of all England was no longer governed to a large extent from her country houses. The passing of the Reform Bill in 1832 had brought to an end the authority of the great Whig families and the building of country seats from which that authority would be exercised. It gave more political power to the middle classes to add to the economic power they were acquiring as a result of the growth of industry and commerce. With the repeal of the Corn Laws in 1846 the ownership of land ceased to be the main source of wealth and influence in spite of the fact that thirty years after this no more than 1200 people still owned a quarter of the land in England.

Luxurious country mansions were being built in some numbers in the later nineteenth century, but mostly for a new kind of owner – the newly rich, who left the cities where they had made their money and set up in country estates. Cragside, Northumberland, was commissioned by Sir William Armstrong the armaments manufacturer in 1870; Waddesdon, Buckinghamshire, for the financier Baron Ferdinand de Rothschild in 1874; and there were many others of like origin. Perhaps Waddesdon should not be given a place in a book on English architecture since it was by a French architect, Hippolyte Destailleur (1822–93), and is wholly French in style, being closely modelled on the châteaux of Blois and Chambord, but the Rothschilds employed English architects elsewhere, for example at Mentmore, Buckinghamshire, in 1852. This was designed for them by Sir Joseph Paxton and G.H.Stokes (a pupil of Sir George Gilbert Scott who became Paxton's chief assistant and married his daughter).

Cragside, near Rothbury, Northumberland, by Richard Norman Shaw; 1870. For the industrialist Sir William Armstrong, this is a romantically situated example of the architect's 'Old English' manner. The house still contains many of Shaw's original furnishings and some of the domestic equipment installed by its owner, which made it technically in advance of its time. It had, for example, water-powered electricity from 1880.

Mentmore was Elizabethan, a style also favoured by the old aristocracy when they did build afresh, as at Eaton Hall, Cheshire, designed for the Marquess of Westminster in 1870 by Alfred Waterhouse. They now preferred it to the Renaissance style they had favoured in the early Victorian period – when, for example, Barry had built his two great Renaissance houses, Trentham Hall, Staffordshire (1834), and Cliveden, Buckinghamshire (1850), both for the Duke of Sutherland. The later Victorians were able to enjoy a new style even more traditionally English than the Elizabethan, the picturesquely irregular 'Old English' style with clustered chimneys, timbered gables and much tile-hanging, of which Cragside was a spectacular example. Another was Leyswood, Sussex (1867), built for a shipping magnate. The architect of both of these was Richard Norman Shaw (1831–1912), who was soon to become the most potent force in English architecture. Equally spectacular was the high-roofed, Dutch-inspired Kinmel Park, Denbighshire, which we shall have to return to later. It was built in 1868 for H.R.Hughes, proprietor of copper mines, by W.E.Nesfield (1835–88).

Besides exhibiting the typical Victorian willingness to cross both national and temporal boundaries when seeking opulent effects – especially the favourite effect, from mid-century onwards, of a striking skyline – the country houses of this time are notable for something other than their appearance: for incorporating technical improvements and comforts which had previously been lacking. In spite of an impressive expenditure on space, the great country houses up to the mid-century – and often well past it – remained surprisingly uncomfortable. Little progress had been made since the first essential luxuries – security and then privacy – had been introduced in the late Middle Ages.

Water-closets had been in use since the eighteenth century, but they did not become really efficient until a succession of technical improvements was made in the 1870s. From early in the nineteenth century a piped supply of water to different parts of the house was increasingly common, and it may be that the fashion for towers, a feature of many of the more picturesque houses both Gothic and Classical, was connected with the need to accommodate a water-tank. Piped *hot* water came later; all through the nineteenth century washing and bathing were normally done in the bedrooms in china basins and

metal hip-baths filled by maids who carried cans of hot water upstairs.

Heating was usually by open coal or log fires, again involving much carrying up and down stairs; but as with plumbing there were early experiments with central heating long before it became common. Sir Walter Scott had steam heating at Abbotsford as early as 1823. More often these experiments employed various methods of circulating warmed air, as the Romans had done. Mentmore, the Rothschild house mentioned above, had a central heating system of hot water pipes when it was finished in 1855. Central heating was however exceptional until well into the twentieth century.

OPPOSITE
Cardiff Castle, South Glamorgan, by William Burges; 1867: the summer smoking room. Burges was a dedicated medievalist with a liking for rich and varied craftsmanship that in many ways looks ahead towards William Morris and the Arts and Crafts Movement. He designed fantastically ornate and colourful interiors in South Wales for the Marquess of Bute, including this apartment in Cardiff Castle, which he recreated, giving it a dramatic but relatively austere exterior resembling some of the medieval reconstructions of the French architect Viollet-le-Duc. (See page 202.)

OVERLEAF LEFT
The Albert Memorial, Kensington Gardens, London, by Sir George Gilbert Scott; 1863–72. Prince Albert died in 1861. His memorial, completed in 1872, consists of a richly decorated Gothic canopy, 175 feet high, containing a seated bronze statue of the Prince at the top of a flight of steps. The base of the canopy has a frieze of figures of artists, poets and musicians sculptured in white marble. At the corners are symbolic groups also of white marble. (See pages 208–11.)

OVERLEAF RIGHT
Natural History Museum, South Kensington, London, by Alfred Waterhouse; 1868. This illustrates the use of differently coloured materials of which Waterhouse and his contemporaries were particularly fond; in this case yellow and blue terracotta with purple-grey slates laid in a striped pattern on the steeply pitched roofs. The style is Romanesque, based for the most part on German examples. The exhibition galleries inside are steel and glass. (See pages 207–8.)

Kinmel Park, Clwyd, North Wales, by W.E.Nesfield;
1868. The first country house to display the high roofs
and white-painted dormers of the style that was to
become known as 'Queen Anne' and was soon to be
popularized by Norman Shaw. Nesfield and Shaw were
partners from 1862 until 1867.

OPPOSITE
Houses in Lower Sloane Street, Chelsea, London. From the
end of the 1870s onwards large parts of the Cadogan
Estate, Chelsea, were built over with tall houses for the
rich and fashionable in a new style, using red brick with
lavish ornaments in terracotta. These bay-windowed
houses are typical. Unlike those in the streets and squares
of Bloomsbury and Belgravia built a generation or two
before, which are unified by shared cornices and
pediments, the Cadogan Estate houses are individually
distinguished by differences in the modelling and the
design of the gables – a characteristic feature. Their
derivation is Dutch, closely related to the 'Queen Anne'
style pioneered by Nesfield and Norman Shaw. A large
proportion of these streets and squares was designed by
Sir Ernest George and Peto, but several other architects
played a part including J.J. Stevenson (1832–1908) and
Norman Shaw himself who designed three separate
richly gabled houses in Cadogan Square.

Luxuries like this, and the inclusion in the plan of a
boiler room to make them possible, were more likely
in the houses of the newly rich industrialists than in
those of the landed aristocracy, not only because the
former liked to employ their wealth in this way but
because they had readier access to new technology.
It was often indeed the source from which their own
wealth came. At Cragside Sir William Armstrong, a
leading engineer, had electric lighting installed in
1880. It was one of the first houses in the world to be
so lit.

Gas lighting came earlier in the century, but it was
smelly, it made the rooms stuffy and it was expensive
until the invention of the incandescent mantle in the
1880s. In the country, moreover, piped gas was
seldom available. Only a large estate justified a
gasworks of its own. Kelham Hall, Nottinghamshire, by Sir George Gilbert Scott (1858),
had a gasworks that also served the adjoining village.
Candles and oil-lamps were the normal source
of lighting throughout the century. Unlike gas
and electricity they did not require special instal-
lations or fittings that were difficult to absorb into
traditional schemes of interior decoration; on the
other hand such an object as a gasolier provided a

new opportunity for ornamental invention and display. The labour involved in keeping a large house with many rooms lighted throughout by candles or oil-lamps encouraged early bedtime in the winter.

The vast houses of the Victorian *nouveaux riches*, only a few examples of which have been mentioned above, were among the more spectacular buildings of the century, but they still have to be regarded as survivals from an earlier style of country life. A development more representative of the late nineteenth century was the spread of the house of small or moderate size from the town into the countryside, resulting from the growth of the middle class and from new means of transport. We saw (in Chapter 10) how, in the seventeenth and eighteenth centuries, the layout of towns was transformed by merchants ceasing to live over their shops or counting-houses and preferring a separate house in a residential area. As such areas became more crowded and the commercial classes more numerous and prosperous, many such families made another move, especially in the early nineteenth century, outwards to the fringes of the larger towns, where they built detached villas in which to live a more gentlemanly life.

This was the start of the low-density extension of the towns which was eventually to create widespread suburbs. At first its extent was limited by the necessary reliance on horse traffic. But it established a new category of domestic architecture: neither the self-sufficient country residence – which could be a great mansion or a modest farmhouse – nor the town house forming part of a built-up street or square. It was no longer necessary to draw an income from land, to work on the land or to possess an unearned income in order to reside in green and peaceful surroundings.

This new style of villa, attached to the town but away from its crowded streets, followed the architectural fashions of the time. It was either

Mentmore, Buckinghamshire, by Sir Joseph Paxton; 1852: the garden front. One of the many extravagant country houses built in the middle and later years of the nineteenth century for industrial and City magnates. This one was for the Rothschild family. Employing a wholehearted Elizabethan style, it is an echo – in fact in many of its parts a direct copy – of Wollaton Hall, Nottingham (see Chapter 7).

Gothic – often with a romantic character such as Nash had given to some of his rustic cottages – or more frequently Italianate; styles that had not, however, been chosen by the occupants but by the speculative builders who arrived on the scene at this time in great numbers and adapted whatever styles might appeal to the social aspirations of the different classes of prospective purchasers.

In the mid-nineteenth century this first tentative move away from crowded urban living was vastly accelerated by the building of the railways, which created for the leisured classes the habit of the country week-end, and for others mass commuter travel and life in increasingly spread-out residential suburbs. The changes this brought are, however, more part of social and topographical history than of architectural. The style of mass-produced nineteenth-century housing, when it aimed at something less basic than the plain, crowded brick and slate terraces run up for the workers in industrial areas, again took the form of some builder's version of one of the lately fashionable styles: a middle- or lower middle-class vernacular usually of plain brick with coarsely modelled stucco ornaments. Among the rare examples of middle-class housing with a sense of architectural quality – the first indication of better things to come – were a number of country vicarages built by William Butterfield and G.E.Street in a more relaxed and homely style, Gothic in spirit but without ecclesiological ornament.

The Queen Anne Revival house referred to at the end of the last chapter, informally planned and based on the type of gabled brick house built in England in the seventeenth century under strong Dutch influence, came as a breakaway from the dreary repetition of these prevalent stiff and conventional styles. One of its earliest manifestations resulted directly from the new commuter transport by rail. When Turnham Green Station was opened in 1873 on the western outskirts of London, on the line between Richmond and the City, an enterprising investor, Jonathan Carr, acquired forty-five acres of land there in order to lay out a residential estate which he called Bedford Park. It was designed to attract people of the professional class with enough discrimination to be discontented with the standardized environment created by the streets of stock brick houses, embellished as described above with tired Italianate or Ruskinian Gothic ornament, that

were going up in such quantities in Finchley and Streatham and the equivalent suburbs of growing provincial towns. He conceived the estate as spaciously planned with wide, tree-lined roads and small gardens between the detached and semi-detached houses – Bedford Park was in fact the first garden suburb and one of the ancestors of the low-density suburban development that became typical of the English scene during the next half century. Carr called in the successful young Norman Shaw to be his architectural adviser and to plan the estate.

Shaw himself designed only a few of the houses, but a church, a shop and a pub, grouped together to give the estate the air of a self-contained village community, were all by him, and the architects who designed the houses followed the new fashion he set. They used red brick, contrasting white-painted woodwork, gables and small-paned windows (the widespread use of plate glass for windows had transformed the appearance and the scale of much domestic architecture earlier in the century). Quaintness was aimed at rather than opulence. The residents of Bedford Park had advanced tastes. They were purchasers of William Morris wall-papers, Liberty fabrics and other consciously artistic furnishings.

The revived 'Queen Anne' style was not however limited to the artistic minority, nor was Norman Shaw its sole inventor. It seems to have been evolved in fact during the time near the beginning of his career when Shaw, after travelling on the Continent and then working as assistant to several in turn of the leading architects of the day – William Burn (master of the Scottish Baronial style), Anthony Salvin and G.E.Street – went into partnership in 1862 with W.E.Nesfield, mentioned above as the architect of the strikingly unorthodox Kinmel Park, Denbighshire, which already showed some Dutch influence. They worked together for six years.

When he set up on his own, Norman Shaw first employed the vigorous 'Old English' style, a style

Lodge at Kew Gardens, near London, by W.E.Nesfield; 1867. The earliest known example of the revived 'Queen Anne' style which Nesfield and Norman Shaw pioneered and which Shaw soon adopted for nearly all his work in place of his previous 'Old English' style. The lodge, although small, has all the 'Queen Anne' ingredients: steep roofs, bold chimneys, moulded brickwork, dormer windows, white paintwork and a generally Dutch flavour.

that made much use of local materials, which has already been noted in connection with houses like Leyswood and Cragside. But the Dutch-influenced so-called 'Queen Anne' style, which Nesfield may have had more to do with originating (see his little keeper's lodge at Kew Gardens with its high central chimney and enormous dormer window, designed as early as 1867, as well as Kinmel Park), brought refinement and sophistication to Shaw's work. He made decorative use of rubbed brick and of wooden balconies and bay windows invariably painted white. His skilfully modulated facades made this style suitable for town as well as country. Nor are all the buildings for which he used it domestic in purpose. They include office buildings (New Zealand Chambers, Leadenhall Street in the City of London, 1872 – now demolished – and the Allied Insurance Building, Pall Mall, 1882) as well as Lowther Lodge, South Kensington, now the headquarters of the

Bedford Park, Turnham Green, London. A typical road in the artistic garden suburb – the first of its kind – laid out by Norman Shaw in 1877. Most of the houses were designed by other architects: E.W.Godwin, Maurice B.Adams (1849–1933), E.J.May (1859–1941) etc., but Shaw designed the church (1878) and set the style for the houses: red brick with a plentiful variety of gables, bays and white-painted small-paned windows.

Royal Geographical Society (1873) and Swan House on Chelsea Embankment (1875). The last has a particularly elegant facade with a variation of the 'Queen Anne' in the shape of mullioned and leaded oriel windows.

Whoever deserves the credit for inventing it, it was certainly Norman Shaw, one of the most prolific of architects, who popularized 'Queen Anne'. It had an immediate appeal, initially perhaps because it offered those with an eye for architecture a refinement that the most recent Gothic Revival buildings seemed to have lost. Soon its appeal spread far beyond those with conscious architectural taste, at first with the help of the schools built in London for the School Board, following the 1870 Education Act, by the Board's architect E.R. Robson (1836–1917), who was a convert to the 'Queen Anne' style. Their tall brick gables stand up prominently above the slate roofs of London terrace houses all over the inner suburbs. The 'Queen Anne' influence then became ubiquitous. Variations of the new style were adopted for commercial buildings, and most strikingly for public houses. Many of the tall, florid pubs with gabled facades incorporating an array of – often clumsily arranged – architectural features like obelisks and turrets, such as were built in great numbers in the 1880s and 1890s, though far from being in the pure 'Queen Anne' style, could not have acquired their exuberant vocabulary without it.

Several eminent architects took up the 'Queen Anne' style more seriously. They included Sir Ernest George (1839–1922), G.F. Bodley (mentioned as a busy church architect in Chapter 14) and Basil

School, Primrose Hill, London, by E.R.Robson. This neo-Dutch style, related to the 'Queen Anne' popularized by Norman Shaw, was freely used for the large number of new schools built as a consequence of the 1870 Education Act, especially those by E.R.Robson who was architect to the London School Board from 1870 to 1889. He had been, surprisingly, a pupil of Sir George Gilbert Scott and of John Dobson of Newcastle, and a partner between 1870 and 1875 of J.J.Stevenson (1832–1908) who worked with him on some of the schools. The steep roofs and prominent gables which are a feature of Robson's schools made them landmarks among the streets of small houses that had recently spread round the fringes of the city.

Swan House, Chelsea Embankment, London, by Richard Norman Shaw; 1875. One of Shaw's most elegant and inventive street facades with many of the characteristics of the 'Queen Anne' style but also such unconventional features as a first floor projecting beyond the ground floor, and the upper floors projecting further still. These represented a return to the practice of several centuries before which is underlined by the design of the leaded oriel windows occupying most of the first floor frontage. They are a close copy of the windows of the early seventeenth-century Sparrowe's House at Ipswich, Suffolk. Shaw used the same type of window elsewhere (New Zealand Chambers, Leadenhall Street, 1872; his own house in Ellerdale Road, Hampstead, 1875), and other architects did so after him (the Six Bells public house, King's Road, Chelsea, by G.R.Crickmay, 1898).

Champneys (1842–1935), whose most appealing building is Newnham College, Cambridge (1875). The change they helped to bring about, from stucco to red brick frequently supplemented by terracotta, led on to a new style of urban street architecture also showing Dutch and Flemish influence and characterized by richly ornamented gabled facades. In parts of inner London, Kensington and Chelsea especially, there are many streets of handsome and opulent red brick and orange-brown houses

Albert Hall Mansions, Kensington, London, by Richard Norman Shaw; 1879. The first block of middle-class flats in London. It stands just east of the Albert Hall and has Shaw's favourite striped brickwork and corner turrets. Shaw studied French apartment blocks before embarking on the design, which initiated a hitherto un-English way of living that was before long to revolutionize the scale and the skyline of many inner residential areas.

(Cadogan Square and Lower Sloane Street are excellent examples), many by Sir Ernest George and his partner Harold Peto (1828–97), in which this Dutch-Flemish style makes a striking contrast to the stock brick and cream-painted stucco of neighbouring Pimlico and Bayswater. Its popularity, like so much at this time, is connected with the growth of rail transport, which made it economical to bring south other bricks than the yellow London stocks and terracotta manufactured in Staffordshire. Terracotta was also welcomed because it was impervious to dirt for which London's, and many Midland cities', atmosphere had become notorious.

Another of the pioneers of the Queen Anne Revival, but at the same time an architect of unusual originality, was Philip Webb (1831–1915), but since

228

he was a pioneer in other respects too with an influence on the next phase of the nineteenth century, he must wait until the next chapter. The hero of the present chapter, Norman Shaw, besides being a brilliant designer, was perpetually fascinated by the technical services – the drains, the plumbing and the heating – that the buildings of his day were beginning increasingly to require. (His campaign for more scientific drainage systems was helped by the near death from typhoid of the Prince of Wales in 1871.) Shaw, too, was the architect of the first prominent example of a new style of middle-class living in towns that was eventually to alter the appearance of large parts of them: the block of flats. In 1879 he built, in his favourite 'Queen Anne' style, Albert Hall Mansions, facing Kensington Gardens, London.

Living in flats had long been traditional all over the Continent and in Scotland. It was new in England but soon – especially in London – it became an accepted alternative to a house both for the well-off classes and for the poorer classes inhabiting central areas. The latter were provided with somewhat grim but hygienic tenements by philanthropic organizations like the Peabody Estates, aimed at combating the disease and lawlessness of the slums. The process of replacing slum streets by tenements had in fact begun in London as early as the 1840s following cholera epidemics in the East End.

Flats were not only a new building type for architects to master but had a greater impact on the London skyline than even the 1870 Board Schools. On only a few occasions, however, did blocks of flats make a positive contribution to the townscape. One that did so was Whitehall Court (by Archer and Green, 1884). Its steep, serrated Early French Renaissance roofs became part of one of London's most picturesque panoramas, that seen looking eastwards from St James's Park.

World's End public house, Chelsea, London; about 1895. A riotous specimen of a familiar style of London pub architecture which, even if it must be called only a caricature of Norman Shaw 'Queen Anne', could not have come into being without it. This building, and the pub vernacular it exemplifies, has many of the 'Queen Anne' ingredients – stripes, projecting bays and moulded brickwork – but a more pronounced Flemish flavour and a more abandoned proliferation of turrets and gables. Architect unknown.

Chapter 17

The Arts and Crafts Rebellion

WILLIAM MORRIS (1834–96) has so far come into this story only in his negative role of defender of medieval churches against the assaults of the restorers, but his positive role was even more significant and its influence far-reaching. The Arts and Crafts Movement, of which he was the central figure, descended from the Gothic Revival and especially from Pugin, who had been as much a designer of furniture and internal finishes as of buildings. He encouraged a new regard for craftsmanship and the sincere use of materials, which were also the basis of the Arts and Crafts Movement's beliefs, for the movement was to a great extent a reaction against the mid-Victorian use of machinery to mass produce ornament and separate the maker from the designer. But the more immediate inspiration Morris drew upon was that of Ruskin, fifteen years older than himself, whose writings – most notably *The Stones of Venice* – Morris and Edward Burne-Jones had read and absorbed with enthusiasm when they were undergraduates together at Oxford.

Morris, like Ruskin, was not an architect, although he spent some time learning about architecture in the Oxford office of G.E.Street. There he met Philip Webb, who was Street's chief assistant. Finding their ideas mutually sympathetic, Morris invited Webb to build him a house – the Red House, near Bexley Heath, Kent (1859), which in its day was revolutionary: simple and unpretentious and more like a farmhouse than the customary gentleman's residence in the Classical or Gothic taste. It was built of plain red brick with an informal arrangement of steep tiled roofs and chimney stacks. Inside were hand-crafted textiles, wallpapers and many other furnishings produced in the workshops of a firm founded by Morris for the purpose in 1861 – the real start of the Arts and Crafts Movement.

The firm was called Morris, Marshall, Faulkner and Co. Philip Webb was one of the founding

Glasgow School of Art, by Charles Rennie Mackintosh; 1898. This is the main frontage. The library wing, with its famous double-height aisled interior, came ten years later. Although Mackintosh is classed as an Art Nouveau architect on the strength of his interiors and furniture, and although his great reputation on the Continent was founded on his contribution to Art Nouveau, this building – his masterpiece – is not decorative in intent but is an exercise in three-dimensional geometry, generated by the spaces within.

231

The Red House, Bexley Heath, Kent, by Philip Webb; 1859. The house Webb designed for his friend William Morris. It was furnished with the hand-crafted productions of Morris and his associates. More revolutionary in its time than it looks today, its style and materials are those of the farmhouses and other anonymous buildings of the English countryside rather than those of the historic monuments, at home and more frequently abroad, from which most contemporary architects sought their inspiration.

directors, and those who helped Morris set it up included also Ford Madox Brown, together with Rossetti and Burne-Jones, members of the Pre-Raphaelite Brotherhood of painters and writers which had shocked and angered the English art establishment a few years before. These attacks on the Pre-Raphaelites had gained them the invaluable support of Ruskin.

At the beginning the Morris firm was a cooperative venture. The artists supplied designs for the textiles, wallpapers, furniture, carpets, stained glass, tapestries and the like produced by the firm, and were paid for their designs in goods. Later it became a normal manufacturing firm with William Morris

holding most of the shares and determining the firm's output. A good, somewhat stolid example of a Morris interior can be seen in the Victoria and Albert Museum: the Green Dining Room (1867). In West Midlands, near Wolverhampton, there is a whole country house, Wightwick Manor, furnished and equipped under the direct influence of Morris and the Pre-Raphaelites. It was built in 1887–93 for a local industrialist by Edward Ould, a Liverpool architect, and includes a 'great parlour' with an open timber roof symptomatic of the medievalizing tendency of Morris and his associates.

The interest the Morris firm's products aroused, in spite of this tendency to look back to the Middle Ages rather than forward towards the design potential of the machines Morris rejected, transformed the domestic interior (and the interiors of churches through the stained glass several members of the firm designed). Its products opened people's eyes to the triviality of much contemporary design and created a market for the work of younger craftsmen-designers pursuing the same objectives elsewhere; for example the furniture-maker Ernest Gimson (1864–1920), who worked in Gloucestershire and whose furniture was conceived

All Saints Church, Brockhampton-by-Ross, Hereford and Worcester, by W.R.Lethaby; 1901. By one of the philosophers of the Arts and Crafts Movement, the biographer of Philip Webb and the first principal of the Central School of Arts and Crafts, London. Lethaby built relatively little and what he built did not always conform to his own rationalist beliefs. This country church is original to the point of eccentricity, yet it achieves a medieval character – Lethaby was an authority on medieval architecture – without copying medieval details. The church is cruciform, with a low stone central tower and a second boarded tower over the south porch. It has a thatched roof and, perhaps to minimize the risk of fire, concrete vaulting over the chancel and transepts – an early use of this material. It is not however *reinforced* concrete, and the piers and arches carrying the vault are stone.

functionally, following traditional country models, instead of being conceived as small pieces of architecture, as was the more self-conscious furniture of the time. Gimson met Morris in 1884. He was a self-taught craftsman, one of whose associates, Sydney Barnsley, began as an architect; another, W.R.Lethaby, remained one.

Philip Webb built several other houses (No.1 Palace Green, London, 1863; Clouds, Wiltshire, 1876; Standen, Sussex, 1891), all of which depended more on practical building than on historical precedent. Webb's use of vernacular forms and materials in the Red House and elsewhere opened the way for similar departures from the conventional range of academic styles on the part of architects like Norman Shaw – his country houses in his somewhat nostalgic 'Old England' style have already been described, since this and the preceding chapter run parallel chronologically. The same example was soon followed by Voysey and Baillie Scott whose cottage-style small houses must be described in a moment; and eventually, in his country houses, by Sir Edwin Lutyens.

Lethaby (1857–1931) was chief assistant in Norman Shaw's office and provides another link between the contrasting worlds of the successful architect with his appeal to the newly rich and the Bohemian world of the minority who responded to the ideas of the Arts and Crafts designers – each world however influencing the other. Lethaby designed a characteristically austere house on Orkney (Melsetter House, 1898) and a highly original church in Hereford and Worcester (Brock-

hampton, 1901). He was an influential writer and the founder (in 1894) and the first principal of the Central School of Arts and Crafts in London.

Charles Annesley Voysey (1857–1941) was likewise an architect not a craftsman, but he took the same all-embracing view as other Arts and Crafts architects and made himself responsible for the design of every detail of his buildings (which were

almost all small houses) down to the light fittings and window fastenings. When given the opportunity, he liked to design the furniture. Voysey's furniture placed emphasis on the basic structure, apart from a few mannerisms of the time such as heart-shaped holes pierced in the vertical surfaces. His textiles and wallpapers, with which he made his first reputation under the guidance of another Arts and Crafts

House at Shackleford, Surrey, by C.F.A.Voysey; 1897. The long roof-lines, the gables, the bay-windows, the quietly harmonious materials (window-dressings of stone with roughcast between) are typical of the style with which Voysey revolutionized English domestic architecture, following local building traditions and relying on good craftsmanship rather than adventitious ornament. Inside, the house has a panelled hall two storeys high with the staircase-landing forming a gallery. Stables were built on to it, and some other additions made, in 1903.

romantic manner than Norman Shaw and on a more cottagey scale, he turned domestic architecture back to its native traditions. His houses, employing the forms and materials to be found in the farmhouses and cottages of rural England, are deceptively simple, with hipped or gabled roofs, white roughcast walls (often with sloping buttresses, one of his favourite devices) and small-paned bay windows. How unorthodox they were is obscured today by the debased imitations of his style out of which a great part of suburbia was subsequently built up.

More unorthodox still was their planning. Voysey – along with Norman Shaw – was one of the first to free the plan of the house from the constriction resulting from the typically Victorian subdivision into separate specialized rooms and to open up the internal spaces so that one flowed into another. His influence, and that of some other architects who worked in a similar style such as M.H.Baillie Scott (1865–1945) – whose houses are rather prettier than Voysey's – and Ernest Newton (1856–1922) – whose houses are rather more conventional – extended far beyond Britain. In the work of these designers, for the first time since the Industrial Revolution, English architecture provided a model for the Continent of Europe to follow. So high was the reputation of the small English house at the end of the century that in 1896 the German government attached a trained architect, Hermann Muthesius, to its embassy in London to keep in touch with, and report on, the English revolution in the domestic arts. His resulting book, *Das Englische Haus*, published in 1906 and illustrating the work of Voysey and a number of his colleagues, launched a new vogue for reasonableness and simplicity first in Germany and then elsewhere in Europe.

Several other English architects were involved, closely or otherwise, in the changes initiated by the

architect, A.H.Mackmurdo (1851–1942), a disciple of Ruskin and a friend of Morris and Webb, had a freshness and gaiety more suited to everyday use than Morris's sober medievalism.

In contrast to the architects of a hundred years before, Voysey distrusted foreign travel, believing that the best architecture of the past had grown out of local requirements and local conditions. In a less

Warehouse, Stokes Croft, Bristol, by E.W.Godwin; 1862.
Designed before the Arts and Crafts Movement got
under way; yet Godwin fits in here because he played a
central part in the widely ranging aesthetic movement of
which the Arts and Crafts Movement was but one
manifestation. He had links also with the Gothic Revival
– he was a friend of William Burges – but this warehouse
was ahead of its time in relying hardly at all on historic
precedent, but instead on the rhythm of the variously
arched openings and the contrasted textures of the
stonework: smooth Bath stone and rustic-surfaced
Pennant stone.

Arts and Crafts Movement and in parallel attempts
to break away from the High Victorian treatment of
buildings as picturesque assemblages of period
motifs. One was E.W.Godwin (1833–86), who
comes into the story at this point, in spite of
belonging to an earlier generation, because of his
connection with the aesthetic movement in the arts
generally, related to the Arts and Crafts Movement
and represented by among others Whistler (for
whom Godwin built a house) and Oscar Wilde.

Godwin occupied a unique position as the link

between this artistic world, the world of the stage,
and the more self-contained world of the professional architects. He was enormously admired by
the young intellectuals of the 1870s. It was with
him that the actress Ellen Terry eloped when she
left her elderly painter husband G.F.Watts. Max
Beerbohm described him as 'the greatest aesthete of
them all'. Like Pugin before him and Voysey after
him, Godwin was concerned as a designer with many
things besides buildings. His leadership of contemporary taste was achieved principally through
his unconventionally spartan interior designs and his
elegant furniture. He was one of the first to become
subject to the Japanese influence that coloured much
English interior design at this time. His first
important architectural work, the town hall at
Northampton (1861, but enlarged later) – the
outcome of a competition – closely followed the
precepts of Ruskin who, along with Burges, was his
mentor. There followed a precociously simple
arcaded warehouse in Bristol (1862), another Gothic
town hall at Congleton, Cheshire (1864), and a castle
– Dromore Castle – at Limerick, Ireland (1867). His
later buildings merge with the Queen Anne Revival
(see the preceding chapter); in fact he was the first
architect to be approached about the design of
Bedford Park and he himself built several plain brick
houses on that estate.

E.S.Prior (1852–1932) was another, though a
sometimes eccentric, architect associated with the
revolution in house design, and like so many of the
leading architects of his time was a pupil of Norman
Shaw. The Art Workers' Guild, an influential

OPPOSITE
*Horniman Museum, Lewisham, London, by
C.H.Townsend; 1902.* Built to house the collections of a
wealthy tea merchant. One of the few truly Art Nouveau
buildings in England, especially the tower with its
plasticity of form and vegetable-inspired ornament. The
mosaic on the main front is by Anning Bell.

OVERLEAF
*Factory, Perivale, near London, by Wallis, Gilbert and
Partners; 1932.* On the Great West Road, an arterial
highway alongside which some large and showy factories
were built in the 1930s. This (for the Hoover Company)
and several of the others followed a new fashion since
labelled Art Deco, employing among its characteristic
tricks of style the rounded windows, the corner
embellishments and the coloured stripes to be seen here.
(See page 258.)

association of forward-looking architects founded in 1884, was largely composed of men from Shaw's office. Prior was also a writer on medieval buildings and a teacher. C. R. Ashbee (1863–1942) was a teacher also. He started the Guild of Handicraft in the East End of London in 1888 but later transferred it to Chipping Campden in the Cotswolds, the home then and afterwards of several offshoots of the Arts and Crafts Movement. Ashbee built little – two adjoining houses in Cheyne Walk, Chelsea (1899), are notable – but his influence was considerable and is the more significant because, although he was a follower of William Morris (in his social as well as his architectural beliefs), he was prepared to accept the changes that the use of machinery would lead to.

Another new influence was discernible in the 1890s in the work of a few architects who, seeking an alternative to the historicism of the academic majority, looked to Europe for new ideas instead of to the vernacular traditions of the English country-side. They looked particularly to the Art Nouveau Movement which had begun to flourish in France and Belgium and in the Vienna of the *Sezession*. This was influential chiefly as a new source of ornament, based on flowing vegetable forms which dissolved rather than accentuated the geometry of structure.

OPPOSITE ABOVE
Highpoint, Highgate, London, by Lubetkin and Tecton; 1935. This block of flats with panel walls of poured concrete (rather than the concrete frame with infill walls of some other material which soon became the normal way of using this material) was regarded as a classic of the international style on account of its rigorously disciplined design and the logic of its planning. Lubetkin, the leader of the Tecton group of architects, was Russian-born with Paris experience. The engineer, Ove Arup, was originally Danish. (See page 264.)

OPPOSITE BELOW
University of York, by Robert Matthew, Johnson-Marshall and Partners; 1962. One of a dozen new universities planned in the 1960s. This was the first to adopt the collegiate system (the picture shows Derwent College). The site was open land on the south-eastern edge of the city of York, and the buildings are informally distributed round a lake and connected under cover by walkways in the roofs of which are the various service pipes and conduits. To save construction time a prefabricated system was used, with precast panel walls, a modification and elaboration of the system first employed (see pages 268–9) for the post-war school building programme.

One English architect who incorporated elements of Art Nouveau in his buildings was Charles Harrison Townsend (1850–1928). His Whitechapel Art Gallery in East London (1897) has a street facade with a boldly arched entrance placed off-centre and friezes of stylized leaf ornament. He also designed, in similar style, the Horniman Museum in south-east London (1902) and a church at Great Warley, Essex (1904), which has an interior equipped with the most startling Art Nouveau furnishings by him and by William Reynolds-Stephens.

In other respects Townsend was wholly charac-teristic of the avant-garde architects of his time: Master of the Art Workers' Guild, builder of houses in Hampstead Garden Suburb (which was laid out in 1907–10 as another manifestation of the urge to escape from urban to rural surroundings) and designer of textiles and wallpapers.

The reference above to Art Nouveau brings us to perhaps the outstanding architect of this epoch – or at least of its more revolutionary productions: Charles Rennie Mackintosh (1869–1928). He is rightly classed as one of the leading practitioners of Art Nouveau – indeed as one of its originators – because his furniture and his ornamental designs in various media made an important contribution to the movement. He was the one British Art Nouveau designer to acquire a reputation on the Continent, especially among the revolutionary young designers of the Vienna *Sezession*. He became more famous there than in his own country. Art Nouveau was in fact far more Continental than English. It never became an accepted style in London or even in Glasgow in the sense that it did in Brussels, Barcelona, Helsinki and Paris.

Mackintosh's one great building, the Glasgow School of Art (1898), nevertheless belongs to Art Nouveau only in the style of its very sparse ornamentation, mostly in wrought iron, and in some of its furnishings. It is revolutionary in a much more fundamental sense, for it represents an architecture of pure geometry generated by the spaces within. It has boldly unsymmetrical facades with large rectangular windows and a handling of internal spaces that justified the advocates of the Modern Movement in the 1930s in looking back to it as a pioneer of functionally lucid planning and of the clear expression of structure. The library especially, a lofty room with galleries on three sides supported by wooden pillars that continue unimpeded from the

*St Mary's Church, Great Warley, Essex, by
C.H. Townsend and William Reynolds-Stephens; 1904: the
chancel screen and pulpit with the apse beyond.* Townsend
designed this memorial church in a modest Home
Counties style: roughcast walls, prominent buttresses
and a bell-turret. He and Reynolds–Stephens designed
the far less orthodox interior, the latter being responsible
for the highly ornate Art Nouveau fittings, executed for
the most part by himself in a great variety of materials –
oxidized copper sheeting, for instance, for the pulpit and
dark green Irish marble, brass, silver, mother-of-pearl
and coloured glass for the screen. The church has a
boarded wagon-vaulted roof with aluminium ribs. The
lower part of the apse is faced with light green Swiss
marble. Its upper walls are faced with aluminium and
decorated with raised aluminium bands in the form of a
stylized grape-vine, the bunches of grapes coloured red.

242

floor to the roof, is a masterpiece of the imaginative
use of structure to create an effective interior.
Mackintosh's career was short and his other
architectural works were few: a handsome house at
Helensburgh (1902) in an austere Scottish vernacular, a school and a number of tea-room interiors in
Glasgow (1897–1907) in which his Art Nouveau
allegiances were seductively displayed. After
Mackintosh gave up work in 1913 Britain's international leadership in domestic architecture and the
applied arts altogether evaporated.

This chapter can conclude with something about
one more architect who belongs also to the next
chapter but must make a first appearance here
because his earlier houses – some would say his best
– are part of the story of the revolution in English
domestic architecture that began with Philip Webb
and Norman Shaw and was carried on by Voysey
and the others mentioned above. This architect was
Sir Edwin Lutyens (1869–1944). Although he
started in the office of Sir Ernest George and Peto
(see Chapter 16), Lutyens set up on his own when he
was only twenty and thus was largely self-taught. He
was helped at the beginning of his career by the
garden-designer Gertrude Jekyll, for whom he built
a house, Munstead Wood, Surrey (1896). He
showed great knowledge and instinctive understanding of English rural traditions, especially those
of the southern counties with their hand-made
bricks, tile-hanging and oak-framed mullioned
windows. He was a master of the apparently casual
but skilfully balanced composition, making use for
this purpose – like Norman Shaw – of tall clustered
chimneys and intersecting rooflines.

Among Lutyens's most notable early houses are
Orchards, near Munstead, Surrey (1897), and
Deanery Garden, Sonning, Berkshire (1899). Their
informal plans and handling of internal space carry
the experiments of his Arts and Crafts predecessors a
stage further. His subsequent predilection for the
neo-Georgian style must be left until later.

*Deanery Garden, Sonning, Berkshire, by Sir Edwin
Lutyens; 1899.* A typical early Lutyens country house,
built for Edward Hudson, the proprietor of *Country Life*
magazine. Like all his houses, it shows masterly and
inventive handling of traditional English forms and
materials; in this case grouped chimneys, red brick and
tiles. The timber-framed bay-window, reminiscent of
some by Norman Shaw, lights a two-storey hall.

Chapter 18

Edwardian Extravagance

In spite of their influence and their significance for the future, the Arts and Crafts and the aesthetic movements described in the last chapter remained only a minority aspect of English architecture as a whole. Their impact was confined to domestic architecture, to interior decoration and to a limited number of church interiors, the latter chiefly through William Morris and his associates' stained glass. The large public and commercial buildings – those buildings which, during the period of increasing prosperity at the beginning of the twentieth century, marked the rapid growth of towns and cities – continued the nineteenth-century practice of wide-ranging historical revivalism. For the most part however the refined scholarship and the marked originality, sometimes amounting to eccentricity, shown by many of the Victorian architects now gave way to a more conventional Classicism, employed with an exuberance, sometimes a vulgarity, that reflected the wealth and self-confidence of a country that found itself the centre of a still expanding empire.

Edwardian architecture also reflected the fact that it was principally a commercial empire. The typical buildings of the period were the banking, insurance and shipping offices in the City of London and in the business centres of other cities, and the city halls and public libraries which advertised those cities' prosperity, together with such new types of building as cinemas and department stores. The architectural treatment of these gave very little sign of the new technologies on which the building industry was coming to rely. Well before the end of the nineteenth century men like Alfred Waterhouse had made use of iron beams. Now the whole structure of many buildings consisted of steel beams and columns, although they were seldom revealed on the outside. The Ritz Hotel in London was the first important English steel-framed building. It was designed in 1904 by a French architect Charles Mewès (1860–

Admiralty Arch, London, by Sir Aston Webb; 1908.
Situated at the end of the Mall, one of London's few processional avenues, laid out in 1660 by Charles II and chosen in 1901 as the site of the national memorial to Queen Victoria. The Mall was embellished by Sir Aston Webb at the western end, facing Buckingham Palace, with stone piers and iron gates and a central island containing a sculptured memorial (by Sir Thomas Brock, 1902) and at the eastern end by this triple archway – the first direct exit from the Mall into Trafalgar Square. It exemplifies Webb's opulent Imperial style which he also employed, though in a stiffer and less exuberant manner, when in the short space of three months he refronted Buckingham Palace (Edward Blore, 1846) for Edward VII in 1912.

Office building, Norwich, by G. J. Skipper; 1903. The headquarters of the Norwich Union Insurance Company, designed by a local architect, G. J. Skipper (1856–1948), who had an obvious mastery of Edwardian Baroque. Business and commercial undertakings in many parts of the country employed a similar full-blooded style to indicate their solidity and self-confidence. The tall building in the background was designed for the same company in 1959 by T. P. Bennett and is typical of the cruder office buildings of that time (see Chapter 20).

1914) and his English partner Arthur J. Davis (1878–1951). It was faced with elegant French Renaissance stonework and crowned with a high slate roof. It is one of the few London buildings with an arcade sheltering the pavement after the manner of the Rue de Rivoli in Paris. Mewès and Davis also designed the Royal Automobile Club in Pall Mall (1910) and Davis was responsible for the sumptuous interiors of several Cunard liners, including the *Aquitania*.

Architectural styles do not necessarily change with a new reign; nor do careers terminate. A number of the architects who have been mentioned as being prominent in the Victorian period were still active in the Edwardian; Sir Ernest George, for

example, who had altered the basic colour of whole areas of residential London with his red-brown terracotta facades in the 1880s, built the Royal Academy of Music as late as 1910. John Belcher (1841–1913), in many ways a typical Edwardian, designed what is perhaps the most satisfying Baroque edifice of its time, Colchester Town Hall, in 1898 and went on to design Whiteley's store in London in 1910. Sir Aston Webb, whose confusingly eclectic Victoria and Albert Museum was designed in 1891, became the leading academic architect of the early twentieth century. In his rather stolid Renaissance style he built the Admiralty Arch at one end of the Mall in London in 1908 and the present principal facade of Buckingham Palace at the other end in 1912.

At the same time as the men of this generation discarded the more exotic of the Victorian styles – Colcutt was perhaps the last of the well-known architects to experiment with these in such buildings as his Palace Theatre, Cambridge Circus, of 1890, and his largely demolished Imperial Institute of 1893 – they also abandoned the use of Gothic, except occasionally for churches. There were a few throwbacks to the Gothic Revival like Temple Moore

Cardiff City Hall, South Wales, by H.V.Lanchester and Edwin Rickards; 1901. One of a group of civic buildings in Cathays Park, laid out on a formal, axial plan (still not complete). Exuberantly Baroque, showing not only these architects' customary adaptations of French styles but also borrowings from the more ornate Austrian Baroque. The City Hall is flanked on one side by the same architects' Law Courts and on the other by the National Museum of Wales (1910), in a heavier style, more Greek in derivation, by Smith and Brewer.

(1856–1920), Sir Charles Nicholson (1867–1949) and – continuing surprisingly late – Sir Ninian Comper (1864–1960), a pupil of Bodley whose Decorated churches with their richly gilt furnishings (St Mary's, Wellingborough, Northamptonshire, 1908) came nearest to a true medieval feeling.

The majority of architects now adopted – and it became the typical Edwardian style – a vigorous Renaissance, most often French in derivation. A list of the most prominent among these would include the following: H.V.Lanchester (1863–1953), a master, with his partner Edwin Rickards (1872–1920), of French ornament, who built the symmetrically laid out Cardiff civic centre (1897–1906), the charming Deptford Town Hall

(1902, in this case with a more Dutch than a French character) and the Wesleyan Central Hall, Westminster (1905), a domed building, very French in style with a handsome elliptical staircase and, like the Ritz, an early example of steel-frame construction; E.W.Mountford (1855–1908), architect of the Old Bailey, London (1900), and of Lancaster Town Hall (1906); F.T.Verity (1864–1937) who, in the footsteps of his father Thomas Verity (1837–91), became a specialist in the design of theatres and cinemas after first designing, in 1890, the pavilion at Lords cricket ground; and Sir John Burnet (1857–1938), who like many of his generation studied at the *Ecole des Beaux Arts* in Paris and was a conscientiously academic architect responsible for many large buildings in Glasgow where he initially practised. He also built the northern extension (Edward VII galleries) of the British Museum (1905) and latterly worked in partnership with Thomas Tait (1882–1954) who will figure in the next chapter, as too will some of Burnet's more adventurous designs.

The same elaborately detailed Renaissance styles still dominated English architecture in the reign of George V. The leaders of the generation that

247

Piccadilly Circus, London : west and north sides, by Sir Reginald Blomfield. John Nash's arcaded Regent Street was replaced in 1913 by buildings of greater height and on a commercially more profitable scale. At the same time the Circus was replanned. Norman Shaw had just completed his Piccadilly Hotel (1905), immediately west of the buildings shown here, in the Baroque revival style he adopted late in his career. He died in 1912 and by then a lighter French Renaissance, first used for the Ritz Hotel further along Piccadilly, was more the fashion. Blomfield used it frequently. His rebuilding of Piccadilly Circus was interrupted by the outbreak of war and the work shown here was not completed until 1930. Blomfield planned to use a similar style in 1932 for rebuilding Carlton House Terrace but that project was frustrated by the first of a number of well-publicized conservation campaigns.

followed those listed above included Sir Reginald Blomfield (1856–1942), nephew of the late Gothic Revival architect Sir Arthur Blomfield (1829–99) and again a devotee of French styles, responsible for the rebuilding (1920) of Nash's Regent Street Quadrant and for the western part of Piccadilly Circus; Sir Herbert Baker (1862–1946), who built all over the Commonwealth and in London the rather cardboardy South African House (1935) and the huge Renaissance pile that rises above the screen-

wall which once enclosed Soane's Bank of England; Sir Edwin Cooper (1873–1942), who designed the guildhall at Hull (1906) and the pyramidal Port of London Authority building near the Tower (1912); and E. Vincent Harris (1879–1971), perhaps the last successful architect with a firm belief in the relevance of Renaissance scholarship. He was a specialist in civic buildings of which his most prominent is Leeds Civic Hall (1930), which has twin towers resembling those on Wren's City churches and also shows perhaps the influence of the later Lutyens (see below).

Vincent Harris was also the architect of that enormous historical anomaly, the Ministry of Defence building in Whitehall, which is said to accommodate five and a half thousand civil servants. It was designed by him in 1913, postponed at the outbreak of war, scheduled for construction in the 1920s, postponed again because of the economic depression, begun in 1935, interrupted by the outbreak of the 1939 war and eventually completed, to a modified version of Harris's original design which had been sedulously retained in the official files, in 1959.

Until the second decade of the century large country houses were still being commissioned, if not on quite the lavish scale of the palaces built a generation earlier by wealthy landowners and successful industrialists. By now Lutyens was the acknowledged leader among designers of country houses; there seemed to be no end to his inventiveness in creating new effects from the elements traditional to the manor house and the farmhouse while at the same time endowing them with a freshness that took them far away from pastiche. Before economic changes, especially those resulting from the 1914–18 war, brought the era of country house building to an end, several other architects – some influenced by Lutyens, some still by the Arts and Crafts Movement – had shown their talent for this characteristically informal English category of design. Among these are Sir Guy Dawber (1861–1938) and the less orthodox E. S. Prior, already mentioned in the last chapter (Home Place, Holt, Norfolk, 1903).

By this time Lutyens himself had turned to the design of substantial urban buildings, mostly for commercial clients. Like Norman Shaw's before him, his later work was less romantic, more formal and conventionally Classical, a change seen also in

Heathcote, Ilkley, West Yorkshire, by Sir Edwin Lutyens; 1906. A contrast to Lutyens's earlier country houses, with their studied informality and affinities with an English rural vernacular. By the time Heathcote was designed he was ready to experiment with Classical formality. He built no other houses quite so Mannerist or so Baroque as Heathcote, though these styles appear in his town buildings. He later designed a number of other Classical, but more Palladian, country houses such as Gledstone Hall, also in Yorkshire (1923).

his later houses. Just as Norman Shaw, towards the end of his life, embarked on Classical exercises like Bryanston, Dorset (1890), and in London the ambitious Baroque of the Piccadilly Hotel (1903), so Edwin Lutyens adopted a formal symmetrical style in houses like Heathcote, Ilkley, West Yorkshire (1906), which contrasts strikingly with the more romantic houses he had designed under the influence of Gertrude Jekyll. And when his great reputation brought him commissions to design important buildings in London, they too were Classical rather than Romantic. He built nothing in the town so picturesquely inventive as Norman Shaw's London masterpiece, New Scotland Yard (1888), a fortress-like block, striped in red brick and stone with round angle-turrets and vigorous Baroque enrichments.

For his town buildings Lutyens chose a more orthodox Classical. They nevertheless mark a break away from the French Renaissance and the opulent Edwardian Baroque of his contemporaries and immediate predecessors; for he introduced a more domesticated style strongly influenced by the work of Sir Christopher Wren. His first experiment with such a style was an office building in Covent Garden, London, for the magazine *Country Life* (1904). It was followed by his most appealing town building, a small bank in Piccadilly (1922) near Wren's St James's Church. Both are in red brick and stone, with their early Renaissance motifs deployed wittily and inventively. Lutyens's more monumental City buildings (the Midland Bank headquarters, Poultry, and Britannic House, Finsbury Circus – both 1924) show a powerful handling of solids and voids and use the Classical Orders dramatically. Nevertheless, leaving aside New Delhi, which is far outside the scope of this book, it may be thought that Lutyens's country houses remain his most admirable contribution to English architecture.

The countryside itself was, however, now changing. It was no longer a place only for agriculture and the residences of the nobility and gentry. Increasingly during the twentieth century the development of the motor car and, in the case of London, the widespread extension of the electric Underground system – above ground when it reached the suburbs –

enlarged the spread of towns far beyond the distance that the fashion for building out-of-town villas had taken it in the nineteenth century. But there was little control over the use of land. The reigns of Edward VII and George V, besides being characterized by extravagantly opulent public and commercial buildings, were extravagant in quite a different sense: in the quantity of land they permitted to be eaten up by sprawling residential estates and – especially damaging to the quality of many people's lives – by ribbon development. The erection of small houses in continuous lines on either side of the existing roads leading out of the towns saved speculative builders the cost of constructing roads and services but resulted in such roads, and thus the newly populated fringes of the towns, being cut off from the green countryside.

The planning deficiencies of this period of rapid urban expansion are not the subject of this book, and in any case the new suburban housing estates were seldom designed by architects. They were the work of speculative builders who evolved a type of detached or semi-detached two-storey house which soon became a recognizable twentieth-century vernacular. It had brick or roughcast walls and tiled roofs and put forward either a vulgarized version of the style developed by the Arts and Crafts architects like Voysey (see Chapter 17) or a miniature version, but with applied instead of structural half-timbering, of the Tudor or Old English style that Norman Shaw had adapted from the traditional manor-house and farmhouse.

Architects had already begun to devote their attention to housing of another kind: to the publicly financed working-class housing in some of the big cities, whose elected authorities were establishing their own architects' departments. The London County Council (LCC), created in 1889, started its architects' department a few years afterwards and set the rest of the country a responsible and forward-looking lead with its Boundary Street Estate, Shoreditch (1896), and its Millbank Estate, Westminster (1898). These were composed for the most part of blocks of flats of up to five storeys (but not yet with lifts). Other estates, from 1903 onwards, were composed of cottages laid out under the influence of the Garden City movement. A notable LCC contribution to low-rent housing was made under the guidance of G. Topham Forrest (1873–1945), who was the council's architect from

1919 until 1935 and therefore during the period when public authorities had to make unprecedented efforts to overcome the housing shortage after the First World War. Topham Forrest evolved a simple but dignified Georgian style, less brutal than that of the multi-storey blocks put up by late Victorian philanthropic foundations. It can be studied in many of the inner suburbs and, for example, alongside Kennington Oval. Other noteworthy low-cost housing in London – also Georgian in style but with a precociously Regency flavour – was that built in 1913 south of the Thames at Kennington by Stanley Adshead (1886–1946) and Stanley Ramsey (1882–1968) for the Duchy of Cornwall Estate.

At this time a few far-sighted architects were beginning to see the need for the profession to encourage and take part in the total design of new residential areas. Among them – and therefore among the pioneers of English town planning – was Sir Raymond Unwin (1863–1940) who, with his architect partner Barry Parker (1867–1941), laid out the first Garden City at Letchworth, Hertfordshire, in 1903 and a similar one at Wythenshawe near Manchester in 1927. Both are more successful socially than architecturally, but another housing layout by the same planners, Hampstead Garden Suburb in north London (begun 1907), has a positive architectural presence to which the part played by Sir Edwin Lutyens makes an important contribution.

For Hampstead Garden Suburb Lutyens designed a pair of distinguished churches balanced either side of the central axis, and a number of small houses. The latter are Georgian in style and they, together with similar groups of Georgian-style houses by a number of architects at Welwyn Garden City (begun 1919), with the LCC housing already mentioned and with the change in taste initiated by Lutyens's town architecture, mark the beginning of the Georgian Revival which was to be one of the dominating influences in the 1920s and early 1930s.

Bank, Piccadilly, London, by Sir Edwin Lutyens; 1922. A lively and wittily perverse adaptation of the Christopher Wren idiom which Lutyens employed for most of his town buildings – all for commercial clients and nearly all designed after the First World War. Of these only Britannic House, Finsbury (1924), follows up the Baroque experiments he had made at Heathcote. Lutyens's town buildings mark the beginning of the Georgian revival which dominated the 1920s.

Chapter 19

Return to Internationalism: the 1920s and the Modern Movement

University Library, Cambridge, by Sir Giles Gilbert Scott; 1931. In the rather nondescript style, derived from several sources, that Scott employed late in his career for monumental buildings. The tower of the library is here seen through the archway, and across one of the courts, of the range of residential buildings (New Court) that Scott had designed earlier (1924) for Clare College. These are of pale grey brick in a refined neo-Georgian – a style he used skilfully, though less boldly than he used Gothic – with Adamesque details.

BEFORE the end of the 1920s English architecture had become strangely fragmented. So great was the variety of styles employed that only a summary of the most significant can be attempted here. At least four main tendencies were observable, some relating to those of the preceding years and some consciously reacting against them. There was no decisive moment of change, and one of these tendencies therefore was a continuation, affected only by minor changes of fashion, of the historical revivalism that had been the basis of the more academic architects' work for more than a century. Such architects still dominated the profession, occupying the senior positions in the Royal Academy and the Royal Institute of British Architects. Their leaders have already appeared in these pages: Sir Reginald Blomfield, Sir Herbert Baker, Sir Edwin Cooper and a few others of like eminence. Most major public buildings were in their hands and their favourite, and by now familiar, neo-Renaissance idiom, with its heavily ornamented facades of Portland stone (which however concealed steel skeletons), was varied only by the somewhat newer Lutyens-inspired neo-Georgian idiom with facades mostly of red brick.

For although Lutyens himself, the most distinguished architect and most inventive designer of that generation, had turned, as described in the last chapter, to a vigorous but formal Classicism for his large city buildings, the more domestic neo-Georgian style that he had done so much to establish was in many circles replacing the grander French Renaissance. For example, a typical building of the 1920s by Sir Edwin Cooper, contrasting with his monumental Port of London Authority building of 1912, was his Star and Garter ex-servicemen's home on Richmond Hill, Surrey, a massive red brick structure with minimal stone embellishments, completed in 1924.

The academic architect most typical of the 1920s,

Star and Garter Home for Ex-Servicemen, Richmond, Surrey, by Sir Edwin Cooper; 1924. On an elevated site overlooking the Thames. A robust example of the Georgian Revival of the 1920s but showing already the tendency that became more evident later to use neo-Georgian for multi-storey buildings, out of character with the style's domestic origins. Note that the third-floor window-shutters are employed decoratively rather than functionally.

however, was one not hitherto mentioned: Sir Giles Scott (1880–1960). He was a member of the Scott family that had played so prominent a role in the nineteenth century and formed an architectural dynasty nearly as influential as the Wyatts. When he was only twenty-three Scott won the competition (judged by Norman Shaw and G.F.Bodley) for an Anglican cathedral at Liverpool. Because of his youth and inexperience he was required to carry out his design in association with Bodley, the veteran Gothic Revival architect who was then seventy-six and had begun as a pupil of Scott's grandfather, Sir George Gilbert Scott, as far back as 1845 – nearly sixty years before. But Bodley died in 1907 four

years after the competition and the design of Liverpool Cathedral is altogether Scott's except for the reredos which is thought to be largely Bodley's.

The cathedral is built of reddish sandstone in a powerful variation of Decorated Gothic which Scott gradually evolved. It is impressive in its vertical scale if a little mechanical in some of its details. It has an original plan with nave and choir of equal length and double transepts. It is wholly traditional in construction, making no use of steel or concrete. Like the medieval cathedrals, its construction spanned several generations. It was finally completed in 1978.

Although this precocious work was begun early in the century, Scott is more characteristically a figure of the 1920s, from which decade, and the following one, the remainder of his important buildings date. They show a willingness, typical of these decades with their uncertain allegiances, to switch abruptly from one style to another. His war memorial chapel at Charterhouse School, Godalming, Surrey (1922) – perhaps the most successful of all his buildings – is in a bold Gothic. His New Court at Clare College, Cambridge (1924), is in a quiet neo-Georgian. In his later work he attempted less orthodox mixtures of

Liverpool Cathedral, by Sir Giles Gilbert Scott; 1903–78: from the south-east. The most ambitious architectural project of the early twentieth century, photographed when the west end was still being finished. Traditionally constructed of reddish sandstone in a version of the Decorated phase of English Gothic, a style evolved, after winning a competition, by the grandson of the eminent Victorian architect; completed to his design eighteen years after his death.

motifs, with less sensitive and rather commonplace results: the University Library, Cambridge (1931); the New Bodleian Library, Oxford (1936). He designed the architectural embellishments of the Battersea and the South Bank power-stations in London (1932 and 1952).

The red brick neo-Georgian style was used also for large business and apartment buildings, but seldom with any success. Its elements were derived from buildings of a domestic scale and did not easily withstand inflation to multi-storey size. Cornices crowning so many tiers of windows and pediments and porticos applied to such vast facades seemed to have too little in common with the role for which they had originally been devised. The neo-Georgian nevertheless, whether used with academic correctness or in the form of some fanciful variation, was thought to be a style well suited to the municipal buildings that were erected in great numbers in the 1920s. These were relatively modest in size, and if a Georgian or Palladian portico was made the central feature of a town hall or library, it gave it the required civic dignity. There was no need to further elaborate the facade and thereby complicate the layout of the spaces within.

255

Park Lane, London; early 1930s. Illustrating the abrupt change in scale that transformed the West End of London in the period between the wars. On the left, surviving bow-fronted private houses of the early nineteenth century; on the right, redevelopment in the form of flats and hotels – neo-Georgian, but with six storeys compressed into the height previously occupied by five. The new building is Grosvenor House (1930). Sir Edwin Lutyens was consulting architect and designed the pavilions housing water-tanks on the roof.

Buildings of this kind were often the subject of a competition and some architects kept themselves fully occupied entering and winning a succession of these: Berry Webber (1896–1963) – town hall at Peterborough, Cambridgeshire (1932); C. Cowles Voysey (1889–1941), the son of the pioneer Arts and Crafts architect Charles Voysey (see Chapter 17) – the White Rock Pavilion, Hastings, Sussex (1924), and the town hall at Worthing, Sussex (1931); E. Vincent Harris – the circular Manchester city library (1929). Harris's larger civic hall at Leeds was referred to in the last chapter.

The buildings named above were composed out of

orthodox Georgian elements, as were the many post offices built at this time. Other civic buildings were in styles of their architects' own contrivance but still incorporated basically Classical elements: Berry Webber – Southampton civic centre (1929); Lanchester and Lodge – Beckenham, Kent, town hall (1932); C.H.James (1893–1953) – town halls at Slough, Berkshire (1934), and Hertford (1939); Sir Percy Thomas (1884–1969) – guildhall at Swansea, South Wales (1934). Municipal architecture was also responsible for introducing into England some fresh variations on the Georgian theme that had been developed in Scandinavia. Swedish work was much admired in England as having a livelier presence than the orthodox neo-Georgian, especially the work of Ivar Tengbom (1878–1968), whose concert hall at Stockholm (1926), with its portico of close-set, elongated columns, was widely imitated.

The most prominent example is the city hall at Norwich (1932) by C.H. James in partnership with S.Rowland Pierce (1896–1966). The latter taught at the Architectural Association School, where many of the staff had been looking admiringly to Scandinavia since the completion of that evocative monument to

Norwich City Hall, by C.H.James and S.Rowland Pierce; 1932. By the 1930s the neo-Georgian style was being given a new flavour by the admiration in England for current Swedish architecture. The elongated columns of the Norwich portico and the tapering tower are evidence of Swedish influence.

a dying romanticism – but one far harder to imitate – the city hall at Stockholm of 1911–23 by Ragnar Ostberg (1866–1945).

This tendency to look overseas for architectural inspiration was new in twentieth-century England if we except the French Renaissance influence on many of the academic architects, which was largely the outcome of study at the *Ecole des Beaux Arts* in Paris. But in the 1920s France again became a source of new fashions as a result of the unexpected success

Peterborough Town Hall, Cambridgeshire, by E. Berry Webber; 1932. Revived Georgian was the approved style for the many town halls and other municipal buildings erected at this time, usually following competitions. The incorporation of shops in this instance presages the later municipal involvement in property finance.

New Victoria Cinema, London, by E. Wamsley Lewis;
1920: the staircase. The Art Deco or Jazz Modern style
was especially popular for the interiors of hotels and
places of entertainment. It made use of stylized
sculpture, of decorative architectural forms invented
rather than derived from history and of glass and metal
products newly made available by industry.

Moderne and then, more lastingly, Art Deco. It had
something in common with the far less flippant
Expressionism (mainly a German movement) and
with equivalent fashions that briefly materialized in
Holland. They spread their influence at the same
time to the newer arts like the cinema.

The Art Deco style was characterized by angular
forms, the use of bright materials such as stainless
steel and mirror-glass and a fondness for certain
non-traditional decorative motifs much in evidence
at the Paris exhibition of 1925 like the stylized
pomegranate – just as the Art Nouveau decoration of
a quarter of a century before had been identified
with the stylized water-lily.

In England Art Deco never became a dominant
style. Its influence was mostly on interior decoration
(with which this book makes no attempt to deal) and
is exemplified by the refurbished salons of such
hotels as Claridges and the Savoy. A brilliant
example was the new entrance to another London
hotel, the Strand Palace (Oliver Bernard, 1929),
which was dismantled in 1969 and acquired by the
Victoria and Albert Museum. Perhaps the best –
certainly the most striking – Art Deco buildings
were the shiny black granite Ideal House (now
Palladium House) in Great Marlborough Street,
near Oxford Circus, London, of 1928 by the
American architect Raymond Hood (1881–1934)
and several factories bordering the Great West Road
by Wallis, Gilbert and Partners.

Stylized ornament related to Art Deco can be seen
applied to a number of other London buildings
designed in the partly denuded Classical style that
also became fashionable at this time: the RIBA
headquarters, Portland Place, of 1932 by G. Grey
Wornum (1888–1957), which – highly eclectic – also
has a Scandinavian flavour, the New Victoria
Cinema of 1920 by Wamsley Lewis (1898–1977),
and many super-cinemas in the London suburbs.
The obvious importance of Art Deco was that it
advertised the possibility (again like Art Nouveau) of
an ornamental architecture that owed nothing to

of the *Exposition des Arts Décoratifs* held in Paris in
1925. Its stated aim was to provide 'the maximum of
novelty and the minimum of traditional influence',
and designers all over Europe found in this
exhibition a whole range of striking new motifs
which seemed to accord with the instinct for seeking
a fresh start at the end of the First World War and
the concurrent urge towards simplification. The
1920s have been labelled the Jazz Age, and the new
style – more a style of decoration than of building –
was called at first Jazz-Modern, or alternatively

Kodak Building (now Gallagher House), Kingsway, London, by Sir John Burnet and T.S.Tait; 1911. A very early example of the business building that derives its architectural character, although remaining Classical in its detail, almost wholly from its steel-frame construction and is thus a forerunner of the style of city building that was to be evolved by the avant-garde architects of the 1930s and afterwards. Kingsway, a wide avenue driven through a slum area, the clearance of which began in 1889, was opened for commercial building development in 1906.

historical reminiscence. Henceforward only the older generation sought their ornamental effects in recreated period styles, whether Gothic, Renaissance, Palladian or Byzantine. The new generation sought new styles of ornament but also, and with more conviction, the greater simplicity that the spirit of the age, and the constraints of its economy, demanded.

Another Continental influence that had a stronger impact on England than Expressionism or Art Deco responded to this last demand uncompromisingly. It came from Holland, specifically from the work of one Dutch architect, W.M.Dudok (1884–1974). His buildings of around 1930 for the town of Hilversum were asymmetrically composed of plain rectangular masses and slabs, with the verticals and horizontals skilfully contrasted. Dudok had a Europe-wide influence which is best represented in England by the work of Thomas Tait (1882–1954). Tait was the younger partner of the eminently academic Sir John Burnet (see the preceding chapter). His later work, designed after Burnet's retirement (Royal Masonic Hospital, Ravenscourt Park, London, 1931), has many of Dudok's mannerisms.

Burnet however must not be unreservedly classified among the academics. A couple of his firm's London buildings, designed when he was still the senior partner, display geometrical forthrightness far in advance of their time and in advance too of Dudok's rather self-conscious stylizations, since although they retain some remnants of Classical embellishment, they clearly express the nature of their frame construction. These are the Kodak Building, Kingsway (as early as 1911), and Adelaide House at the approach to London Bridge (1924), the latter given a somewhat Egyptian flavour.

Another architect to contribute to the simplification of the multi-storey urban building and at the same time to express its new plan-forms as well as its cellular nature was Charles Holden (1875–1960): the London Transport Headquarters in Broadway, Westminster (1927). He began as an assistant to C.R.Ashbee, which again illustrates the link between the new architecture emerging in the 1920s and the pioneers of the Arts and Crafts Movement. More monumental in conception and therefore not so typical of the changes then taking place were Holden's Senate House and Institute of Education for London University (1932), which were subsequently regretted by many because of the way they

The Senate House, University of London, Bloomsbury, by Adams, Holden and Pearson; 1932. Massively built (solid stone, without the steel skeleton usual at this time) with a 210-foot tower; proclaiming its allegiance to new architectural fashions by its regular pattern of plain unornamented windows (Georgian however in shape, and some with vestigial balconies) and by its replacement of Classical cornices and string-courses with plain horizontal bands. The building was barely finished at the outbreak of war in 1939 when it served as the Ministry of Information. It was occupied by the University in 1946.

had been superimposed on the linked sequences of squares and terraces that made Bloomsbury the best exemplar of eighteenth- and early nineteenth-century town planning ideals.

Holden (with his partners Adams and Pearson) did other work also for London Transport, which in

the 1920s was one of the few public corporations with a positive design policy, given it by its chairman Frank Pick. The lead he set was more effective in industrial and typographical design than in architecture, but Holden designed for him a number of suburban stations of which Arnos Grove (1932) is a good example, based on a simple functional geometry, and relying on plain brick walling and reinforced concrete slab roofs.

The neo-Georgian (incorporating the neo-Scandinavian), the Art Deco and the simplified smooth-walled Classic are thus the first three of the four phases most plainly distinguishable in 1920s and 1930s architecture. The fourth phase, too, was an importation from the Continent. England, having been the incubating place of a revolution in domestic architecture with the Arts and Crafts Movement of the 1880s – a revolution which later spread across the Western world – had soon afterwards reverted to her previous insularity; but she was now ready, as she had not always been, to absorb new ideas from outside if not to initiate them.

This new phase, now generally referred to as the Modern Movement, had only a small impact on the style of buildings put up in England until after the Second World War, and none at all before 1930. It was nevertheless a movement of major significance from the beginning because of the wider view it took of the architect's responsibilities. The Modern Movement was not just another style or fashion in spite of the new vocabulary of forms and materials it introduced, based on its insistence on a close relationship between appearances and techniques and on various influences it absorbed from parallel developments in the other arts. The architects who became devotees of the movement in fact turned their back on style; that is, on the form of a building being imposed by the choice of one of a number of ready-made styles or by some predetermined set of personal mannerisms.

They advocated instead a return to first principles and demanded that the form of a building should emerge, as Gothic architecture for example had emerged, as part of the process of satisfying its functional programme. Their first priority, however, was that architects should involve themselves in matters like mass-housing, the location of industry and the growth of towns, from which the architectural profession had kept aloof in spite of the increasing influence these were exercising on

Arnos Grove Underground Station, North London, by Charles Holden; 1932. One of the brick and concrete suburban stations which, by discarding references to past periods of architecture, helped to give a new-style image to the London Underground system, along with its sign-posting, advertisements and typography.

contemporary living conditions and on the environment of almost every building constructed.

In England the notion of conscious control of the environment in the public interest was not altogether new. It had been the basis of the work of the pioneer town planners like Sir Raymond Unwin, which had led to the passing of the Town Planning Act of 1925. On the Continent there was a tendency to approach notions like this by way of politics, but in England they were already established in many architects' consciousness as moral rather than political issues because an identification of architectural with social ideals had been postulated in the previous century by Ruskin and William Morris, who in this sense had prepared the ground for the Modern Movement.

The influence of both these men was restricted by their preoccupation with the past. An altogether fresh start to architecture founded on a direct analysis of social needs, at the same time discarding the meaningless historicism of the academies, was the new twentieth-century conception. It first emerged as an organized movement with clearly defined principles in 1928, at La Sarraz in

261

Crawford Offices, Holborn, London, by Frederick Etchells; 1930. One of the earliest English examples of the uncompromisingly functional style that had been pioneered some years before in Europe. The continuous strips of window are characteristic, subdivided by stainless steel mullions.

The principle of reinforced concrete construction: (1) the stress set up in a beam; (2) a heavy load will break a plain beam owing to concrete's low tensile strength; (3) in a reinforced concrete beam the tensile stress is taken up by steel rods inserted where the stress occurs; (4) when the beam passes over intermediate supports, the stresses change their positions; (5) reinforcement rods follow the stresses.

Switzerland. A meeting there of architects from several countries set up the *Congrès Internationaux d'Architecture Moderne* (known by its initials CIAM) with the purpose of supporting and propagating the tenets of the Modern Movement. It was led by such seminal figures as the French-Swiss Le Corbusier (1887–1965), the German Walter Gropius (1883–1969), the Dutch Cornelius van Eesteren (b. 1897), head of the town planning department of the

city of Amsterdam and, from 1923, a member of the influential Dutch abstract art movement *De Stijl*. Its general secretary was the Swiss art historian Sigfried Giedion (1888–1968).

In the early history of CIAM England played no part. Its aims and objects nevertheless need stating here because before long it began to make quite a powerful impact on English architectural thought. The policies it stood for were rooted in three beliefs:

in the conscience about architecture's failure to fulfil its social responsibilities already described; in an eagerness to exploit new technologies; and in a desire to move nearer to what was conceived to be the spirit of the age than adherence to the traditional styles allowed. Loyalty to the last two beliefs inevitably led, in spite of the movement's rejection of applied styles, to the use of a common idiom that was hardly to be distinguished from a style. This idiom was derived from the technique and materials employed (for reasons either of utility, economy or fashion) and from a natural tendency to imitate the work of the pioneer architects of the movement.

A number of young English architects, inspired by these and by Le Corbusier especially, began to make some headway at the beginning of the 1930s. The first substantial English building that can be recognized as an example of the new idiom was not however by an architect associated with this group. It was an office building in Holborn, London (1930), by Frederick Etchells (1887–1973) and had the characteristic smooth white walls and horizontal bands of windows. Etchells had been the translator into English, in 1927, of Le Corbusier's epoch-making book *Vers une Architecture*. His subsequent work was mostly concerned with the restoration of medieval churches. Other pioneer modern buildings were being designed at this time by a Welsh-born engineer, Sir Owen Williams (1890–1969), whose bold combination of reinforced concrete and glass (pharmaceutical factory at Beeston, Nottinghamshire, 1930) was far more advanced, structurally and aesthetically, than anything built in the modern style before.

In 1933 the young architects mentioned above formed themselves into the Modern Architectural Research Group (known as MARS). It was to be the English branch of CIAM and was therefore to bring England into regular contact with the experiments being undertaken by the latter. Initially the most active architect members of the MARS group – its membership also included some writers and critics – were Wells Coates (1895–1958), E. Maxwell Fry (b. 1899) and F. R. S. Yorke (1906–62). But they had few opportunities to build. The traditional architects were too strongly established and public and official opinion too conservative. There was no interest in architectural ideas in high places like that which had, for example, inspired the Stuart kings to bring the architecture of the Italian Renaissance to

Pharmaceutical factory, Beeston, Nottinghamshire, by Sir E. Owen Williams; 1930. Independently of the avant-garde architects, this structural engineer, who had made his reputation with the 1924 British Empire Exhibition at Wembley, designed buildings, like this factory for Messrs Boots, that were admired by the devotees of the Modern Movement for their bold use of advanced construction methods – in this case reinforced concrete columns with cantilevered concrete slab floors and all-glass curtain walls.

England and which was currently giving government backing to forward-looking architectural policies in Scandinavia.

Most of the commissions the English modern architects obtained were for small private houses, a type of building that offered them the least scope for the spatial innovations that their interest in the new technologies and in geometrical experiment demanded, and no scope at all for social amelioration and urban improvements. They were thus driven further towards placing the emphasis on aesthetic revolution, and although they continued to declare that they were not trying to establish a style, the idiom they shared with their colleagues on the Continent became more important to them – and more nearly a chosen style – than their principles allowed them to acknowledge. Although their principles

263

House at Amersham, Buckinghamshire, by Amyas Connell; 1928. Connell (1901–78) and his partners Basil Ward and Colin Lucas were the most notable designers in England of the type of white-walled concrete house associated with the theories and practice of the French-Swiss architect Le Corbusier. This example, called High and Over, built for a university professor, aroused controversy when it was completed as to the merits, and the suitability to England, of the so-called international style it represented.

centred round the modern architect's social obligations and his belief in the dominance of science, the picture they had in their minds of the architecture that would emerge on the day when they were given the opportunity to put these principles into practice was a clear and uniform one, almost identical with the picture that was coming into focus on the Continent through the work of Le Corbusier and his Dutch and German associates.

It was a picture of white walls, flat roofs and large windows, and it provided for them and their admirers a stimulating alternative to the prevailing but outworn architectural language based on history. There was no technical reason why, in a new language, walls should be always white, but their conscientious use of a language common to all who shared their beliefs, wherever they might be, helped to create among them a sense of unity, essential while a small minority in each country was struggling for recognition.

The connection of the English modernists with the maturer work of their colleagues on the Continent was facilitated by the presence in the English MARS group of a number of architects of European origin, notably Berthold Lubetkin (b. 1901) – a Russian – Serge Chermayeff (b. 1900) – originally Russian but trained in Paris and London – and Ernö Goldfinger (b. 1902) – a Hungarian trained in Paris. This non-English element was dramatically enlarged after about 1933 when several of the leading European modernists arrived in England as refugees from the persecution of modern artists and architects (whether Jewish or not) by the Nazi regime in Germany. Walter Gropius and Erich Mendelsohn (1887–1953) were only the best known of a number of highly skilled and experienced Central European architects who by their presence raised the morale of the native English modernists and increased their sense of being part of an international movement. But even the most famous of the refugees from Germany, for the same reasons that had denied the modern English architects the support of those with the resources to become their patrons, were given few opportunities to build and soon moved on to America.

Their only substantial buildings were an entertainment pavilion at Bexhill-on-Sea, Sussex, by Erich Mendelsohn in partnership with Chermayeff – the outcome of a competition held in 1935 – and a college at Impington near Cambridge (1937) by Walter Gropius with Maxwell Fry. Notable English buildings in the style of the Modern Movement by the members of the MARS group, other than private houses, are the gorilla house (1934) and the penguin pool (1935) at London Zoo and Highpoint flats, Highgate (1935), all by Lubetkin and Tecton (the latter being a team of half-a-dozen younger architects whom Lubetkin formed into a partnership in 1932); flats in Hampstead (1934), Brighton (1936)

Entertainment Pavilion, Bexhill, Sussex, by Erich Mendelsohn and Serge Chermayeff; 1935. The outcome of a competition won by Mendelsohn, one of the best known of the Central European architects who came to England as refugees but soon moved elsewhere, and his Russian-born partner who had worked in England since 1927. Constructed in reinforced concrete, it was one of only a few public buildings in the pre-1939 international style.

thought generally prevailing in the twentieth century. Architectural writers and historians have subsequently come to regard its manifestation in the 1930s as a key episode – in fact *the* key episode – of that decade; not because of the buildings it produced but because it nurtured, for better or worse, nearly all the significant developments that were to take place when building resumed after the war.

and Kensington (1938) by Wells Coates; some working-class housing in Kensal Green, London (1936), by a team led by Maxwell Fry, and the Peter Jones store, Chelsea (1937), by William Crabtree (b. 1905).

How soon the modern idiom might have become more widely accepted and firmly established if it had not been for the outbreak of war in 1939, which brought all civil building to a stop, is impossible to determine. Although the Modern Movement was then still in an experimental stage and supported only by a minority, it put forward the only clear and confidently formulated philosophy of architecture since Ruskin wrote in the middle of the nineteenth century. Its intellectual impact was perhaps more comparable with that of the Palladians early in the eighteenth century and was the more effective because of the contrast between the Modern Movement's positive if somewhat didactic pronouncements and the confusion of architectural

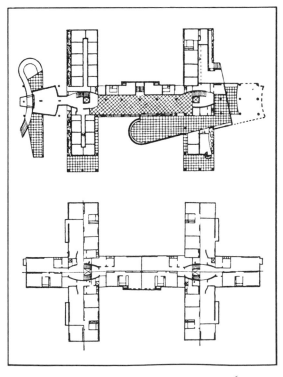

Entrance floor (above) and typical upper floor (below) of Highpoint, London (see page 240). On the upper floors one flat occupies the whole of each wing.

265

Chapter 20

The Post-War World: Welfare State and Commercial Developer

Barbican Development, City of London, by Chamberlin, Powell and Bon; begun 1955. The largest area in the City of London, among those devastated by bombing, to be rebuilt as a whole. Circulation within the site is wholly pedestrian. Housing for six thousand people is provided in horizontal and tower blocks (background of picture) linked by high-level walkways. Among them are placed a school (four-storey building in front of tower) and an arts centre. On the left is the medieval church of St Giles, Cripplegate. It stands between two of the Barbican's central spaces, one of which is also bounded by a section of the old Roman wall.

THE Second World War performed wonders for the changes in architecture that had been so slow in coming in the 1930s, even in the face of the revolutionary efforts of the Modern Movement. This was not however because all architects and their clients had suddenly been converted to a belief in the movement's principles; nor because its buildings had belatedly acquired an aesthetic appeal for more than a small minority. It was because there was no alternative to change, practically, technically and economically. When the war ended Britain was faced with an enormous reconstruction programme arising out of the six-year period during which all civil building had been suspended, further increased by the need to repair the damage caused by air raids. Such a programme could not be undertaken except with the use of modern technical methods capable of combining economy with speed of construction. Consequently after 1945 there was very little attempt, except in small houses, to revert to the neo-Georgian and other styles, dependent on traditional methods and skills, that had dominated the architectural scene before the war.

In addition, the spirit of the times demanded a new start. There was a general urge to reject all that was associated with the past and look only to the future. The same spirit inspired a quantity of new social legislation, including that which created the welfare state in its various manifestations and that embodied in the 1947 Town and Country Planning Act. The state now took responsibility for much that had previously been left to private enterprise: land use and town development (including the programme of new towns envisaged in a report issued while the war was still being fought by the town planner Sir Patrick Abercrombie, 1879–1957); housing and education.

To push these forward, public authorities – the city, borough and county councils as well as the organs of central government – were given unpre-

Primary School, Welwyn Garden City, Hertfordshire, by the county architects; 1949. Typical of the large number of prefabricated schools built in the post-war years, first by this county and then by others. The use of standardized parts – light steel columns and beams and wall-panels of various materials – allowed the many new schools required after the war to be built quickly and cheaply, and yet to be differently planned to suit the needs of each site.

cedented responsibility for building programmes and established their own large architectural offices. For a time much of the more advanced architectural thinking took place in these offices, rather than in private offices as it had in the past. The switch to new technologies was however slower than this switch to a new professional structure, because for some years after the war the building industry was still largely composed of small firms trained only in craft techniques and for political reasons the government was unwilling to enforce a rapid reconstruction of the industry. Hence, although there was some experimentation with prefabricated houses, house building was still limited to traditional methods. The houses comprising the new towns, for example, were mostly of orthodox construction and appearance, two-storey with brick walls and tiled roofs.

By contrast, in another type of building for which in the post-war circumstances there was an unprecedented demand – schools – unconventional techniques were adopted unequivocally. In the Home Counties especially, with their expanding populations added to the need for more school places created by the Butler Education Act of 1944, the demand was such that traditional methods could not have supplied it in a reasonable time. In Hertfordshire the county architect C.H.Aslin (1893–1959) and his schools architect Stirrat Johnson-Marshall (b. 1912) evolved, in partnership with industry, a system of school construction using factory-made components assembled on the site that was yet flexible enough to allow the design to be varied according to the needs of individual schools and the peculiarities of their sites. In the first fifteen years after the war this one county, with a relatively modest architectural office, was able to complete nearly two hundred of these prefabricated schools.

They became famous all over the world as evidence of the utility – and proof of the potential – of properly studied industrialized architecture. The Hertfordshire schools and those of several other public authorities which followed their lead were the most successful outcome of the post-war enthusiasm for allowing technology largely to determine the direction in which architecture should develop. At the same time the schools, when in use, served to accustom a new generation to inhabiting a style of architecture that owed little to past epochs.

In spite of the success of these schools and of other experiments of a similar kind, the use in them of so many untried materials and methods caused a number of technical shortcomings, some of which were only revealed several years later. These shortcomings were especially evident when industrialized methods were applied to multi-storey housing. Such housing was to some extent the product of architects' enthusiasm for planning theories that favoured it, or of their reaction against the wasteful sprawl of low-density housing estates; but more often multi-storey housing was the outcome of local authority, rather than architectural, decisions arising from three different sources: political pressure to increase the number of people rehoused; the persuasiveness of the proprietors of industrialized building systems and the fact that the government subsidies paid to local authorities encouraged the inclusion of tower blocks in housing schemes.

Tower blocks proliferated especially in the 1950s and 1960s. Their unpopularity, which was aggravated by the unattractive environments most of the new housing estates provided – the result of local authorities trying to save money on landscaping and the provision of services – did much harm to the reputation of post-war architecture. The public moreover, since these heartily disliked buildings showed no visible relationship with the familiar architecture of the past, associated their failings with the changes initiated by the Modern Movement

although in many ways they contradicted its principles. This led, at the end of the 1960s, to a nostalgic urge to return to something more familiar and traditional.

Dislike of the new tower blocks and of the social defects of most central area housing estates was paralleled by dislike of other architectural developments not directly connected with the Welfare State, particularly the dominating part played, from about 1950, by speculative property developers. This began when the government offered financial incentives of various kinds to persuade developers to invest private capital in the rebuilding of cities, but failed to impose controls sufficient to ensure that the public interest was paramount. The result was a great quantity of new building – especially office building – that was ill adapted to the sites it occupied and ignored the opportunities of civic improvement that the process of rebuilding offered. At one stage legislation was passed aimed at ensuring that excess profits from commercial development should be returned to the community through a 'betterment tax' but a Conservative government repealed this. As a result building development – especially of offices – became exceedingly profitable. The property millionaire was as typical a financial figure in the 1950s and 1960s as the iron master and the railway king had been in the 1850s and the great landowner in the 1750s.

The architectural disasters resulting from excessive and irresponsible property speculation appeared in two main forms. First, old city centres, since to rebuild them on a twentieth-century scale paid handsome profits, were torn down in the post-war years more comprehensively than enemy bombs had knocked them down, in order to replace their modestly planned, mostly Georgian or Victorian buildings with office blocks and supermarkets (Worcester and parts of Newcastle are instructive examples), thereby destroying all sense of local identity and historical continuity. Secondly, towns and cities were burdened with many new buildings of abysmal architectural quality, crude and clumsy and in a style that was 'modern' only in the sense that period forms and decorations had been discarded. The main reason for their disappointing architectural quality was the absence of discriminating patronage on the part of the developers and boards of directors who chose and briefed the architects. These had no tradition of cultural responsibility and selected architects for their skill and experience in estimating the profitability of sites, negotiating their way through town planning procedures and supervising building contracts rather than for their talent and judgement as designers.

Familiar townscapes up and down the country were thus transformed in less than a generation. In previous eras the buildings dominating the skylines of towns and cities had been those having some communal significance. When not an inheritance from the past they were conceived most probably by the most distinguished architects of their day. But by the 1960s the overpowering features of the urban scene were either multi-storey housing that was the outcome of political pressures as much as architectural aspirations, or commercial buildings with the profitable exploitation of sites the first consideration – all new and most second-rate. This caused a further disillusionment with contemporary architecture and a decline in the public regard for architecture as an expression of contemporary culture.

It was impracticable for the architects of the 1950s to seek fresh guidance in the rules and disciplines of the traditional styles; the enlarged size of so many buildings precluded this and technical developments, especially in the use of concrete, made reversion to the historic styles increasingly a masquerade. Lacking either a ready-made vocabulary or the humility to keep a low profile (as did, for example, the builders of Georgian streets) on occasions that did not call for the creation of new centres of interest, architects were tempted to follow one ephemeral fashion after another. Some, in an effort to make fresh contact with an alienated public, sought it in reference back to vernacular practices. All suffered from the loss of the conviction and sense of direction they had relied on in previous centuries.

The mediocrity of much mid-twentieth-century architecture is not however the subject of this book. In the midst of all the confusion just referred to some buildings were erected in which the timeless attributes of good architecture were still evident. The best of these, because of their sense of architecture as a service to the community or because of their expressive use of the new technology, were indeed more to be admired than most building of the period just before the war. They were

for the most part by architects who had absorbed the principles and disciplines of the Modern Movement but no longer felt bound to imitate its mannerisms, still less to partake in its mistaken enthusiasm for sweeping away everything that belonged to the past and beginning afresh.

In the 1950s and 1960s some of the most responsible building was the collective work of architects who had submerged their personalities in one or other of the public offices. In all the preceding chapters – at least those dealing with epochs later than the Middle Ages – it has been possible to summarize the course architecture has taken by naming the leading architects and discussing their successive buildings. The rise of the public architectural office around 1950 meant that henceforward some of the best architecture would be anonymous.

Among such offices that of the London County Council was, for several years after 1950, outstanding. First under Sir Robert Matthew (1906–75) and then under Sir Leslie Martin (b. 1908), and especially in the field of housing and schools, the architects employed by the LCC set the standard for many others. Their housing at Roehampton (1952–59) is a typical example of the mixture much favoured at this time of high and low blocks arranged in a green landscape according to the precepts of Le Corbusier. The virtues of this and similar schemes have since been obscured by the effects of poor maintenance and vandalism – each more a social and economic problem than an architectural one – but they can still be admired as being far removed in conception from the workers' housing that had created the slums of the nineteenth century. Good examples of the LCC schools of the 1950s, a time when the main task was to preserve intelligibility and humanity in comprehensive schools serving as many as two thousand children, are those at Catford (1954) and Tulse Hill (1956). Among the most spectacular was the densely planned concrete and glass Pimlico comprehensive school of 1967.

High-density housing schemes were also built in great numbers by the architects' departments of the Metropolitan boroughs. Characteristic examples are Acorn Place, Peckham (1961), by the Borough of Camberwell and the Alexandra Road scheme (1972) – monumental to the point of megalomania – by the Borough of Camden. A contrast to these and to the earlier LCC estates is Grahame Park, Hendon,

Public Authority Housing, Roehampton, West London, by the London County Council architects; 1952–59. The acquisition for housing of a large tract of land (previously the gardens of middle-class mansions) alongside Richmond Park offered the opportunity of planning a large landscaped estate of mixed housing types: the eleven-storey blocks seen in the picture, widely spaced; five-storey blocks of maisonettes and a few terraces of individual two-storey houses. The buildings have brick walls clothing reinforced concrete frames.

Middlesex (1974), on the site of the pre-war aerodrome – also by the LCC and also composed of mixed houses and flats. Its dark brown brick (replacing the cold concrete used in the 1950s) and

its varied layout and landscaping together represent the attempts in the later 1970s to create a more humane and sympathetic environment.

For quite a time after the war the best public authority architecture was all in London except for the Hertfordshire schools and for other schools elsewhere (for example in Nottinghamshire) that followed the same pattern. A few provincial cities – among them Sheffield – built notable, but not always environmentally attractive, high-density housing. Several of the new towns experimented with schemes that achieved a high density without rising beyond two or three storeys. One private architect, Eric Lyons (1912–80), in designing small housing estates for a speculative builder, achieved an idiom

that acceptably combined vernacular elements with the simple geometry of the Modern Movement. His brick and timber houses at Twickenham and Blackheath, planned in groups with careful attention to planting, did much to revitalize the design of the suburban house.

In London some private architects were given opportunities to design housing schemes under local authority sponsorship. Churchill Gardens, Pimlico, by Sir Philip Powell (b. 1921) and Hidalgo Moya (b. 1920) was one of the earliest and best. It was the outcome of the first big architectural competition after the war, in 1946, and is typical of its time in being boldly functional in its use of structure and materials but in lacking subtlety with its diagrammatic repetition of rectangular blocks. Later on Pimlico provided the setting for housing schemes in red brick with a more irregular style of landscaping, by Darbourne and Darke (b. 1935 and 1929). At World's End, Chelsea, Eric Lyons and H. T. Cadbury Brown (b. 1913) built in 1967–75 for the Borough of Kensington one of the last of the high-density public authority housing schemes in the form of an elegant cluster of red brick towers growing out of courtyards surrounded by lower ranges of flats and shops.

The most ambitious of all London's urban redevelopment projects was the Barbican scheme in the City (begun 1955), by Chamberlin, Powell and Bon (Peter Chamberlin, 1919–78). It occupies the only substantial area of the City of London to be rebuilt to one design after wartime bombing had

LEFT ABOVE
Private housing, Blackheath, near London, by Eric Lyons; 1956. Suburban houses for sale, planned round small, well-planted courtyards. One of several schemes by the same architect (others are at Twickenham and Cambridge) using simple, traditional materials to create a domestic style fresher and more relaxed than the fussily pretentious styles usually employed by speculative builders.

LEFT
Public Authority Housing, Lillington Street, Pimlico, London, by Darbourne and Darke; 1967. One of the first low-rent schemes to try to break down the rigid geometry and visual monotony of tower-block housing. Irregularly planned blocks of flats of varying heights, using a warm red brick, enclose small paved and planted spaces. Built for Westminster City Council.

Concert Halls, South Bank, London, by the London County Council architects; 1949–68. The clearance of a stretch of the south bank of the Thames, occupied for the most part by derelict industrial buildings, was undertaken in the early post-war period to provide a site for the main exhibition of the 1951 Festival of Britain and eventually for a group of cultural buildings aimed at extending London's entertainment area across the river and opening up the region beyond. The latter purpose was soon frustrated by commercial development in the form of the solid cliff of buildings (the Shell Centre, by Easton and Robertson) seen, with its tower, in the background of the picture. On the river front is the Royal Festival Hall (completed 1951), the first important official building in England in the modern style; to the left is a later group comprising two more concert halls (the Queen Elizabeth Hall and the Purcell Room) and an art gallery (the Hayward Gallery), all of reinforced concrete in the massively impenetrable style fashionable around 1960. These riverside buildings are linked by raised pedestrian terraces.

cleared it of buildings. It reintroduced housing into the business centre of London, which had totally lost its residential population. The Barbican is an essentially urban conception, accommodating six thousand people in a complex arrangement of high towers and rectangular blocks linked by pedestrian pathways at various levels. The central area contains schools and an arts centre (theatre, concert hall, library, etc.). Within the Barbican complex are preserved parts of the bastioned stone wall that once surrounded Roman London and the medieval church of St Giles, Cripplegate, an early instance of the practice of weaving old buildings into the pattern of the new which was to be more frequently adopted in the 1960s and 1970s after the defects of the post-war enthusiasm for comprehensive redevelopment had become evident.

In the initial period of post-war reconstruction a monumental character, though inappropriately aimed at in some commercial buildings, was generally eschewed by the more thoughtful modern architects as being foreign to the conception of architecture as an anonymously performed social service. It was attempted however on two occasions that indisputably called for it. The first was the Royal Festival Hall (1949) on the South Bank of the Thames, by the architects of the London County Council led by Sir Robert Matthew and Sir Leslie Martin. This was the first officially commissioned public building in England in the modern style – as little as ten years earlier it would almost certainly have been neo-Georgian. It is functionally planned in the sense that foyers and restaurants surround the auditorium to protect it from external noise; the latter is therefore not seen behind the symmetrical stone-faced facade. The Festival Hall was later given as neighbours a cluster of concert halls and art galleries (1967 and 1968), also by LCC architects, of

273

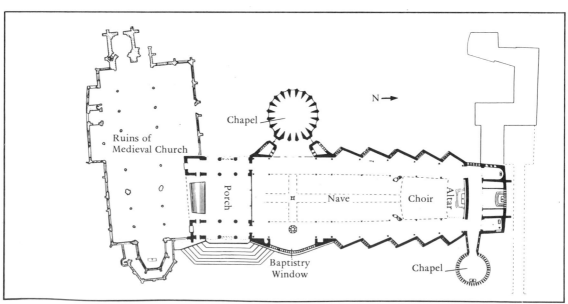

Ruins of
Medieval Church

Chapel

N →

Porch

Nave

Choir

Altar

Baptistry
Window

Chapel

Coventry Cathedral, West Midlands, by Sir Basil Spence; 1951. On the left the burnt-out shell of the medieval cathedral, destroyed by bombs in 1941 and serving as the approach to the new cathedral, which is planned at right angles to the old and entered through the porch in the centre of the picture. To its right is the curved baptistry window with glass by John Piper. The walling material is red sandstone. The sculpture alongside the window is by Jacob Epstein.

The plan of the cathedral is shown below the picture.

exposed concrete in a deliberately heavy style that became fashionable at the beginning of the 1960s – a by-product of the theory that all materials should display their intrinsic nature.

The second monumental building of the post-war years was the new cathedral at Coventry, West Midlands, built in 1951 on the site of the large medieval parish church, promoted in 1918 to the status of a cathedral, which had been destroyed in a 1941 air raid. The architect was Sir Basil Spence (1907–76), who won the competition with a design which preserved the tower and the burnt-out shell of the old church as an approach to the new. Though far from being conventionally Gothic, the load-bearing stone walls link the new cathedral with the orthodoxies of ecclesiastical building, its main contribution to contemporary design being the

works of art that embellish its interior, notably a tapestry by Graham Sutherland and stained glass by John Piper.

A somewhat later public building with a monumental presence is the National Theatre (1967–73) built on a Thames-side site in London just downstream from the group of LCC buildings referred to above. It was by Sir Denys Lasdun (b. 1914), one of the English architects who remained most faithful to the principles and the disciplined geometry of the Modern Movement. He had made his mark ten years before with a distinguished block of luxury flats overlooking Green Park in London, boldly modelled and yet in keeping with the rhythm of the older houses on either side. The National Theatre, like the earlier

The National Theatre, London, by Sir Denys Lasdun; 1967. On the south bank of the Thames, downstream from the group of concert halls, etc., shown on page 273 and separated from them by Waterloo Bridge, from which this picture was taken. The building contains three self-contained auditoria, with shared foyers and bars on several levels. The strongly marked horizontal lines of the exterior are created by the foyers extending on to outdoor terraces. The material is smooth, light grey, board-marked concrete.

LCC concert halls and art gallery nearby, is in exposed grey concrete but with a more precise finish. It reads from the outside as a series of horizontal layers, representing outdoor extensions of the several foyers. It is remarkable inside for the varied spaces created by the sequence of foyers and the unexpected views from one into another; also for the scale and sweep of the larger, open-stage auditorium, an effect typical of those that the new structural techniques evolved in the preceding years had made possible.

Other architects who continued to pursue the ideals of the Modern Movement included H.T.Cadbury Brown – the Royal College of Art, South Kensington, 1959, with Sir Hugh Casson – and Powell and Moya, whose housing in Pimlico has already been mentioned and who were responsible also for several hospitals (for example at Swindon, 1957) which again illustrated the benefits of placing the newest architectural and planning techniques at the disposal of the welfare state. Outstanding among a somewhat younger generation of architects were

James Stirling (b. 1926) and Norman Foster (b. 1935). All the foregoing designed some of their most notable buildings for universities, where most of the significant new architecture outside London was to be found at this time.

Outstanding new buildings added to the older universities included student residences at St John's College (1965) and Queen's College (1975) at Cambridge, and the totally new postgraduate Wolfson College at Oxford (1966), all by Powell and Moya; a new women's college, New Hall, at Cambridge (1962) by Chamberlin, Powell and Bon; a group of specialist libraries at Oxford (1964) by Sir Leslie Martin; a striking red brick and glass engineering building at Leicester (1959) by James Stirling in partnership with James Gowan (b. 1924); and a library in George Square, Edinburgh (1966) by Sir Basil Spence and J. Hardie Glover.

But the most significant advance in this type of building came after 1961 when the government instituted a programme of university expansion and founded a number of totally new universities. Three were especially interesting and consistent architecturally: Sussex (1961) by Sir Basil Spence, laid out on a traditional courtyard plan using throughout an identical idiom of red brick with segmental-arched concrete lintels; York (1962) by Matthew and Johnson-Marshall, more openly planned in a purposely planted landscape and employing one of the prefabricated structural systems that had been evolved for school building programmes; and East

Anglia, near Norwich (1963), by Sir Denys Lasdun. The last, wholly in concrete, has a more concentrated plan and is remarkable for the stepped pyramidal residences at the centre. To the same university Norman Foster added in 1975 the Sainsbury Arts Centre in steel, aluminium and glass which carried precision building as far as it would go.

It was chiefly in commercial buildings that England became aware of the powerful American influence that had been felt all over the world in the years after the war, reflected especially in framed city buildings with precisely detailed steel and glass facades of the kind pioneered in Chicago by the German-born architect Mies van der Rohe. Castrol House, Marylebone Road, London (1960), was the first English city building to employ this idiom in a moderately successful echo of Lever House, New York (Skidmore, Owings and Merrill, 1950). The most distinguished building in the same idiom, attaining as few did the standard of the best American business buildings, was the Commercial Union building in the City of London (1964) by the same architects as Castrol House: Gollins, Melvin and Ward (James Melvin, b. 1912). A similar combination of steel and glass was dramatically exploited in a number of industrial buildings and shopping centres, notably in the largest and most ambitious of the new towns, Milton Keynes, Buckinghamshire (1977).

Engineering Building, Leicester University, by Stirling and Gowan; 1959. A bold answer to the relatively new problem of building for teaching and research into one of the practical sciences. The two nearer buildings, faced with red tiling, contain offices, seminar rooms, etc., and two lecture theatres identifiable by their sloping floors. The more distant single-storey building, constructed wholly of patent glazing, contains the workshops.

Plan of York University (see page 240).

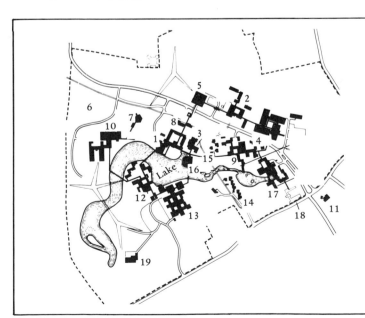

1. Vanbrugh College
2. Alcuin College
3. Language centre
4. Music room
5. Library
6. Housing
7. Music centre
8. Computer building
9. Langwith College
10. Biology laboratories
11. Lecture hall
12. Goodricke College
13. Physics laboratories
14. Housing 'A'
15. Housing 'B'
16. Central hall
17. Derwent College
18. Heslington Hall
19. Sports centre

Civic Centre, Hillingdon, Middlesex, by Robert Matthew, Johnson-Marshall and Partners; 1970. A new headquarters building for a large borough on the western outskirts of London. A deliberate attempt to create, by means of broken surfaces, pitched roofs and vernacular brick detailing, a human-scale idiom which, while not imitating the styles of the past, is yet sufficiently familiar in appearance to overcome the sense of chilliness and aloofness engendered by many of the buildings of the Modern Movement.

Before the latter was built there was, however, some reaction against the unresponsiveness and the impersonality of glass and steel – also against untreated concrete – similar to the reaction already described against the tower blocks prominent in high-density housing. A new generation of architects tried to develop a style that would exploit the traditional appeal and familiar associations of brick and tiles and timber, of pitched roofs and other long-established forms, while preserving the freedom gained when direct imitation of the historic styles was discarded. This tendency is well illustrated by the civic centre at Hillingdon, Middlesex (1970–78), designed by some of the younger partners in the Matthew, Johnson-Marshall firm in a style that echoes the intricacy, and reverts to the domestic scale, of the suburban tradition.

Such conscious attempts to recreate a popular vernacular faced the obvious danger that, in exploiting for this purpose the idiom of the now departed handicraft age, they would lose the impetus that had always driven architecture forward to meet new challenges with new solutions. And yet there was nevertheless a deeply felt need in the 1970s, which many architects were endeavouring to meet, for some means of halting the increasing divergence (which must have been evident also at the beginning of the Renaissance) between a style of architecture with which people felt at home and the new styles that were emerging, as the best architecture has always done, refreshed and revitalized by inevitable changes in technical, social and aesthetic aspirations.

Glossary

aisle. One of the lateral divisions of the nave or chancel of a church.

ambulatory. Aisle round the east end of a church.

apse. The (usually semicircular) termination of the east end of a church.

arcade. A range of arches supported on piers or columns. A *blind arcade* is one attached to a wall.

arch. A curved structure of wedge-shaped blocks spanning across an opening or between columns. It may be semicircular, segmental (i.e., forming less than half a circle) or pointed.

architrave. See *entablature*.

ashlar. Stonework laid with a smooth face in regular horizontal courses.

attic storey. The topmost part of a Classical building above the *cornice*.

bailey. A walled area outside the keep or central fortifications of a castle; also called a *ward*.

bar-tracery. See *tracery*.

barbican. A fortified outwork of a castle, often defending the entrance.

barge-board. A board protecting the edge of a sloping roof or gable, especially when ornamented in some way.

Baroque. The late phase of Renaissance architecture which followed the first simple, rational phase. It originated in Italy around 1600 and is energetic and often theatrical, with flowing lines.

barrel-vault. See *vault*.

bartizan. A small turret projecting from the corner of a castle tower.

bastion. Projecting portion of a castle, or other fortified wall.

batter. The slight inward slope sometimes given to a wall or tower.

battlements. The parapet of a building with regular openings for defence; also called *crenellations*.

bay. A subdivision of a building or of the space inside a building, especially meaning, in for example the nave of a church, the space between one set of columns or piers and the next; also a projecting window.

boss. A projection, usually carved, at the intersection of the ribs of a vault.

brise-soleil. A screen, usually of horizontal or vertical slats, on the facade of a building to protect the interior from the sun.

broach spire. A type of church spire that rises straight from the tower without a parapet. Sloping half-pyramids make the transition from the square shape of the tower to the octagonal shape of the spire.

buttress. Masonry projecting from a wall to add strength and resist the outward thrust of a roof or vault above. A *flying buttress* is an arch serving the same purpose, sometimes resting on a detached pier.

campanile. A tower, usually slender, to hold bells.

cantilever. A beam etc. projecting beyond the wall and supported at one end only.

capital. The uppermost element of a column or pilaster, on which the beam, or *architrave* of the *entablature*, rests.

casement window. One that opens by being hinged at the side.

chancel. The eastern portion of a church, reserved for the use of the clergy and containing the main altar; also called the *choir*.

chantry. A small chapel, attached to or built inside a medieval church, endowed in order that masses shall be said for the donor.

chapter-house. A building attached to a cathedral etc. as the meeting place of the ruling body or chapter.

chevet. A ring of chapels round the apsidal east end of a cathedral.

choir. See *chancel*.

Classical. Architecture of a style that originated in ancient Greece or Rome.

clerestory. The uppermost of the three superimposed ranges of arches forming the nave or chancel walls of a cathedral or other large church; the clerestory windows admit light over the aisle roofs. The lower range of arches is the *nave arcade* and the central (usually the smaller one) the *triforium*.

cloisters. An arcaded walk surrounding an open space; in a cathedral or abbey it served as a promenade and as a passage between the church and the other buildings.

concrete. A mixture of pebbles etc., sand, cement and water poured into a mould. It hardens when dry into a stone-like substance. *Reinforced concrete* has steel bars inserted where the tensile stress is greatest to give extra strength.

Corinthian. One of the Classical Orders; it is the most

ornamental, and is identified by the capital of the column (which is usually fluted) being carved with a leaf motif based on the acanthus.

cornice. The upper of the three main parts of a Classical entablature, projecting the furthest. It is also used by itself, when the word simply means the moulded projection along the top of a wall, an opening etc.

cottage ornée. Rustic-style cottage designed as a picturesque or romantic ornament in the landscape.

crocket. Carved and foliated knob decorating the sloping sides of Gothic spires and pinnacles.

crossing. The space where nave, choir and transepts meet in a cruciform church.

crucks. Pairs of timbers leaning together to create the triangular form of the roof and upper walls of a primitive framed house.

crypt. Chamber or other space beneath the floor of a church.

cupola. A small dome perched on a roof or crowning a dome or turret.

curtain-wall. The fortified wall enclosing the central buildings of a castle and providing the main defence.

cusp. A pointed projection on the inner face of the tracery bars of a Gothic arch or window. This is formed by the intersection of the foils and is the basis of the system of decoration that tracery creates.

dais. The raised platform at one end of a medieval hall where the owner sat.

Decorated. Name given to the second of the three main periods of English Gothic. It followed the Early English and preceded the Perpendicular. Also called, in the nineteenth century, Middle Pointed.

Doric. The simplest (and earliest) of the Classical Orders, identified by relatively sturdy proportions and a plain capital and, in the case of Greek Doric, a column with shallow flutings and no base.

Early English. The first of the three main periods of English Gothic, relatively unornamented and with narrow sharply pointed arches; sometimes called *lancet.*

entablature. The upper horizontal member of one of the Classical Orders. It has three main parts: the *architrave,* the *frieze* and the *cornice.*

escutcheon. Metal plate surrounding the keyhole of a door.

fan vaulting. See *vault.*

fenestration. The arrangement of the windows on the facades of a building

flèche. A slender spire rising from a roof.

flying buttress. See *buttress.*

framed building. One whose structure consists of a skeleton of columns and beams rather than of continuous walls.

frieze. The middle section of a Classical entablature.

gable. The triangular area of walling enclosed by the sloping edges of a roof.

Galilee. A large porch projecting from a medieval church (usually from the west end), for use as a chapel by penitents.

Greek cross. A cross with arms of the same length.

groin vault. See *vault.*

half-timber. A form of (usually house) construction in which a vertical and horizontal timber frame (sometimes with diagonal members also) is filled in with brick or other material. See *nogging.*

hall church. A church in which the aisles are the same height as the nave.

hammer-beam roof. A timber roof, found especially in Perpendicular-period churches, in which the main timbers spring from short beams, often carved, projecting from the top of the wall.

hipped roof. A roof with sloping ends as well as sides.

Ionic. One of the Classical Orders. It was evolved after the *Doric,* than which it is more elegant, and before the *Corinthian.* It is identified by the volutes (or spiral scrolls) that decorate the capitals of the columns.

keep. The central stronghold of a castle, usually containing the owner's living-quarters.

Lady Chapel. Chapel projecting eastwards beyond the chancel of a cathedral or other church and dedicated to Our Lady.

lancet. A sharply pointed window or other arch, of slender proportions, typical of Early English Gothic.

lantern. A turret, with windows, crowning a roof or dome. At Ely Cathedral the term is used for the octagonal roof structure over the crossing.

Latin cross. A cross with one arm longer than the others.

louvre. Inclined slats set horizontally in an opening to admit air but not rain.

Mannerist. Description of the work of those sixteenth-century Italian Renaissance architects who evolved a style that played with, rather than conformed strictly to, the Classical rules. It led on to the *Baroque.*

Mansard roof. One with two contiguous slopes.

mezzanine. A low storey fitted in between the main storeys of a building.

motte. The artificial earthen mound on which the central stronghold of the most primitive type of medieval castle was built. It was surrounded by a *bailey.*

mullion. The upright member (stone or wood) subdividing a window opening.

nave. The main (western) part of a church in which the congregation sits; usually flanked by *aisles.*

Neo-Classicism. An eighteenth-century style involving a return to the disciplines of Greek and Roman architecture after the freedom and exuberance of the Baroque. In England Neo-Classicism culminated in the strict scholarliness of the Greek Revival.

nogging. Brick infilling between the framing of a half-timbered building.

obelisk. A tall square pillar tapering towards the top and ending in a pyramid.

ogee arch. One composed of a convex and a concave curve,

appearing principally in late Gothic and Tudor buildings.

Orders of architecture. The standard elements of a Classical building and their proper arrangement. An Order consists principally of a column (with base, shaft and capital) and *entablature* (with architrave, frieze and cornice). See *Corinthian; Doric; Ionic.*

Palladian. Modelled on the work of, and the rules recommended by, the Italian architect Andrea Palladio (1518–80).

pargetting. Ornamenting external plaster surfaces with patterns, incised or in relief; a technique commonest in East Anglia.

pediment. A triangular topmost feature in Classical architecture, frequently crowning a portico etc.; also the triangular mouldings over windows and doors. *Broken pediment:* one in which the apex is omitted; a favourite Baroque device.

Perpendicular. The latest of the three main periods of English Gothic, following the *Early English* and the *Decorated.* The Perpendicular merged into the Tudor.

piano nobile. The first floor of a mansion or palace, especially a Renaissance mansion, when that floor is loftier than the others and contains the main reception rooms.

Picturesque. A term used in the eighteenth century, relating to the composition of a landscape, when the aim was to give buildings and landscape together the controlled irregularity of a picture.

pier. A heavy stone support in a colonnade etc.; usually square (as distinct from a column, which is round).

pilaster. A flat projection on a wall with subdivisions and ornaments like those of a Classical column and used in conjunction with it.

plate tracery. See *tracery.*

podium. The base on which a Classical building stands.

portico. The colonnaded entrance to a building.

quoin. The stones (or bricks) forming the corners of a building.

refectory. Dining hall of a monastery, college, etc.

Renaissance. Literally rebirth. Used to describe the reintroduction of Classical learning into European culture in the fifteenth and sixteenth centuries and the styles of architecture that derived from this.

reredos. A carved or otherwise ornamented screen behind the altar in a church.

ribs. The structural members of which Gothic vaulting is composed and the ornamental members that divide the spaces between the structural ribs. See also *vault.*

rood-screen. Openwork screen of stone, wood or (sometimes in the nineteenth century) metal separating the chancel of a church from the nave or crossing and designed to carry a rood (crucifix).

rotunda. A circular building.

rustication. Masonry with recessed joints, often used to emphasize certain parts of a building.

sash window. One in which the opening parts slide vertically, controlled by counterweights, as distinct from the hinged opening of the earlier *casement* window.

soffit. The under-side of any architectural feature.

solar. The upper chamber at one end of a medieval hall, usually the private chamber of the owner.

spandrel. The triangular space formed between two arches or between an arch and a wall.

strapwork. Decoration applied to panelling, plasterwork, etc., especially in the Jacobean period, consisting of interlacing flat bands.

string course. A projecting band or moulding running horizontally along the face of a building.

stucco. Plaster of a smooth quality as used, especially in England in the eighteenth and early nineteenth centuries, for facing brick buildings.

terracotta. Clay baked in moulds to make building components and ornaments.

tie-beam. The main horizontal member of a timber roof, spanning from wall to wall.

tracery. The subdivisions of a window in Gothic architecture, for ornamental purposes and to enable its width to be increased. The most primitive was *plate tracery* in which flat stone plates have shaped openings cut in them. Then *bar tracery* was introduced and made to form increasingly complex patterns (see *cusp*). Certain elaborate tracery is called flamboyant because of the flame-like shape of the apertures created. *Reticulated tracery* (usually early fourteenth-century) has a net-like pattern of identical ogee shapes.

train-shed. In a large railway station, the roofed area containing the platforms and the tracks between.

transepts. The north and south arms of a cruciform church, the other two arms being formed by the *nave* (west) and the *chancel* or choir (east).

transom. Horizontal member (stone or wood) subdividing a window opening.

triforium. The intermediate of the three superimposed arcades that flank the nave of a Gothic cathedral or large church. Below it is the *nave arcade* and above it the *clerestory.* Behind the triforium is sometimes an ambulatory or passageway.

truss. (i.e. *roof-truss*) Timbers framed together to span a distance greater than the length of any one of them.

tympanum. The space within the arch of a doorway above a square door opening. In medieval churches this is often the place for sculpture.

vault. An arched roof of various forms, especially in Gothic architecture. A *barrel-vault* is a continuous semicircular arch. A *groin-vault* is formed when two barrel-vaults intersect at right angles – these are used in Renaissance as well as medieval (i.e. Romanesque) architecture. *Ribbed vaults*, formed of pointed arches, can take different forms according to how the surfaces formed by the ribs are subdivided into star and other geometrical shapes. A *lierne vault* is one in which secondary ribs (liernes), not springing from the wall, further subdivide the space between the main ribs. In a *fan vault* the ribs radiate outwards from the wall, creating a fan-like form.

Venetian window. One consisting of an arched central opening flanked by narrower rectangular openings. Much used by English Palladian architects.

wainscoting. A timber lining to the walls of a room, usually in the form of panelling.

wattle and daub. An early form of wall construction consisting of branches or thin strips of wood woven together (wattle) and plastered with mud or clay (daub). It was also used to fill the spaces between the uprights of half-timbered buildings.

weatherboarding. Overlapping horizontal boarding covering the walls of a, usually timber-framed, house.

Recommended Further Reading

A few of the books in the first three categories below cover European architecture as well as English. Such books are included when they give an especially useful account of the latter; also because the wider background is helpful. For particular regions of England there are the indispensable volumes of Nikolaus Pevsner's *The Buildings of England*. The books listed below are arranged, as is customary, alphabetically under authors except in the case of the last, biographical, list which is arranged alphabetically under the architects dealt with for the greater convenience of the reader.

GENERAL HISTORIES

Clifton-Taylor, A., *The Pattern of English Building*, 1972.
Kidson, Peter, Murray, Peter, and Thompson, Paul, *History of English Architecture*, 1962.
Lancaster, Osbert, *Here, of All Places*, 1959.
Pevsner, Nikolaus, *Outline of European Architecture*, 1943.
Riseboro, Bill, *The Story of Western Architecture*, 1979.

BOOKS ON PARTICULAR PERIODS

Clapham, A.W., *English Romanesque Architecture*, 1930.
Clark, Kenneth, *The Gothic Revival*, 1928 (revised 1962).
Crook, J. Mordaunt, *The Greek Revival*, 1972.
Dixon, R. and Muthesius, S., *Victorian Architecture*, 1978.
Dannatt, Trevor, *Modern Architecture in Britain*, 1959.

Davey, Peter, *Arts and Crafts Architecture*, 1980.
Girouard, Mark, *Sweetness and Light: the 'Queen Anne' Movement, 1860–1900*, 1977.
Harvey, John, *The Medieval Architect*, 1972.
Hitchcock, Henry-Russell, *Architecture: Nineteenth and Twentieth Centuries* (Pelican History of Art), 1958.
Hitchcock, Henry-Russell, *Early Victorian Architecture in Britain*, 1954.
Hussey, Christopher, *The Picturesque*, 1927 (reissued 1967).
Lees-Milne, James, *The Age of Adam*, 1947.
Lees-Milne, James, *Tudor Renaissance*, 1951.
Muthesius, S., *The High Victorian Movement in Architecture: 1850–1870*, 1972.
Pevsner, Nikolaus, *Pioneers of Modern Design from William Morris to Walter Gropius*, 1949.
Richards, J.M., *Introduction to Modern Architecture*, 1940.
Salzman, L.F., *Building in England down to 1540*, 1952 (revised 1967).
Service, Alastair (ed.), *Edwardian Architecture and its Origins*, 1975.
Steegmann, John, *The Rule of Taste: from George I to George IV*, 1936.
Summerson, John, *Architecture in Britain, 1530–1830* (Pelican History of Art), 1953.
Summerson, John, *Georgian London*, 1945.
Webb, Geoffrey, *Architecture in Britain: the Middle Ages* (Pelican History of Art), 1956.
Whiffen, Marcus, *Introduction to Elizabethan and Jacobean Architecture*, 1952.

White, J.F., *The Cambridge Movement: the Ecclesiologists and the Gothic Revival*, 1962.

BOOKS DEALING WITH PARTICULAR BUILDING TYPES

Barley, M.W., *The English Farmhouse and Cottage*, 1961.
Barman, Christian, *Railway Architecture*, 1950.
Betjeman, John (ed.), *Pocket Guide to English Parish Churches*, 1968.
Braun, H., *English Abbeys*, 1971.
Braun, H., *Parish Churches*, 1970.
Clark, B.F.L., *Church Builders of the Nineteenth Century*, 1938 (reissued 1969).
Cox, J.C., *The Parish Churches of England, 1937*.
Fitchen, John, *The Construction of Gothic Cathedrals*, 1961.
Girouard, Mark, *Life in the English Country House*, 1978.
Girouard, Mark, *The Victorian Country House*, 1971.
Girouard, Mark, *Victorian Pubs*, 1975.
Glasstone, Victor, *Victorian and Edwardian Theatres*, 1976.
Harvey, John, *The English Cathedrals*, 1950.
Hussey, Christopher, *English Country Houses* (three vols.: Early, Mid and Late Georgian), 1955–58.
Johnson, Paul, *The National Trust Book of British Castles*, 1978.
Lindley, Kenneth, *Chapels and Meeting Houses*, 1969.
Lloyd, Nathaniel, *A History of the English House*, 1931 (reissued 1975).
Meeks, Carroll, *The Railway Station*, 1956.
Mercer, Eric, *English Vernacular Houses*, 1975.
Morris, Richard, *Cathedrals and Abbeys of England and Wales*, 1979.
O'Neil, B.H.St J., *Castles*, 1953.
Penoyre, J. and J., *Houses in the Landscape*, 1978.
Richards, J.M., *The Functional Tradition in Early Industrial Buildings*, 1958.
Whiffen, Marcus, *Stuart and Georgian Churches*, 1948.
Wood, M., *The English Medieval House*, 1965.

BIOGRAPHIES OF ARCHITECTS

Robert Adam and his Circle, John Fleming, 1962.
Thomas Archer, Marcus Whiffen, 1950.
John Francis Bentley, A.S.G.Butler, 1961.
Capability Brown, Dorothy Stroud, 1950.
Isambard Kingdom Brunel, L.T.C.Rolt, 1957.
William Butterfield, Paul Thompson, 1971.

Sir William Chambers, John Harris, 1970.
Wells Coates, Sherban Cantacuzino, 1978.
Life and Work of C.R.Cockerell, David Watkin, 1974.
Thomas Cubitt: Master Builder, Hermione Hobhouse, 1971.
George Dance, Architect, 1741–1825, Dorothy Stroud, 1971.
Life and Work of James Gibbs, Bryan Little, 1955.
The Conscious Stone: the Life of Edward William Godwin, Dudley Harbron, 1949.
Hawksmoor, Kerry Downes, 1959 (enlarged 1969).
Henry Holland, Dorothy Stroud, 1950.
Inigo Jones, John Summerson, 1966.
Life of Sir Edwin Lutyens, Christopher Hussey, 1953.
Mackintosh and the Modern Movement, Thomas Howarth, 1952.
The Work of William Morris, Paul Thompson, 1968.
John Nash, John Summerson, 1935 (revised 1949).
The World of Sir Joseph Paxton, G.F.Chadwick, 1961
John Loughborough Pearson, Anthony Quiney, 1979.
Pugin, Phoebe Stanton, 1971.
John Rennie, C.T.G.Boucher, 1963.
Humphry Repton, Dorothy Stroud, 1962.
The Work of Sir Gilbert Scott, David Cole, 1980.
Richard Norman Shaw, Andrew Saint, 1976.
Robert Smythson and the Architecture of the Elizabethan Era, Mark Girouard, 1966.
Sir John Soane, John Summerson, 1952.
Thomas Telford, L.T.C.Rolt, 1958.
The Life and Work of Alexander Thomson, Ronald McFadzean, 1979.
Vanbrugh, Kerry Downes, 1976.
Seven Victorian Architects (Burn, Hardwick, Smirke, Pearson, Bodley, Waterhouse, Lutyens), Jane Fawcett (ed.), 1976.
C.F.A.Voysey: an architect of individuality, Duncan Simpson, 1979.
Philip Webb and his Work, W.R.Lethaby, 1935.
William Wilkins 1778–1839, T.W.Liscombe, 1980.
Sir Christopher Wren, John Summerson, 1953.
James Wyatt: Architect, Anthony Dale, 1936.
Matthew Digby Wyatt, Nikolaus Pevsner, 1950.
The Wyatts: an Architectural Dynasty, John Martin Robinson, 1979.
Henry Yevele, John Harvey, 1944.

Biographical Dictionary of British Architects, 1600–1840, H.M.Colvin, 1978.

Index